A STORY OF HOPE

IN A TIME OF DESTRUCTION

By
Reverend William F. Maestri

Foreword by
Archbishop Alfred C. Hughes

ÉDITIONS DU SIGNE

Table of Contents

Introduction

Words are powerful. The book of Genesis recounts the stories of creation. God brings order out of chaos. The heavens and the earth, and all therein, are *spoken* into existence through God's powerful, creative words. The Hebrew prophets were God's messengers, their voices clearly proclaiming, "Thus says the Lord…" They proclaimed God's words for the causes of conversion, repentance, fidelity, justice and peace. In the fullness of time the Word, the Logos who is God, becomes flesh in the Person of Jesus the Christ. Jesus proclaimed the Kingdom of God and empowered his disciples to preach and teach to the ends of the earth.

The power of words is not confined to the sacred realm. History is filled with great oration that moved hearts, nations, and profoundly influenced world events.

The history of this nation owes as much to words as to bullets. The bravery of Nathan Hale and the thundering defiance of Patrick Henry expressed a love for liberty and the need to defend freedom with the ultimate sacrifice. The words of

Lincoln at Gettysburg touched the soul of a nation with its declaration of the equality and dignity of each person. In times of testing, from Franklin Roosevelt to John Kennedy and from Dr. Martin Luther King Jr. to Ronald Reagan, powerful words roused a nation to meet the lofty ideals and values of freedom, justice, and the courage to build a more peaceful world.

Along the Louisiana Gulf Coast, few words are as powerful as "hurricane." At the mention of the word, images and emotions fill the mind – crashing waves, swirling wind, driving rain, empty streets, broken signs and downed power lines, bumper to bumper traffic, shelters filled with the displaced and newly made homeless, and those who could return walking in shock and sadness through what remained.

Part of the history of life on the Gulf Coast involves stories about hurricanes. Among the most unwelcome arrivals include Audrey, Betsy, Camille, and, more recently, Georges, Gustav, Rita and Ike. For the greater metropolitan New Orleans area, Hurricane Katrina is the defining storm. The scars – visible and invisible – have yet to heal and may not heal for generations to come. One thing is clear. As long as there is a New Orleans, Hurricane Katrina will forever be part of its story. And not as a minor subplot, but as a major, if not defining, event which fundamentally altered the Crescent City.

What follows, however, is not so much about Hurricane Katrina, for which so much has already been written, but rather about what has gone too often unreported, misunderstood, and unappreciated – a story of abiding faith, unconquerable hope, and enduring love. What will unfold is the story of the Archdiocese of New Orleans' response to

© yegorius - Fotolia.com

Hurricane Katrina. In the aftermath of massive destruction and a great loss of life, the archdiocese began a concerted response to massive needs in circumstances never before encountered. There was simply no blueprint to follow in trying to put New Orleans and the surrounding areas together again. Response, recovery, and rebuilding were truly works in progress. The archdiocese played a significant role in writing this book, which contains information previously unreported, about confronting the ravages of this super hurricane.

The story that will unfold in the coming pages is not an exercise in institutional self-congratulations. Even less is it a boast that the archdiocese alone accomplished great things. There are many hands that joined with the archdiocese in its response to Katrina: people of different faiths or no expressed faith at all, civil authority agencies, military authorities, secular agencies, and private individuals who came together in the face of a massive challenge. They were united in a common desire, namely, to help in some way.

Old divisions, walls of separation, and lingering suspicions were breached just as the waters after Katrina burst through the levees. The days after Katrina could be likened to that first Pentecost in the Acts of the Apostles in which various peoples came together in a common understanding. The need for recovery and the imperative to recover would require a renewed sense of the common good. Recovery was too important and massive to be left to any one segment of society or a single power player. The hard work, creative intelligence, and the willingness to take risks and make mistakes were essential in the early days of recovery. Above all, in the face of so many basic needs, with the temptation to despair, the need for hope was indispensable. There was a fundamental need to *believe* that recovery was possible, indeed, would be achieved.

Genuine hope requires words and action. Words without action can easily lead to disillusionment. Action without words, vision, and goals can lead to fragmentation and various efforts competing at cross purposes. The Archdiocese of New Orleans combined action with words, often the words to bring hope in a time of destruction. This witness to hope was the essential medicine of grace to invite many to become part of the "unofficial family of the archdiocese." Action and conversation invited more action and conversation, often among those who were once on terms of indifference or hostility. Once improbable partnerships were now forged. The forging of new alliances never imagined took shape. Without false pride or the inflation of memory into myth, the archdiocese played a crucial role in the forming and encouraging of such partnerships and alliances.

From the beginning, the archdiocese was present providing help and hope without pre-conditions. Through the tireless work and spirit-filled energy of the staff of Catholic

Charities Archdiocese of New Orleans, immediate pressing needs were met. All the basics – from food to mobile medical services – were delivered to the displaced in shelters that dotted local and state areas, as well as those who were in need beyond Louisiana's borders. The Office of Catholic Schools opened the area's first schools just weeks after the storm. Clergy, many of whom stayed at their churches, held religious services, offered the Eucharist, administered the sacraments, and provided counseling and support to all in need regardless of religious affiliation. Scores of laity worked as never before in archdiocesan recovery projects. Many religious men and women and their communities continued their presence in the greater New Orleans metropolitan area and, in some cases, even took on increased ministerial responsibilities. The archdiocesan Finance Office was faced with the challenge of meeting so many needs while also having to repair those archdiocesan properties damaged by the storm. Adding to the archdiocese's concerns was a significant reduction in financial contributions due to so many churchgoers having evacuated and not being able to return quickly. There was also a significant gap between insurance coverage and damage to archdiocesan facilities. The need for prudent stewardship and the drafting of economic priorities became more essential than ever. In order to coordinate these many and complex activities, communication was vital. Correct information is vital during times of crisis. Rumors and misinformation easily fill the information vacuum when news is severely limited. The challenge to convey information was severely compromised by the extensive damage to the ordinary means of communication upon which we greatly depend. The need not only to inform those *within* the archdiocese but also those in the larger *outside* community was essential. In addition to its own means of communication, the archdiocese turned increasingly to the secular media as a way of providing for the free flow of information. In the pages that follow, we will explore in greater detail how these immense challenges were confronted by various departments of the archdiocese.

The heart of this book is *not* primarily about Hurricane Katrina, though its destructive effects are present throughout. This book is a narrative of the largely untold account of the archdiocese's response to one of the greatest natural disasters in American history. While framed in institutional terms, the story is about ordinary people confronted with extraordinary circumstances and called upon to perform unexpected tasks. There is no need to enlarge their dedication by this writing beyond what it was in the doing. The power of their witness is known to the countless lives that were touched and made better.

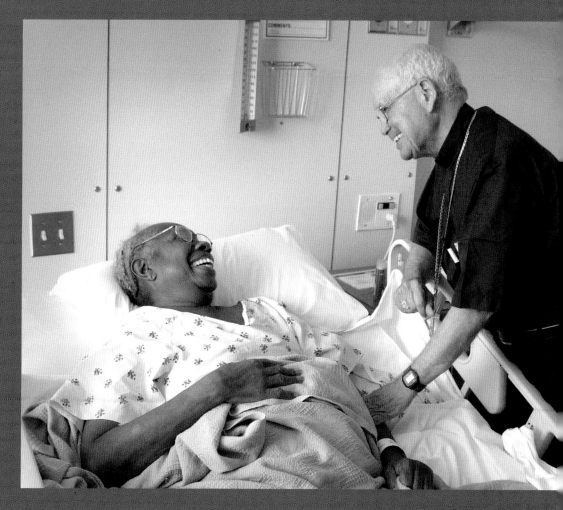

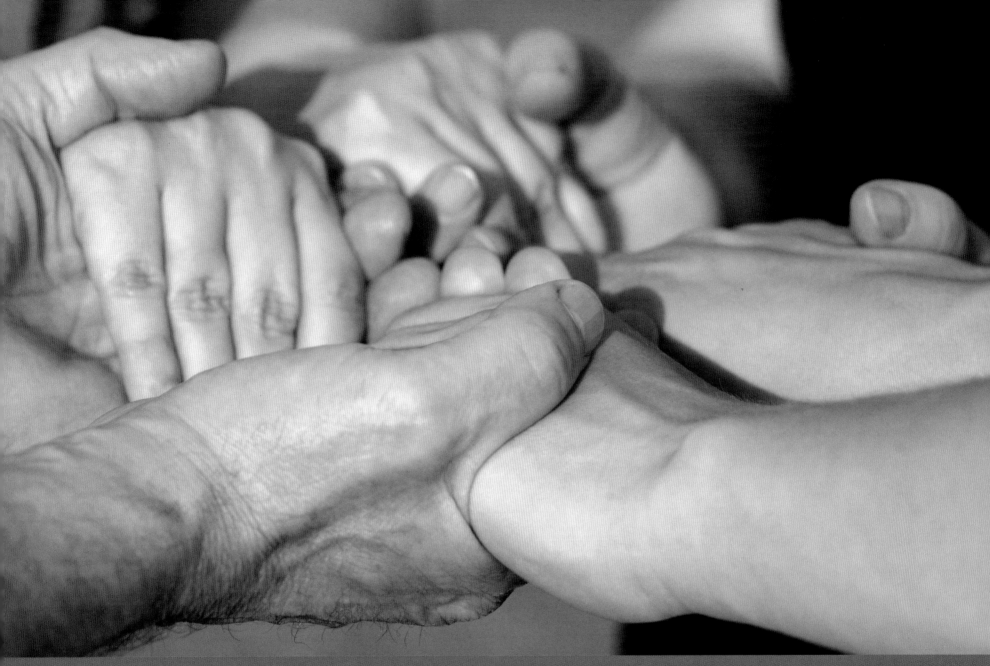

The expression of gratitude is a welcomed opportunity, especially for a writer. Profound gratitude and admiration are extended to the countless men and women who made up the "official" and "unofficial" family of the archdiocese. Their individual and collective witness to hope deserves a permanent place in our city's and church's histories. I am personally grateful to all who took time to participate in this project and read various segments. Their suggestions and corrections improved the text in ways beyond my limited power. My gratitude also requires a note of regret; namely, so many specific individuals and stories had to be left out. My regret is balanced with the realization that all is known to God. Their names and stories are recorded in a book not kept in a human library.

I am deeply grateful to Elizabeth Rouillier for her invaluable expertise with the initial research for this book. Her willingness to participate in this project laid the foundation for the book's completion. Words are not adequate to express my indebtedness to Bettina Buval. From research to editing to production, Miss Buval's skill and devotion to this project are evident on every page. It is not an exaggeration to say that without her extraordinary work there would be no book.

A special word of gratitude is extended to Archbishop Alfred C. Hughes. His spiritual and pastoral leadership for the common good served as an inspiration for those inside the archdiocese and leaders of the wider civic community. I am at once humbled and grateful to Archbishop Hughes for entrusting me with the writing of this book. The idea for this project belongs to Archbishop Hughes.

I am most appreciative to Archbishop Gregory M. Aymond, who succeeded Archbishop Hughes, for his willingness to support this project. Archbishop Aymond's commitment, with words and resources, to the completion of this book was a significant blessing.

The writing of this book was placed under the patronage of St. Gabriel, the Archangel of the Annunciation and the intercessor for those in communications. This acknowledgment of St. Gabriel's direction is not a display of threadworn Catholic piety. It is an expression of genuine gratitude to the one who guided this project throughout. Without St. Gabriel's intercession, the completion of this book would not have been possible. Of course, all the shortcomings are my own.

No acknowledgments would be remotely adequate without an expression of deep gratitude to the staff of the Clarion Herald. Peter Finney Jr., executive editor, made available the relevant materials that are so evident throughout this book. A special word of appreciation is extended to Frank J. Methe, whose photographs have enriched not only this book, but the whole of the archdiocese and places beyond.

I think it is appropriate to end this brief introduction before we commence our story with a dedication. This book is offered in honor of all those brave, generous, and faith-filled members of the archdiocese, along with those partners with whom we joined hands for the common good. A dedication through prayers is offered in memoriam for all who lost their lives in the storm.

It is to the Archdiocese of New Orleans and Hurricane Katrina, a witness to hope in a time of destruction, that we now turn our attention.

_____ *Reverend William F. Maestri*
Archdiocese of New Orleans
New Orleans, Louisiana

Archdiocese of New Orleans

Office of the Archbishop

7887 Walmsley Avenue New Orleans, LA 70125-3496

Tel : (504) 861-9521

Fax : (504) 314-9614

www.archdiocese-no.org

Greeting *Archbishop Gregory M. Aymond*

Dear Sisters and Brothers in Christ:

It is truly a privilege to share with you some reflections as you begin reading *The Archdiocese of New Orleans and Hurricane Katrina: A Story of Hope in a Time of Destruction*.

We remain so grateful to Archbishop C. Alfred Hughes for initiating this book and to Father William Maestri for his excellent work in recounting the tragedy of Hurricane Katrina and the story of hope that has resulted.

As a native New Orleanian, I am quite familiar with tropical depressions, hurricanes and the anxiety that is a part of our lives during the hurricane season. In fact, in 1965 our family home was flooded by Hurricane Betsy, and we left home in a boat.

Though I was not present in New Orleans for Katrina, I painfully watched the news accounts of horrific flooding, homes demolished and people's belongings left in shambles. I do not claim to know the pain and loss experienced by the people of the archdiocese. However, through prayer and reflection, I was able to compassionately walk spiritually with them during their time of crisis.

Today, people still talk of losing loved ones to death and the fear of losing their own lives as if the hurricane were yesterday. Yet, the stories and those who tell them have a genuine spirit of hope, assurance of God's compassion in times of tragedy, and commitment for the continued rebuilding of our communities.

As you read this account and reflect on this story, please join me in thanking thousands of people who came from other parts of the United States to help in the clean-up and rebuilding efforts. Also, many people in our area, with the guidance of Catholic Charities Archdiocese of New Orleans, used their hands and hearts to make the hope of Jesus visible.

New Orleans, in its nearly 300-year history, has experienced fires, hurricanes, floods, a yellow fever epidemic and other disasters. We do not lose hope. God is faithful and he gives us the wisdom and strength to rebuild with him.

Wishing you God's blessings, I am
Sincerely in Christ,

+ *Aymond*

Most Reverend Gregory M. Aymond
Archbishop of New Orleans

Foreword Archbishop Emeritus Alfred C. Hughes

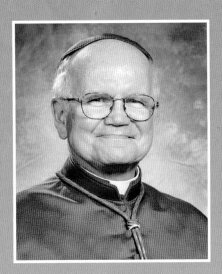

In *The Archdiocese of New Orleans and Hurricane Katrina: A Story of Hope in a Time of Destruction*, Father William Maestri offers us a masterful account of the efforts of the Archdiocese of New Orleans in the first years after Hurricane Katrina. In his introduction, he rightfully locates these efforts in the broader context of a truly remarkable response on the part of so many people representing varying churches, different faiths or no faiths at all, secular non-profits, civil and military authorities and committed individuals working on their own. In this book, he relates the Catholic story and thereby makes a further contribution to the historical accounts already available.

It is evident that Father Maestri has made painstaking efforts to assemble the detailed data to ground his work in the facts. Then he has brought the facts to life with a series of stories which provide human accounts of people delivering or receiving disaster assistance.

Father Maestri was himself the central protagonist in the efforts reported in Chapters Five and Six, although he never mentions his own name. As archdiocesan director of communications and superintendent of schools, he assumed responsibility for these two linch pins in the archdiocesan works of recovery. He urged and provided for the maximum use of the means available through the media at a time when a creative approach to communication was imperative, given the fractured state of the ordinary means for human contact.

Father Maestri also developed a strategy for the relocation of Catholic students and then the reopening of Catholic schools. Within two months, 95 percent of all Catholic school students had been relocated in a Catholic school somewhere in the country, thanks to the generosity of bishops, superintendents, principals and teachers in so many dioceses. He then developed a vision which he describes in the book as the "magnet" versus the "big tent" approach. He won national acclaim as the archdiocesan Catholic School Office reopened one school after another, beginning with the St. Louis Cathedral Academy, and welcomed all students, whether Catholic or non-Catholic, whether previously in Catholic schools or not, whether able to pay or not. This magnanimity of spirit made it possible for some 2,000 students who had never been in a Catholic school before to salvage a year of education. All were welcomed by school administrators and faculty, themselves attracted back by this innovative plan to form hybrid teaching staffs for that first year. Chapter Six offers a sampling of the ingenious models developed to make Catholic education available to all who wanted to avail themselves of it during the first year following Katrina.

Chapters Nine and Ten offer reflective insight: the first, philosophical; the second, theological. Each renders a real contribution to post-Katrina analysis. A correct understanding of the role of church and state can help us be more realistic about what we should expect of each in a time of crisis. Realistic expectations free both for constructive collaboration in service to the common good.

In a time of disaster, faith and hope are essential. Faith enables us to see God's presence despite the fog of confusion and disorientation. Hope grounds us, not in transitory expectations, but in the ultimate guarantee of victory under God.

In my pastoral visits to those recently rescued or those traumatized in public shelters, I was constantly inspired by the thirst for a word of faith and hope. After receiving the basic needs of food, drink, medicine and shelter, many wanted some sign that God cared. They welcomed a listening ear, a prayer, a Bible or a religious article.

One woman held up a small plastic bag and said: "This is all I could save. The Lord has given and the Lord has taken away. I guess I now have to try to bless the name of the Lord." She was obviously struggling but uttered a powerfully realistic prayer in a time of severe deprivation. Another survivor, a man, wrestled with intense anger as he reported how he dragged his emotionally traumatized wife to the roof of his home, only to lose her from his grasp and see her swept away by the flood waters. He struggled with God, with himself and with those he considered responsible for the breach of the levee. He needed a listening heart, a word of consolation and hope.

When the 82nd Airborne Division came to New Orleans to help to bring order, they engaged, as is their custom, in one symbolic good will gesture to signal their desire to bring peace. They decided on their own to clean up the St. Anthony Garden behind St. Louis Cathedral. They discovered that a tree had broken fingers from one hand of the Sacred Heart statue which dominates the garden.

After finding the broken fingers, they presented them to Archbishop Philip Hannan, retired Archbishop of New Orleans and a former World War II chaplain in the 82nd Airborne Division. At the first Mass at St. Louis Cathedral after the storm on October 1, 2005, I recounted that story to the standing-room-only congregation and suggested that the image of the Sacred Heart expressed powerfully the Lord's faithful love for us. But then I noted that the broken fingers could be interpreted as a symbol of the Lord's desire to solicit our partnership in bringing about recovery. For that reason, I determined not to reattach the fingers until the recovery would be complete. That moment now lies in the hands of my good successor, Archbishop Gregory Aymond.

Please read Father Maestri's account, a story of how religiously motivated, dedicated and competent people became the Lord's fingers in promoting the work of recovery in metropolitan New Orleans.

• A shard of stained glass pierced the side of the Corpus at Immaculate Conception Church in Marrero

Newly arrived
Archbishop Philip
Hannan surveys
Hurricane Betsy
damage in 1965

HURRICANE KATRINA AND NEW ORLEANS: AN OVERVIEW

To live on the Gulf Coast requires dealing with a number of givens: heat, humidity, rain, mosquitoes, and hurricanes. To those outside the South, the headshaking question is often asked – who would want to live there? And why do they stay?

The often-heard answer goes something like this. We live along the Gulf Coast for the same reason people live in California with its earthquakes, in the Midwest with seasonal floods, and in the Northeast with its frigid temperatures and snowbound lifestyle – we like it. We determine that the benefits outweigh the burdens. Many people do enjoy the weather, especially when compared to images of drifting snow. Residents participate in the varied outdoor hunting and fishing activities, both for recreational enjoyment as well as economic necessity for their livelihood. Scores of individuals and families are greatly enriched by the "southern way of life" with its stories, folklore, dialects, and mores. Simply put, living and raising a family anywhere but in the South is unthinkable.

To say that hurricanes are part of the Gulf Coast landscape is not to trivialize the massive impact these destructive forces inflict on individuals and whole communities. Death, destruction, and dislocation never become routine. Broken lives and homes yield broken hearts. The very young, the poor, the sick, and the elderly often suffer the most. Still, in the face

of all these consequences, Gulf Coast residents refuse to leave. Along with hurricanes, hardcore Gulf Coasters have come to accept stocking up storm supplies, boarding up houses and businesses, contraflow evacuation routes, scrambling for hotel rooms out of harm's way, and an overall disruption of one's taken-for-granted world. For many residents with years of hurricane exposure there sets in a kind of "automatic pilot" response. For some, there is more a feeling of annoyance, or even complacency, rather than fear. Such feelings were pre-K (before Katrina), but in our post-K world the very beginning of hurricane season is enough to spark heightened vigilance.

Prelude to a Storm

In the years before Katrina, veteran Gulf Coast residents had witnessed an increase in the number and intensity of storms. For residents of Southeast Louisiana, another element concerning hurricanes has emerged – namely, an attitude

The threat of hurricane damage is something area residents learn to live with in New Orleans

• Archdiocesan priests tour Hurricane Betsy damage in 1965

of complacency born of having dodged so many direct hits. A feeling of invincibility is usually expressed in this way – "it's going to turn at the last minute." To a large extent this belief proved to be accurate. Why should the next storm be any different? Evacuation, with its long lines out of town, added expense seemingly for no good reason, and the idea of leaving one's property unguarded tipped the scales in favor of "riding this one out."

The danger of rolling the dice is clear: you are gambling with your life and the lives of loved ones that the storm will veer away or produce limited life-threatening consequences. Maximum vigilance must be the standard operating procedure.

With the memory of Hurricane Ivan still fresh, Gulf Coast residents remembered the hysteria surrounding a hurricane that turned out to be more like a typical summer squall rather than a major hurricane. Why would the next hurricane be any different? The reports of a newly developing tropical storm were assigned to the recesses of residents' minds.

• Storm survivors help others to higher ground

Into the Gulf

With hurricanes, small beginnings do not always signal the devastating power that can emerge over time given the right conditions. Such was the case with Hurricane Katrina. This storm formed as a result of three elements converging: a tropical wave, an upper-level trough, and the mid-level remains of Tropical Depression 10. On August 23, 2005, a tropical depression formed in the Caribbean about 200 miles southeast of Nassau in the Bahamas. The initial track of this new depression was northwest, and it became Tropical Storm Katrina on August 24, 75 miles east-southeast of Nassau. From August 24 through 25, Katrina sprinted westward in the direction of southern Florida. Katrina became a hurricane just before striking Florida near Miami-Dade/Broward counties during the evening of August 25. Due to lack of developmental time between hurricane status and landfall, Katrina arrived in Florida as a Category 1 storm (wind speeds of 75 mph or greater). Katrina emerged the next day, August 26, into the eastern Gulf of Mexico.

Katrina storm track

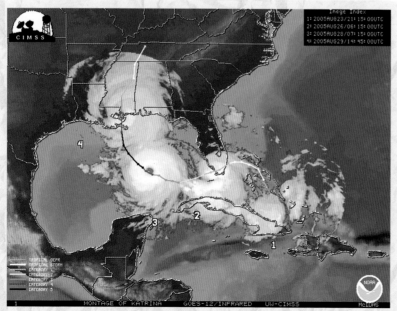

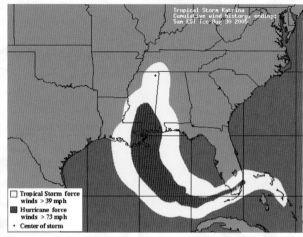

Weather stations track the path of the killer storm

A stranded man signals for help

Where Will She Go?

After entering the Gulf of Mexico, Katrina proceeded to move westward. Gulf Coast residents began to pay attention. It should be kept in mind that Katrina moved quickly across the southwest tip of the Florida peninsula, traveling seven hours over land with winds gusting above 90 mph. The winds were not significantly reduced; hence, Katrina had a rapid re-intensification from the warm Gulf waters.

Weather conditions over Texas would play a major role in Katrina's final destination. As the storm moved into the Gulf on its westward march, a mid-level weather ridge centered over Texas weakened and moved westward. This weakening allowed Katrina to slowly turn to the northwest and fill the upper-level weakness which developed over Texas. In addition to this upper-level weakness, the warm Gulf of Mexico waters and an upper level anti-cyclone over the Gulf greatly aided the intensification of Katrina.

During the next 48 hours, Katrina continued its northward movement, growing in intensity and size. On Sunday, August 28, Katrina reached a maximum wind speed over 175 mph and a minimum central pressure of 902 millibars (mb),

Katrina Facts: Hurricane Katrina spun off 62 tornadoes in eight states from Florida to Pennsylvania. Maximum storm surge was 26 to 28 feet along the Mississippi coast, 10 to 15 feet near New Orleans, and 10 to 12 feet along the Alabama coast.

Levee breach floods neighborhood around St. Mary of the Angels Church in New Orleans

gone, the panic to "get out" was in full force. Unfortunately, all major evacuation routes were in gridlock. The Interstate highways resembled huge parking lots. Any movement of traffic made the proverbial snail's pace seem fast. Cars were running out of gas. Other cars were stalled due to various

• An Air National Guardsman unloads MREs at the New Orleans Naval Air Station

the fourth lowest on record for an Atlantic storm. The intensity of Katrina's winds reached that of Hurricane Camille's. However, Katrina was significantly larger and affected a much broader area.

The forward movement of the storm and its massive size made it clear to everyone that Louisiana, especially New Orleans and surrounding areas, would not enjoy another "hurricane wobble," shifting the storm surge effects to another destination. Katrina showed no signs of veering to the west or to the east. This time New Orleans was in the eye of the storm. The rush, even the panic, was on to evacuate the city.

Leaving the metro area would not be easy. For too many, it would prove impossible and deadly.

Too Many, Too Late

With Katrina bearing down on southeast Louisiana and packing winds of 175 mph, and all hope of the storm turning

• A National Guard truck delivers supplies to the Superdome on August 31, 2005

mechanical failures. Knowledge of seldom-used roads and well-kept secret shortcuts were of little use. All the while Hurricane Katrina continued her relentless march toward New Orleans. Many residents simply viewed television and decided to stay, or risk their safety in a public shelter of last resort. Few could have imagined the terror that awaited those who sought safety at the Louisiana Superdome and the Ernest N. Morial Convention Center.

• Storm victims wait on I-10 for rescue in the wake of Hurricane Katrina

• Young and old seek shelter on St. Mary of the Angels School roof waiting for rescue

Tragically, there were the poor, elderly, and sick who depended on the government for transportation away from the storm. Unfortunately, for many, a way out would not arrive. Those who waited out the storm – or stubbornly refused to leave with family members – were trapped in their homes or various designated drop-off locations. Public transit buses designated as pickup and delivery vehicles, in most instances, never left their staging areas or were unable to move through the heavily congested traffic. Individuals most at risk and the needy had to either ride out the storm where they were or make their way to a shelter as best they could. Poor preparation and planning by public officials, along with residents' decision to wait and see if the storm turned, only added to the tragedy that was Hurricane Katrina.

• Unidentified woman keeps high spirits despite tragedy

August 29, 2005: Katrina Arrives

On Sunday, August 28, Katrina reached a wind speed of 175 mph. Category 5 storms reaching that status seldom maintain such intensity because of internal dynamics which weaken the inner structure of the eye wall. So it was with Katrina. Drier air and an opening of the eye wall on the south and southwest reduced Katrina to Category 4 status.

On the morning of August 29, Hurricane Katrina slammed into Grand Isle, La., packing winds of 125 mph – a strong Category 3 storm with a central pressure of 920 mb (the third lowest on record for an Atlantic storm that actually made landfall in the United States). Katrina turned after this initial contact at Grand Isle to the northwest and north with the center making landfall around Buras, La., with maximum winds holding at 125 mph. By the time Katrina reached New Orleans, wind gusts just west of the eye were recorded at over 100 mph.

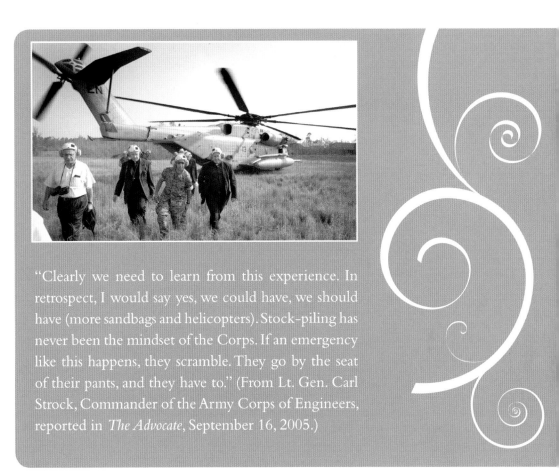

"Clearly we need to learn from this experience. In retrospect, I would say yes, we could have, we should have (more sandbags and helicopters). Stock-piling has never been the mindset of the Corps. If an emergency like this happens, they scramble. They go by the seat of their pants, and they have to." (From Lt. Gen. Carl Strock, Commander of the Army Corps of Engineers, reported in *The Advocate*, September 16, 2005.)

After passing through New Orleans, Katrina continued its northward path and made a second landfall near the Louisiana/Mississippi border. The storm moved through Laurel, Mississippi, with hurricane force winds (120 mph/ Category 3 status) still holding. It wasn't until Katrina reached the Tennessee Valley on August 30 that she was downgraded to a tropical depression. By August 31, Katrina was classified

USAF and US Army Police assist New Orleans evacuees

as an "extra tropical low." Later on the same day, Katrina was absorbed by a frontal zone over the eastern Great Lakes.

• Archbishop Alfred Hughes reviews Katrina's damage over the Greater New Orleans area

Katrina — Act II: Now the Water

After Katrina left the metropolitan area, heading north, plans were being formed by civil authorities and residents for the long road home. Rain and wind damage would be evaluated. Basic services had to be restored. Businesses supplying essentials such as food, electricity, and medical services would be given priority in reopening. Waves of residents would return, take stock of the damage and begin the difficult cleanup process and restoration. Dealing with insurance companies and contractors was just part of the recovery process. Veteran metro area residents had been through all this before, and Katrina would be no different.

Not quite. While the storm had long passed, the high destructive winds were now replaced by high water and even greater destruction. One of the worst fears of metro area

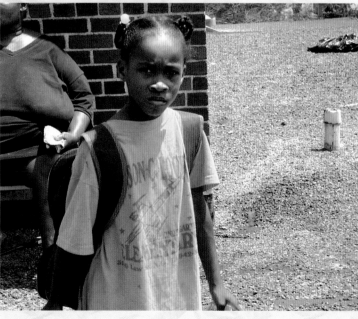

Young girl waits anxiously for her turn on the rescue helicopter

• 17th Street Canal levee breach

- 24 -

residents is massive flooding. Greater New Orleans faces sea level challenges, as well as being surrounded by numerous bodies of water. An elaborate set of levees and locks was all that separated the metro area from the destructive strength of rising waters.

• Hurricane surge pushed this barge onto a levee

The strong Katrina winds, heavy rainfall, a 10-to-20 foot storm surge, and human engineering errors all combined to weaken, breach, and finally break crucial parts of the levee system. It was estimated that more than 80 percent of New Orleans was under water. In some places the water reached 20 feet high. The "soup bowl" reference of New Orleans had come to pass.

A Bitter Brew

The saucer that is New Orleans remained filled with the toxic brew of water for weeks. Stagnating water contained a mixture of chemicals, gasoline from flooded vehicles, sewerage waste, and bio-hazards created from decomposing animal and human bodies trapped in destroyed homes. Major sections of the Greater New Orleans area were impacted by the breach and levee break. Eastern sections of New Orleans, major parts of the city, and almost all of St. Bernard Parish did not escape major flood damage. Large sections of

neighboring Jefferson Parish experienced damage but other areas were spared from the extensive flooding experienced in New Orleans. In addition to major property damage, estimated to have exceeded well over $100 billion, there was a significant loss of life. Louisiana and Mississippi suffered the loss of 1,200 lives (1,000 in Louisiana and 200 in Mississippi).

• Many evacuees returned to their homes despite many obstacles

However, such figures are misleading. An exact number may never be known due to the chaos and record-keeping breakdown in the days following Katrina and the subsequent flooding. It should be noted that not every Katrina-related death occurred immediately and could be directly attributed to the storm. Many sick and elderly individuals died weeks and months later. Many evacuees were so severely depressed that in the words of one returning resident, "My mother just gave up. She couldn't face returning to all the loss. She decided to die."

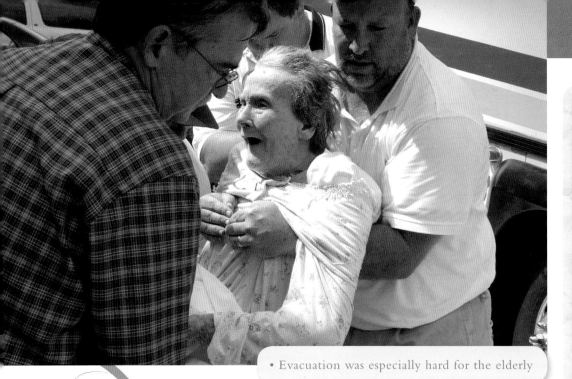

• Evacuation was especially hard for the elderly

• Murphy Oil Refinery

As horrific as the loss of life attributed to Katrina was, it was far from the deadliest storm in the United States. In terms of deaths, the Galveston hurricane of September 8, 1900, claimed more than 8,000 lives. Of course, at that time, there were not the advanced warning systems of today. Residents were caught by surprise. Yet, even with today's modern technology, many who perished in Katrina were caught by the rising waters after levees were breached and finally gave way, unleashing devastation.

Katrina was not the strongest storm to make landfall. The following storms were more powerful:
• The Labor Day Hurricane in the Florida Keys (9/2/35); Category 5 with almost 200 mph winds
• Hurricane Camille in Mississippi (8/17/69); Category 5 with almost 190 mph winds
• Hurricane Andrew in Southeast Florida (8/24/92); Category 5 with 165 mph winds
• Hurricane Charles in Punta, Florida (8/13/04); Category 4 with 150 mph winds

The deadliest hurricane on record was in Galveston, Texas, on September 8, 1900. More than 8,000 lives were lost. Reported deaths after Katrina reached 1,200.

Collateral Damage

In addition to the tragic loss of life and the horrific property and infrastructure damage, other major aspects of the area were affected. As a result of Katrina there was also a critical demographic loss. Pre-Katrina, the New Orleans metropolitan population was 1.3 million people. Post-Katrina, the population fell to a low of approximately 700,000 before rebounding to nearly 1.2 million by 2010.

Various economic sectors suffered in the aftermath of Katrina. Specifically, the oil, gas, tourism, transportation, and maritime sectors were derailed by the breakdown in vital links locally, statewide, and nationally. The oil industry is important not only to Louisiana, but also to the nation as a whole. Oil production in the Gulf of Mexico was reduced by 1.4 million barrels per day. In percentage terms, this translates to 95 percent of daily production.

A major industry driving the economy for the Greater New Orleans area is tourism. New Orleans has long been a "must-visit" destination for those in nearby areas, as well as, for world travelers. Katrina severely impacted travel access to New Orleans. Louis Armstrong International Airport and the New Orleans Lakefront Airport were closed on August 30, 2005. The Interstate 10 system heading east was destroyed. To compound matters, a vast majority of coastal highways along the Gulf Coast were impassible in places, as were minor roads near the shore. The storm's rainfall, more than 10 inches across the region, which fell in a very short period of time, along with pumps that no longer operated, hampered travel for those seeking safety by heading inland. Tourism was greatly curtailed due to transportation being severely disrupted, along with media images of widespread destruction and mass flooding being broadcast worldwide.

Long a vital part of the New Orleans economy, the Port of New Orleans was seriously damaged by Katrina. Both imports and exports were greatly reduced in the months after Katrina. Each category of shipping declined by over one million tons. Even before Hurricane Katrina, the port was facing challenges from competing port facilities along the east and west coasts, as well as from other Gulf Coast ports. Katrina greatly compounded the challenges.

Out of the Water and the Rubble

Initially after Katrina, there was serious talk in some quarters, most troubling by some politicians in Washington and elsewhere, that New Orleans should not be rebuilt. Their thinking went something like this: With the increase in the number of "super hurricanes," the seeming inability to protect the city built like a saucer from major flooding, and the tremendous drain on the nation's resources, it was both foolish and wasteful to rebuild. The best thing to do was to cut our losses.

Of course, the same argument could be said of those parts of the country that must deal with earthquakes, flooding, snow, seasonal fires, and tornadoes. Few have suggested we no longer support or rebuild California counties because of brush fires and earthquakes. When more rational voices gained control of the conversation, the notion of "canceling New Orleans" was quickly dismissed. In addition to severely impacting the tourism industry, Katrina dealt a severe blow to the offshore oil and gas industries of south Louisiana. Exploration and production declined significantly after Katrina, which cost Louisiana much-needed revenue. This loss of oil and gas from the Gulf of Mexico added to the costs of these resources throughout the nation. While the prices for oil and natural gas are extremely volatile, having

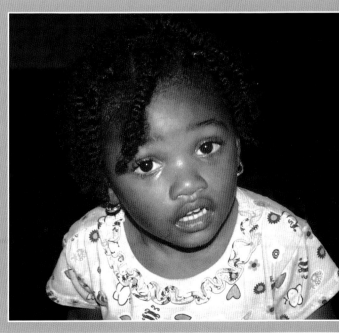

After Katrina, there are proportionally fewer young people, notably the 5- to 14-year-old group. Not surprisingly, their parents (the 25- to 44-year-old range) were also significantly lower in number. The middle-aged group, 45 to 64 years old, has grown the most. (From the Metropolitan Report, University of New Orleans, March 2009.)

Churches adopted Katrina families

• Baton Rouge Bishop Robert Muench greets young evacuee

spiked upward in 2008 and holding steady in 2009, there has been a significant recovery in this industry. This rebound helped the region fare better than the rest of the country in the face of the severe 2008-09 recession, but the massive BP oil spill in the Gulf of Mexico in 2010 created new economic concerns.

In the years since Katrina, there have been encouraging signs of recovery affecting major areas of public life. The local population has risen to approximately 1,150,000 or 85 percent of the pre-Katrina level. And the population continues to grow. Projections for the 2010 census place the population figure at 1,190,000. Tourism has enjoyed significant revitalization. By the end of 2008, tourism returned to approximately 75 percent of pre-Katrina figures. Of importance is the word-of-mouth testimony by those

who visit and return home. Of significance, major areas of the region, along with familiar tourist attractions, have reopened. Images and memories of Katrina's devastation are hard to erase. However, the word is getting out that New Orleans is once again a magical place to visit. The positive experiences by tourists are helping to balance the images of horror immediately after the storm.

Port activity is down by an average of 3.7 percent, but a significant factor is the worldwide recession. Even with that decline there has been a notable recovery in activity since the early months after Katrina. As the global recession recedes it would be expected that the port will participate in the rebound.

Ursuline Academy Elementary students replant trees on school campus

"How appropriate it is for us to gather as a community of faith.... Our prayers and readings from the texts sacred to the Hindu, Jewish, Muslim, Protestant, and Catholic faiths have led us through expressions of lamentation, thanksgiving and hope. We lament the loss of lives, homes ... a way of life. We thank God for his providential care. We dare to lift our hearts to a vision of hope." (Archbishop Hughes' Prayer of Lamentation, Thanksgiving, and Hope, St. Louis Cathedral, 2005)

There are other welcomed signs of recovery. In the face of a general economic downturn worldwide, the employment statistics in the metro area have fared well. Pre-Katrina, the metropolitan area had about 610,000 jobs. After Katrina, employment sank to 426,000 jobs (76 percent of pre-Katrina employment). In 2009 the metropolitan job market showed a return to 526,600 jobs. The University of New Orleans forecasts a 4,000 job gain by 2010. This job gain would return employment to 97 percent of pre-Katrina levels. As might be expected, construction has been robust throughout the metro area. The major sector of construction growth is in the area of non-residential building. Major projects to repair the area's infrastructure have contributed to a strong construction sector. Another important area of recovery is retail sales. The overall taxable sales level continues above pre-Katrina levels. Much of these sales are related to continued efforts to rebuild after Katrina. Orleans and St. Bernard parishes, the most heavily damaged areas, have experienced the largest sales-related revenue.

Flood and Waves

The crashing waves and flood waters of Katrina were soon replaced by a new, and this time welcomed, wave and flood of generous hearts that simply saw a great need and wanted to help. While, unfortunately, some political leaders were simply overwhelmed, squabbled over turf, and entered into useless debate, the metro area was awash with waves of goodwill by those who donated helping hands and resources necessary for recovery. Most heartening was the influx of young people from across the country and

• Student volunteers

world who put their lives on temporary hold in order to make a difference. In addition, the Hispanic and Latino population grew, as many of the early and difficult cleanup jobs were undertaken by these newly arrived workers. Their contribution to bringing New Orleans back was invaluable.

Along with the numerous private organizations which donated time, talent, and treasure to rebuilding New Orleans, the faith-based communities – the churches – made an indispensable contribution. Motivated by a mission that comes from beyond this world, countless individuals and communities showed their love for God by serving those with acute needs. The Body of Christ extended beyond our familiar denominational labels. Unity in the Spirit replaced the divisions which too easily divide members of the one Family of God.

With this overview of the details leading up to and beyond the great natural disaster that we call Hurricane Katrina, we now turn our attention to the efforts of one such faith-based community, a particular church, namely, the Roman Catholic Church of the Archdiocese of New Orleans. It is a story which must be told, and retold, to succeeding generations. It is a story which transcends a storm and even a city. It is the story of hope in a time of destruction. It is a story of God's amazing grace calling forth new life amid the ruins.

Celebrating Christmas in a FEMA trailer

• Josephite Father Joseph Campion rededicates
St. David Church in the lower 9th Ward

Chapter 2

HURRICANE KATRINA AND THE ARCHDIOCESE OF NEW ORLEANS: AN OVERVIEW

"Hurricane Katrina has been an enormous catastrophe of epic proportions. The suffering it has caused is overwhelming in loss of life, loss of homes, churches, and schools." This concise and powerful statement was penned to cardinals and bishops by Archbishop Alfred C. Hughes soon after Katrina from his temporary office established in Baton Rouge.

The wind and the water of Katrina made no distinction between city and church, civic and religious. All were affected. All would be needed in the long, daunting work of cleaning up, rebuilding, and recovery. The Archdiocese of New Orleans, like the entire region, had been through storms before, but nothing like Katrina. This "super storm" would challenge the vitality, creativity, imagination, determination, and yes – the faith of individuals and an institution that

Archdiocese of New Orleans
Coat of Arms

has played such an integral part in the history of the region. There was no reference book to guide the archdiocese in responding to the challenges of Katrina. Plans and actions would have to be directed by native intelligence, prudent judgments, guess work, luck, and an abundance of grace. To be sure, there were missteps and mistakes, hesitations and over-reaching, but these actions always were motivated by fidelity to a mission, namely, to be Church and serve in the name of Jesus.

Abiding Presence

• Original Church of Saint Louis   • Arrival of the Ursulines, 1727

The Catholic Church and the State of Louisiana, especially the southern part of the state, and in particular, the metropolitan New Orleans area, enjoy an historical

relationship of great depth. The first Mass was offered on Louisiana soil in 1699. In 1727 the first Ursuline nuns arrived from France. It was not until 1850 that New Orleans became an archdiocese, 47 years after the Louisiana Purchase and 38 years after Louisiana became the 18th state in the Union.

Archbishop John Shaw blesses ground for the new Notre Dame Seminary, February 8, 1922

In addition to this impressive historical pedigree, the Catholic Church has been in every part of the state. The Archdiocese of New Orleans extends far beyond the boundaries of Orleans Parish. The archdiocese reaches into eight civil parishes: Orleans, Jefferson, St. Bernard, Plaquemines, St. Tammany, St. Charles, St. John the Baptist, and Washington. Hurricane Katrina most severely affected the parishes of Orleans, Jefferson, St. Bernard, and Plaquemines due to the track of the storm, the extensive flooding in these areas. The archdiocese has significant physical presence in these parishes.

• Archbishop Philip Hannan and the 82nd Airborne in St. Anthony's Garden behind St. Louis Cathedral, September 2005

Before Katrina arrived on August 29, 2005, the archdiocese consisted of 142 parishes and eight missions with a Catholic population of 490,898 (the total population within the boundaries of the archdiocese totaled 1,361,488). In 2005, there were 148 active diocesan priests, along with 195 religious order priests, for a total of 343 active priests for service within the archdiocese. The school year had just begun before Katrina's destructive call. The archdiocese operates one of the most comprehensive school systems in the nation. At the beginning of the 2005 school year, there were 109 elementary and secondary schools with a student population of nearly 50,000. The archdiocese offered numerous social services, including, but not limited to, medical care, housing assistance, individual and family counseling, and a wide variety of programs aiding the elderly. Due to this extensive presence, the archdiocese is responsible for a significant number of properties. Finally, the archdiocese is one of the largest private employers in the metro area. The number of active employees, allowing for seasonal fluctuations, ranged between 8,000 and 10,000 individuals.

• Second Harvest volunteers package food for distribution to the hungry

• Two stranded ships in Plaquemines Parish

• Upended pews at St. Ann Chuch in Empire show destructive power of Katrina

The vastness of the archdiocese's presence proved to be a blessing as well as a major challenge after Katrina. The archdiocese suffered significant damages – more than 300 flooded properties – which greatly reduced the capacity to provide those services upon which so many had come to depend. At the same time, the complexity of the archdiocesan network would prove invaluable immediately after the storm, as well as for long-term recovery. Consider the impact of the storm: in addition to the number of water-damaged facilities, the number of active priests serving in the archdiocese declined from 343 in 2005 to 289 in 2009. Operating parishes decreased from 142 to 108 parishes post-Katrina. The Catholic school system faced a significant decline in the number of schools, as well as in the overall student population. To date (2009), 86 schools – both elementary and secondary – have reopened with an approximate population of 40,000 students. (The remarkable story of Catholic education after Katrina will be dealt with in greater detail in Chapter Eight.) The overall financial challenges facing the archdiocese were staggering. The archdiocese suffered $287.8 million in property loss to church-owned facilities (more on the financial challenges facing the archdiocese will be presented in Chapter Seven).

Helicopters drop sandbags to fill a levee break

Archdiocesan office building on Howard Avenue

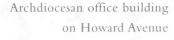

Archbishop Hughes and Deacon David Warriner survey
damage at a Protestant church in Gentilly before
an interfaith news conference

• Outdoor Mass at Our Lady of
Prompt Succor, Chalmette, in 2005

• Everyone thought things would
be back to normal after Katrina passed

long-term health care facilities suffered over $5.9 million in losses; and various community centers, which provide for the basic needs of the poor, experienced almost $1 million in losses. (The heroic efforts of Catholic Charities Archdiocese New Orleans will be recounted in Chapter Three.)

It is important not to get ahead of our story. Katrina was at our doorstep, and the lives of so many would be forever changed. For too many, life would be ended.

Where to Go? What to Do?

As it became clear to just about everyone, Katrina was a massive storm, and it had its sights set on the metro area. The weekend of August 27 and 28 would be anything but business as usual. It was time, long past time, for many to evacuate or anchor down as best they could. Religious services and other archdiocesan activities were officially canceled. Thoughts and prayers were offered for safety, minimal damage and loss of life, and the long road back home. No one could have imagined just how long and steep that road would be.

• Katrina quieted many churches
in the metro area

Traditional sources of revenue, mainly offerings at weekend Masses, were severely curtailed due to churches not being able to reopen, the corresponding decline in church attendance, and the need of many parishioners to divert money to their own recovery needs. Despite the heroics of the Archdiocese New Orleans to continue its mission of humanitarian aid to the wider community, the archdiocese experienced major challenges to its mission. Serious losses (more than $36 million) were experienced by Christopher Homes, which sustained damages to 70 percent of its units;

In the aftermath of the storm, the many people who are part of the archdiocesan family were scattered in varied directions. Communications (to be discussed in Chapter Four) in the hurricane strike areas was next to impossible. The city of New Orleans was not only heavily damaged and under water, but civil society had been washed away. For the most part, there was an absence of law enforcement personnel, except for the small number of brave men and women who kept watch. There seemed to be only two groups left in the city – victims and criminals. It was not until the military entered the area that a sense of order returned. Not since the Civil War had New Orleans been occupied and placed under martial law by federal troops. It was now!

Like so much of the metro area, the archdiocesan administration building on Walmsley Avenue experienced significant wind and water damage and could not be adequately secured. Even if the city had been reopened, the administration building could not be occupied. A crucial challenge arose – where to go? Where and when could the archbishop and his administrative council gather in order to formulate a program for re-entry and recovery?

• Katrina could not bring down flags, windows, or the cross at St. David Church

The most logical choice for relocation was the Diocese of Baton Rouge. It was close to New Orleans which would ease travel and facilitate communication. The Baton Rouge Diocese was not as severely damaged by Katrina's winds, and massive flooding was not a major problem as it was in the New Orleans area. The Catholic Life Center, the administrative office building for the Baton Rouge Diocese, was large enough to meet the personnel, administrative, and ministry needs of the archdiocese as plans for recovery were being formulated.

The logic of proximity and the ability to accommodate archdiocesan requirements should by no means suggest that a great sacrifice would not be required of the Baton Rouge Diocese. The need to find space for archdiocesan staff often required both staffs working out of the same office space. However, under the leadership of Baton Rouge Bishop Robert W. Muench, the Catholic community as a whole, and the various offices of the Baton Rouge Diocese in particular, made "the strangers welcomed" in a true

"The vitality of the churches of New Orleans and Baton Rouge and the cooperation is great. I have never seen the Church more alive; especially under these testy circumstances…With the loss of material things, the growth in Spirit, dependence upon one another and on God will make us stronger than ever before." (Baton Rouge Bishop Robert W. Muench, October 10, 2005, news conference)

spirit of fraternal charity. From office space, to temporary housing, to making diocesan media outlets available, to the many daily needs of the archdiocesan staff, the Catholic community reached out and made this temporary displacement a home of hope. The words of Bishop Muench should be kept in mind, not only as they apply to Katrina, but for the moments of trial yet to come: "In this tragedy, may we unite ourselves to God and one another. For what we have, let us give thanks. For what we need, let us have hope. In the midst of all the challenges we face, may we demonstrate faith and keep perspective and balance. Let us realize God will see us through these difficult days…We as Church, and community need to continue to be at our best."

• Damage to St. Mary's Academy

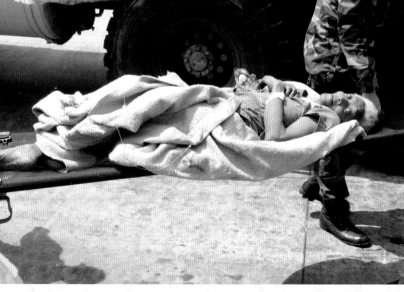

Many of the sick and elderly had to be carried to safety

In the early days and weeks after Katrina, the Baton Rouge Diocese and the wider Baton Rouge area played host to more than 200,000 evacuees. This influx of the displaced caused a tremendous strain on diocesan resources and the region in general. Activities such as driving, eating out and shopping – once taken for granted - became major tasks. Trips that usually took a few minutes now took an hour or more. Restaurants and malls were bursting with people. All this was great for merchants, but it put a strain on nerves and city services. It was as if Baton Rouge had doubled in size in a few weeks.

With so many families displaced for an unknown period of time, it was only natural that parents would begin looking for schools. Parents began a rush to diocesan elementary and secondary Catholic schools in order to continue the education that had just begun before Katrina. This challenge was met with creativity, hospitality, and understanding. Baton Rouge Catholic elementary schools welcomed hundreds of students who were in need of uniforms and supplies.

Many students were not able to provide vital records, and parents often could not pay tuition. Nonetheless, students were accepted and made a part of the school community. Education continued, which was vital for students who needed routine and some sense of normalcy and for parents who needed reduced anxiety over the possibility that the school year would be lost.

Beyond directing students to area Catholic schools, several dislocated New Orleans Catholic high schools took a different approach. In cooperation with St. Michael the Archangel High School, a satellite secondary school was established at its campus with a late afternoon into evening schedule, which provided education to hundreds of New Orleans-area students. Some New Orleans religious-sponsored schools re-opened at affiliated schools to accommodate their displaced students. These early signs of the important role of schools in a time of displacement would only grow as the return to metro New Orleans became possible. In the words of one parent, "I know my child is safe and in a learning environment. I've begun to think about home and everything that it will take to be together again. For now, my family is sleeping a little better."

"My second (and perhaps, most lasting) observation was that the people with whom we met were inspirational. They were tremendously strong, resilient, and optimistic. Faith united people of different religious traditions, socio-economic classes, and ethnic background…There was still love for the city and hope for its future." (Letter from Rev. John J. Jenkins, C.S.C., President of the University of Notre Dame, on the involvement of the university community in the recovery work in New Orleans.)

Not only was there cooperation between the two diocesan school offices, but with so many evacuees in need of basic and special care it was imperative that there be coordination and collaboration between the Catholic Charities offices. And such was the case in splendid fashion. Catholic Charities of Baton Rouge provided office and service space for such basic needs as food, clothing, and shelters. Both offices worked together in providing medical, counseling, and special needs services to countless displaced persons. In addition to the joint efforts of both diocesan offices, much-welcomed assistance was provided by Catholic Charities USA, Catholic Relief Services and the American Red Cross. This massive joint humanitarian aid effort was critical, especially for those who were confined in shelters. (In the next chapter, a detailing of Catholic Charities Archdiocese of New Orleans will be presented.)

These examples of cooperation among diocesan departments, as well as with agencies within and outside the state, would prove essential for the care of those in need. It cannot be stated often enough the extraordinary nature of the response by the Diocese of Baton Rouge to those in need. The genuine hospitality and Christian charity shown were authentic embodiments of Gospel values. Doors, departments, homes, and hearts were swung wide open to receive those who suffered a great loss. No expression of gratitude is sufficient in response to the love shown. Those who showed such a love would no doubt say that none was necessary. Perhaps there is one sign of gratitude that may arise from the Katrina experience, namely, to follow the example of Christian hospitality exhibited by the church community of Baton Rouge. To whom much is given, much is expected. Imitation is the highest tribute.

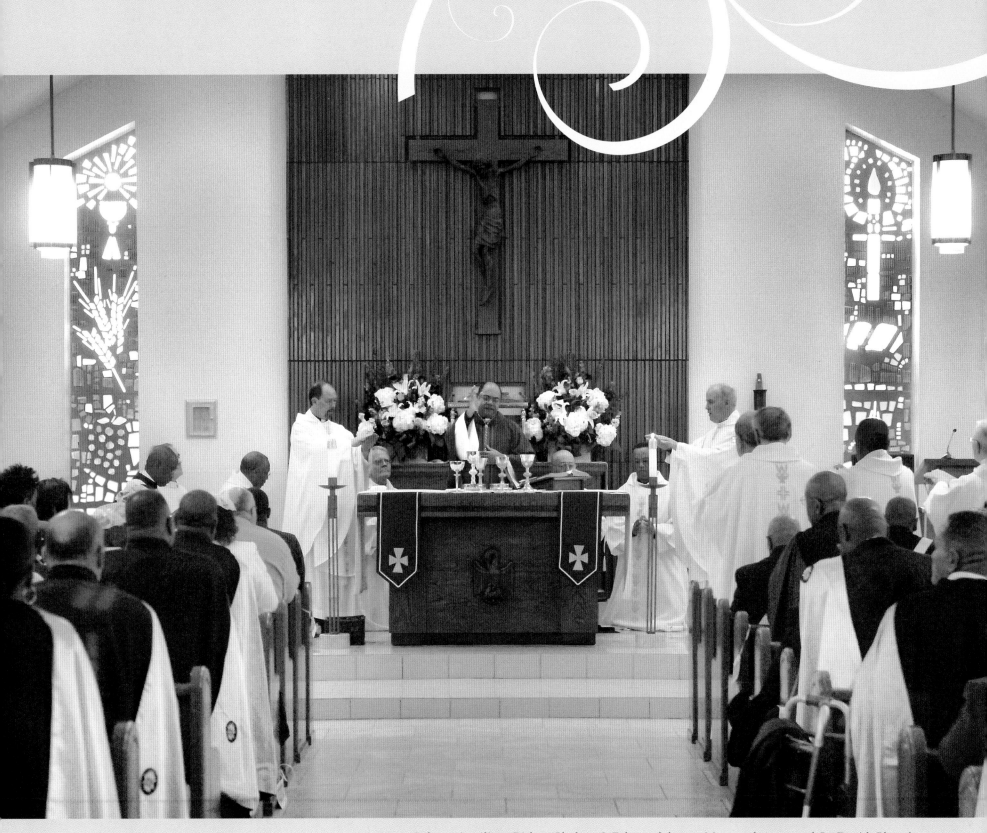

New Orleans Auxiliary Bishop Shelton J. Fabre celebrates Mass at the restored St. David Church

Now that a new, though temporary, location was secured, the pressing need was formulating an overall plan of action and setting priorities for going forward. From the first, under the leadership of Archbishop Hughes, the primary priority, guided by Gospel principles, was "for people." From this "People First Principle," specific objectives became clear. Those still in harm's way needed to be rescued and accounted for, and a safe shelter found. The physical needs for food, water, and clothing had to be provided; proper medical services for individuals in need had to be dispensed; and it was crucial that those separated from loved ones make contact.

The spiritual needs of people became more acute after the storm. In order to meet these pressing needs, it was crucial to make contact with priests who themselves had to evacuate and were scattered over several states. With communications practically non-existent, making connections was no easy task. However, many priests were able to reach archdiocesan officials in Baton Rouge. A pastoral plan was formulated to provide priestly ministry and presence to significant numbers of evacuees in Baton Rouge, Lafayette, Lake Charles, Alexandria, Houma, Thibodaux, Shreveport, Jackson, Houston, Dallas, and Atlanta. In cooperation with the local bishop of each diocese, a priest was assigned as a liaison in each diocese to reach out to New Orleanians in need of pastoral care. Some bishops went so far as to offer a number of their priests to provide ministerial services.

Catholic Charities Archdiocese New Orleans, working with religious and secular partners, was charged with the monumental task of responding to a wide range of human needs, from basic physical requirements to the more complex and specialized needs (usually those related to medical needs). It should be kept in mind that Catholic Charities is uniquely qualified and structured to respond to this wide range of needs because of its 45 different programs. As will be recounted in a future chapter (see Chapter Three), Catholic Charities Archdiocese of New Orleans would come to play

The critical work of implementing the numerous responses by the archdiocese to Katrina was assigned to Auxiliary Bishop Roger Morin. Bishop Morin was well-suited to lead the effort to help people in need. He accomplished his duties with great professional competence, all the while directly suffering from Katrina himself. Bishop Morin had to be rescued from Notre Dame Seminary and transported to Baton Rouge. In the first days after Katrina, Bishop Morin's residence was burned to the ground, and much of his priestly memorabilia was lost to the flames. His chalice was severely damaged but recovered. Bishop Morin's chalice was restored and used for the offering of Mass at many church parishes he visited after the storm.

Parishioners of Our Lady of Lourdes in Slidell give prayerful thanks for faith, life and each other

an even more vital role as the shock of Katrina wore off and people began the agonizing process of returning home and rebuilding.

Now that the immediate needs of evacuees were addressed, attention could be focused on the archdiocese's employee family. The Archdiocese of New Orleans is a major employer in the metro New Orleans area. Archbishop Hughes wanted to exercise the utmost care and responsiveness to staff members and their families. With over 9,000 employees, a number of employment issues arose, adding to the anxieties of employees. Among the concerns of employees the following were uppermost: would employment continue after the storm? If so, to what extent would employees be retained? If an employee had to be let go, would any compensation be offered? Also, if an employee would not be retained, what would become of his or her medical benefits and retirement? Would any help be offered to those seeking new employment? The Office of Human Resources was responsible for working with employees during this tense time. The comment of one employee, Ava, was representative of a number of employees' feelings: "I was very nervous about my job. I really needed my medical benefits and salary. The people I spoke to for the archdiocese were professional and really tried to lower my anxiety. They really listened to me." These questions, real and urgent, would be answered shortly.

Several days after the storm, Archbishop Hughes and his administrative team (members of the administrative council, along with various office heads) were holding daily meetings for the purpose of information – updating the status of ongoing projects and planning the next steps. It became increasingly clear that issues surrounding employees were becoming more urgent. This was especially the case after erroneous media reports indicated the archdiocese was going to lay off all of its employees. Of course, this caused a good deal of distress among people already heavily burdened. In order to set the record straight, Archbishop Hughes used his daily news briefing to calm fears and to inform employees and the general public of plans concerning employment issues. Specifically, there were to be NO wholesale layoffs. Of the 9,000 employees, a small minority would not be able to continue with the archdiocese. The archbishop went on to explain that due to the shrinking size of some parishes, schools, archdiocesan agencies, and the central administration, a number of positions would be eliminated or would not be filled at that time. Furthermore, the archdiocese was eager to assist those employees who could not be offered either their old job or a new one in another department. The archdiocese was also active in working with state unemployment agencies and FEMA officials to obtain assistance until new employment could be secured. Archbishop Hughes, after consultation with officials from the Finance Department, decided employees would be paid through October 1, 2005, in addition to receiving health benefits through October 30. At the end of the day, the Archdiocese reluctantly laid off 881 employees.

Time Toward Home

As more and more demands were being placed on both New Orleans and Baton Rouge dioceses, it became evident that the Catholic Life Center, the Baton Rouge diocesan administrative headquarters, could no longer accommodate both staffs. It was time for the archdiocese to find new temporary administrative headquarters. A location in the Baton Rouge area, close to the Catholic Life Center – Bon Carré – was leased until the end of the calendar year. An important objective was to establish an administrative presence back in New Orleans in the new year.

"Being exiled from our homes and workplaces is not easy. Even as we express appreciation for the provision of a home away from home, I share with you the challenge of exile. Like the Jews of old, we long for a return to our holy city. I pray for you. I ask that you pray for me. I believe that God calls us to move from being victims to victors in Christ Jesus." (Message from Archbishop Alfred C. Hughes to evacuees, September 27, 2005)

By the end of October, there was a significant increase in activity within the archdiocese as it related to the metro area. Priests were offering Mass in parishes, as well as in makeshift locations. More schools were reopening, which facilitated the return of families, the opening of more businesses, and encouraged an increase in the general rebuilding activity of the region. Catholic Charities Archdiocese New Orleans was increasing its presence in the metro area as needs increased with the growing number of people returning home. More and more, the archdiocese was in the process of closing down one phase of its post-Katrina operations – evacuation and temporary administration – and beginning a new phase or post-Katrina II – a return to New Orleans and the reopening of administrative offices at the chancery building on Walmsley Avenue.

The return to the chancery would take time. The building experienced extensive damage to its interior structure as well as to the electrical and computer networks. The time had come to return to New Orleans. With the pace of recovery both for the metro area and the archdiocese increasing rapidly, the return to the chancery would have to be delayed until the facility was fit to occupy. The decision was made to find another temporary headquarters within New Orleans proper. The decision was made to use the Incarnate Word School buildings, which had not been in operation for some time, as the location for operations. It was close to the chancery, and since the property belonged to the archdiocese, an added financial burden could be avoided. A major transformation of the buildings was required. Nonetheless, the archdiocese had returned from the diaspora. The next, and, hopefully, last move would be a grateful, joyful homecoming to the chancery. This important event was accomplished in April 2006.

Light in Darkness

Lights needed to be restored. Not just the lights of the city by means of electrical power, but that light which shines in the darkness of despair and is not overcome. It is that Light and Life which glows in every heart through grace. In the days and months after Katrina, there was much darkness of a physical and spiritual kind. The temptation to despair was intense. A paralyzing fear filled the city to a depth beyond that of flood waters. Above the needs of the body, people were hungry for that which would nourish the soul. In addition to food, clothing, and shelter, people needed light, hope, and encouragement. These items could not be shipped in or manufactured by intellect or will. Such essentials of the soul come as gifts from beyond and enliven the drooping spirit, quench the thirsty soul, and sustain the weary body. Who will provide such gifts? What will serve as a channel for this light and hope? When will such gifts come?

• St. Dominic Church in Lakeview made a remarkable recovery

As to the question of the Provider, for the person of faith, the answer is obvious – Almighty God. The testimony of Scripture, Church tradition, and general human experience holds that God is the giver of all good gifts and graces. In bright days and star-drenched nights, in dark and starless nights, the providential care of God is present, ordering all things to their proper end. God is involved in human history with us and for us. Nothing is beyond or hidden from the mind and will of God. Even in those days of great suffering, perhaps most especially in those times of tears, God is not only with us, but God also acts on our behalf. The Cross of the Suffering Servant reveals God's solidarity with the broken-hearted. The empty tomb of Easter offers a hope against hope with its message of new life. The God who took on our poor flesh, died our human death, and who now lives at the right hand of the Father does not leave us orphans. God is faithful. The Holy Spirit is sent to dwell in each heart, and in the people of God – the Church.

It is through the Church, the historical and tangible sacrament of Jesus' faithful presence, that those gifts for the soul and body are ministered. The Church is not only the Mystical Body, but also incarnational, a physical presence. Where people are hurting and without hope, displaced and desperately longing for home, bewildered and searching for meaning, devastated and in need of comfort, the Church

• Catholic schools continued
education and worship

• Archbishop Gregory Aymond and Father John Arnone distribute
Communion at restored Our Lady of Lourdes Church in Violet in 2009

must be there because Jesus Christ is there. The Church was present ministering in the name of Christ to those in need. The ministry of the Church varied in mode as well as location: from the archbishop who visited evacuees in shelters and offered Mass at St. Louis Cathedral; to priests providing pastoral support, administering sacraments, and opening their parish churches; to members of Catholic Charities working to reconnect families, and providing for the most basic of physical, medical, and financial needs. Schools played their part by reopening and providing students and parents with a sense of routine, security and normalcy. In all of these ways, the Church was present, and the underlying motivation was the same – to respond to the hidden presence of Jesus in the hurting among us.

As to the question of when – a question of time – the answer of faith is not the solving of a problem but an invitation to enter a great mystery – God's providential care for all that exists. God's ways with the world do not fit our demand for clarity and predictability. We lack direct access to the mind of God. This is not to say that we are without "a rumor of angels" and "signals of transcendence." They are all around and deeply embedded in human experience. The gifts that nourish the soul, the gifts of grace, come from the "Eternal now" and "the Beyond in our midst." These gifts for the soul are for *every* time and season. They are beyond our poor powers to create or will. They are ours to *receive* with gratitude. And they come from the One who bestows every blessing and grace. These gifts are mediated, passing through what St. Thomas Aquinas termed "secondary causes" – individuals, institutions, communities, and events by which the God who dwells in unapproachable light becomes present to and for us. Each time the Gospel is preached, the Eucharist offered, a cup of water given, food shared, a hand extended, an embrace of solidarity and consolation shown, and silent presence and prayer lifted up, the Beyond is in our midst, the Eternal is now; the gifts of the Spirit are shared. (More will be discussed about these themes in our final chapter.)

The Vietnamese in New Orleans East were hard hit by Katrina

Smaller in Size, Not in Zeal

The archdiocese, like the metro area, not surprisingly, has shrunk in size and resources. Equally not surprising, this down-sizing has not affected the intensity of commitment to Gospel service. In this post-Katrina world there are fewer priests, religious, and deacons providing ministerial service. There are fewer schools and parishes, especially within the most affected areas. The workforce of the archdiocese has been reduced because of necessity, as well as a reduction in resources to sustain pre-Katrina levels. Economic realities have also reduced the number of services that can be offered. While the archdiocese is smaller, one thing is clear — the work goes on, and the determination to serve in the name of Jesus will never die. A reduction in size and resources calls for a renewed sense of stewardship and prudence. However, the guiding principle of all archdiocesan efforts, as articulated time and again by Archbishop Hughes — "people first" — has never been compromised.

This chapter and the preceding one have been overviews of the New Orleans metropolitan area and the Archdiocese of New Orleans. These overviews are written in broad strokes and generalities. It is said "the devil is in the details." But so are the angels, saints, and ordinary people called to do extraordinary things in unprecedented circumstances.

It is to the details of the archdiocese's response to the devastation of Katrina — a response of hope — that we now turn.

Auxiliary Bishop Fabre blesses the holy water font at the restored St. David Church

Chapter 3 ———————

CATHOLIC CHARITIES ARCHDIOCESE OF NEW ORLEANS: EARLY RESPONDERS IN LOVE

The horrific images of the September 11, 2001, terrorist attack are forever part of this generation's collective memory, much like the pictures of December 7, 1941 (Pearl Harbor) were to a previous generation.

A stunned America and a shocked world could not believe what was unthinkable to civilized people – using commercial airliners filled with passengers as weapons of terrorism. These innocuous planes were used as death missiles targeting government buildings and the World Trade Center (WTC), a symbol of America's global power. Again and again, we saw planes being flown into the sides of the WTC. There were images of black smoke, collapsing towers, the Pentagon on fire, smoke and ashes rising from the island of Manhattan, panic in the streets as people were in full flight from Ground Zero and a genuine fear across the nation, as we were left to wonder where and when next.

There was another image that will forever remain, namely, that of men and women, mostly in uniforms, rushing into the danger. Against all common sense, these heroes were in the grasp of an uncommon valor. Numerous men and women, termed "first responders," charged toward the fire, the smoke and rubble, the cries of the injured, and the bodies. Theirs was the task of caring for the injured, rescuing the trapped, and marking the location of the dead – all without a thought for their own well-being.

How do we get such people? How are we blessed by those who give their last full measure for strangers? Obviously, from God's grace, building on character. Expert training is also essential, especially in a crisis for which there is little time to think and plan. One must simply act. Lives are to be saved. Not to be discounted is the desire to make a difference and not just exist – to add life to days and not just days to life. Simply put, the meaning of life is to live a meaningful life. Those first responders of 9/11 – police, fire, and medical personnel, to name but the most visible – turned Ground Zero, in the words of New York's Cardinal Egan, into "Ground Hero."

• Volunteers from all over the country, including Steubenville, Ohio Bishop R. Daniel Conlon, far left, helped rebuild Louisiana and the Gulf Coast

Volunteers and employees of Second Harvest Food Bank unload water from a military helicopter. Photo courtesy of Second Harvest Food Bank of Greater New Orleans & Acadiana.

by the archbishop. There were three crucial reasons for its selection. First, CCANO is poised to respond to everyday and specialized human needs, employing its standing network of social services (housing, counseling, medical services, education, emergency relief services, youth and senior citizen care, and a host of family services to address critical needs). Not only does CCANO possess a vast network of service providers, but it has been doing such ministry since 1727, when the Ursuline nuns began such ministry in the Lower Ninth Ward.

Fast forward to 2005. This time the destruction was not the deranged raging of terrorists but the fury of nature. It was once again time for those "first responders" to charge into danger. They would be the first ones who would meet the needs of those reeling from Katrina. For the Catholic Church, the task fell to members of Catholic Charities Archdiocese of New Orleans (CCANO).

When it became clear that Katrina would not bypass the metro area, public officials requested the aid of the archdiocese to meet the many needs that would arise after the storm passed. No one could have imagined just how great the level of need was, especially with 80 percent of the city under water. Just three days after the storm, Archbishop Hughes, members of the Administrative Council and the co-presidents of Catholic Charities were able to meet in Baton Rouge for an initial strategy meeting.

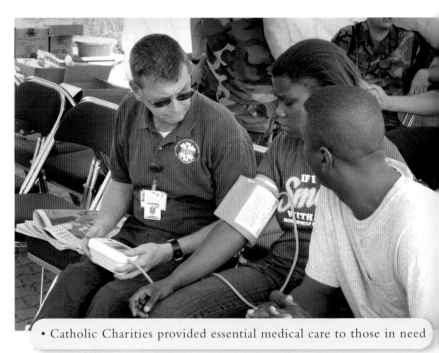

• Catholic Charities provided essential medical care to those in need

Why Catholic Charities Archdiocese of New Orleans?

Some may wonder why Catholic Charities Archdiocese of New Orleans was designated as an "early" responder

Secondly, those who participate in the work of Catholic Charities Archdiocese of New Orleans are highly trained. The needs of those seeking assistance often call for expertise in such areas as medicine, finances, education, and counseling. Highly qualified and specialized members of CCANO, both employees and volunteers, were needed to care for those suffering from Katrina.

A member of Catholic Charities' Hispanic Apostolate Community Services team at a Partners for Healthy Babies Fair. Photo courtesy of Catholic Charities Archdiocese of New Orleans.

Thirdly, and most importantly, is the mission which guides all the work of Catholic Charities. It reads as follows:

Respecting the dignity and potential of each person, Catholic Charities Archdiocese of New Orleans collaborates with the wider community to serve them in need. Impelled by the love and teaching of Jesus Christ, we offer life-giving programs, advocate for the voiceless, and empower the poor and vulnerable to foster a more just society.

Dignity through respect

Service through love

Justice through advocacy and empowerment

Unity through prayer

Catholic Charities serves people of all faiths and employs people of all faiths.

Without a mission, a common vision and core set of values, an organization will perish; the individuals within the organization will be off doing their own projects. Without a sense of a common purpose and the common good, such individualism often leads to a dispirited community working at cross purposes and feeling isolated. This becomes acutely evident during times of crisis. The effectiveness of Catholic Charities Archdiocese of New Orleans, which has been widely praised, grew out of ministries grounded in a common mission.

The grounding mission of CCANO, along with the core values of respecting each person's dignity as made in the image of God, energized the three-fold work of the CCANO. In response to Katrina, CCANO exemplified the values of loving service, seeking an ever greater sense of justice by speaking for and with those who are often marginalized, promoting a true freedom through empowerment, and finally, by building a sense of solidarity through prayer. The three-fold work of CCANO involved an early response, post-Katrina recovery, and the ongoing work of rebuilding. To each of these we now turn our attention.

"Rebuilding should be carried out in a manner that treats the area's poorest citizens with the same respect and dignity as the more affluent…Without government intervention and assistance, the market will not be kind to the less fortunate … their brave spirits are in need of hope – of a plan for tomorrow, next week, next month and next year." – CCANO co-president Jim Kelly's testimony before Congress, January 2006)

Early Response

Members of Catholic Charities Archdiocese of New Orleans did not wait for the storm to strike and pass. When it became evident that Katrina had designs on the metro area, Gordon R. Wadge and James R. Kelly, co-presidents of CCANO, went to the Superdome to distribute food and water which had been sent earlier in preparation for shelter evacuees. As events unfolded, this action turned out to be a real godsend. Branching out from the Superdome, CCANO,

through its affiliated ministry, Second Harvest Food Bank, reopened food distribution centers where possible.

Along with meeting immediate physical needs, CCANO responded to the spiritual and psychological needs suffered by survivors from the aftermath of Katrina. CCANO counselors brought comfort, information about loved ones, authentic news about the condition of the city, and provided a grace-presence through prayer, Scriptures, and a simple calming and soothing presence which offered hope. One of the places most in need of their grace-presence was the Louis Armstrong New Orleans International Airport, where many of the frail and elderly were transported in order to meet their special needs. It also fell to CCANO counselors to minister to those who minister. Many first responders had worked to the point of physical and emotional exhaustion. They were in need of rest, renewal, and time to just be with others who were engaged in a common work.

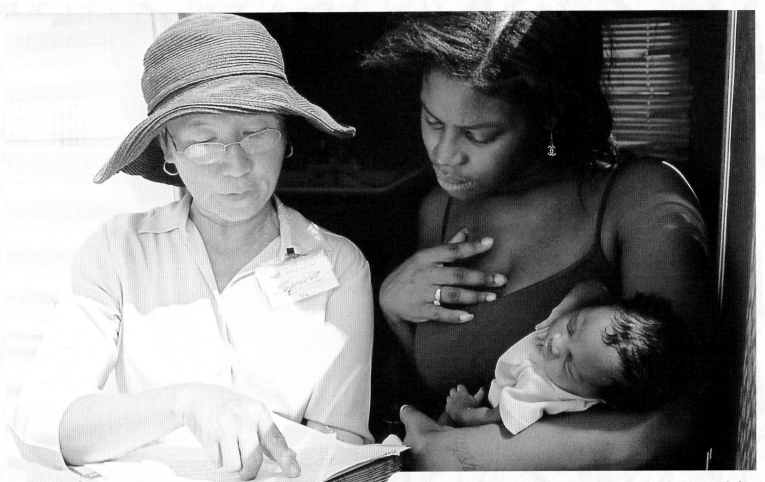

A Catholic Charities' Louisiana Spirit staff member shares resources with a young mother living in a FEMA trailer in New Orleans after Hurricane Katrina. Louisiana Spirit provided crisis counselors who went door-to-door in the community to help people in need, and was a Catholic Charities program through 2007. Photo courtesy of Catholic Charities USA.

Shaula Lovera (left), Dr. Elmore Rigamer, Medical Director for Catholic Charities (center), and an unidentified responder discuss the Catholic Charities Archdiocese of New Orleans emergency response in Baton Rouge shortly after Hurricane Katrina
Photo courtesy of Catholic Charities USA.

Within days after the storm, two things became clear: first, the destruction in the metro area was more extensive than initially thought; and second, CCANO would have to relocate its operational headquarters in order to effectively respond to the crisis. All of this would require more than Catholic Charities Archdiocese of New Orleans could muster on its own. The national office of Catholic Charities USA dispatched significant personnel and replenished various resources which were depleted or in danger of being exhausted. A center of operation was set up in a Baton Rouge hotel ballroom. The largest humanitarian effort in American history was about to commence.

Local restaurants, such as Drago's, prepared daily meals for first responders in front of St. Dominic Church in Lakeview.

• Saints owner/executive vice president Rita Benson LeBlanc spends time with two clients at the PACE Center named for her grandmother, Shirley Landry Benson.

centers was highly problematic. CCANO provided mobile kitchens so the food could be distributed to those in need. Throughout this initial phase of operation, CCANO was tested, time and time again, to find new and creative ways of doing its ministry. What is most extraordinary is the realization that these early responders of CCANO were themselves victims of the ravages of Katrina. They had loved ones with whom they had lost contact or hadn't seen for days. Staff members were left to wonder about their own homes and the extent of damages to their belongings. Counselors from CCANO were not immune from anxiety and fatigue. Yet the multi-faceted ministry of CCANO continued, to a remarkable extent, in both scope of services and depth of genuine compassion.

From this Baton Rouge operations center a myriad of services were set in motion: a clinic was organized to treat first responders with immunizations, medical care, counseling, and rest from long hours of physically and emotionally taxing work. CCANO sent teams of counselors into evacuation shelters, motels, and other sites where the displaced were holing up. Providing food was crucial, especially to the poor, yet the ability to reach distribution

Volunteers work to clean out an elderly woman's home as part of Catholic Charities' Operation Helping Hands. The program was started in November 2005, about three months after Hurricane Katrina. Operation Helping Hands initially brought volunteers from around the country to gut flooded homes of the elderly and disabled, and currently brings in volunteers to actually rebuild homes for people. Helping Hands has welcomed more than 25,000 volunteers from colleges, church groups and businesses since Hurricane Katrina.

The first few days and weeks went by like the winged chariot of time. So much to do and so much left undone. So much still lay ahead. This first phase of response was coming to an end. It became clear that Phase II, recovery, was crucial if the metro area had any realistic hope of rebuilding. Phase III, Catholic Charities Archdiocese of New Orleans' own "road home" plan, would become a key component in the region's overall rebuilding efforts.

Recovery

Staff members of CCANO, who had been acting out of the temporary operations center in Baton Rouge, began returning to the metro area. What they found was like nothing seen on television – it was worse! It seemed as if a nuclear bomb had been detonated. CCANO workers, with mouths wide open, eyes filled with tears, and shaking heads unable to speak, saw destruction in all its forms. Some houses were left intact but were now resting blocks away from their foundations. Other houses were completely destroyed. It was not uncommon to see cars and machinery resting atop a house. Canals were filled with debris. Electrical poles and lines were lying about the streets. In some places, the Katrina waters were still in standing pools. It seemed as if there was no part of the metro area that was left unaffected. At night, the city was in almost complete darkness, providing an eerie sign of what many felt inside. The magnitude of the destruction could easily dispirit even the most cockeyed optimist. And the military, on the ground and in the air, seemed to be everywhere – thank God.

Like most of the metropolitan area, CCANO's headquarters in New Orleans were severely damaged and uninhabitable.

• College student volunteers help with cleanup

Archbishop Hughes, second from left, thanks Steubenville Bishop R. Daniel Conlon for helping to gut the home of Melanie Ally, left, and her son Alan

In making a virtue of necessity, the work of CCANO had to continue, but in non-traditional ways and unexpected places. People and their needs after Katrina were highly mobile, and for good reason, since many had to change residency

A Padua Pediatrics resident gets a visit from her parents and a staff member.
Photo courtesy of Catholic Charities Archdiocese of New Orleans.

a number of times. Therefore, CCANO had to be on the move as well. Temporary offices were established where available. CCANO employees made their homes available so the ministries of CCANO would not be interrupted. Some employees operated out of their cars, delivering much-needed goods and services to those in need.

Phase III of Catholic Charities Archdiocese of New Orleans' response to Katrina was the most ambitious, and would require a long-term commitment to rebuilding the metro area. It would require money – and more. It would call for significant numbers of volunteers, skilled and unskilled, to pledge a major donation of time. Creativity, imagination, the ability to collaborate with others of diverse backgrounds, and the grace of patience for the long and winding road ahead, became essential qualities. It is to this third and continuous phase that we now turn our sights.

Rebuilding

Catholic Charities Archdiocese of New Orleans set for itself an ambitious three-year rebuilding plan. Better yet, the enormous array of human needs made it imperative that bold thinking, coupled with prudent action, be the order of the day. This three-year plan would include five major areas: response and recovery, housing, healthcare, education, and economic development. A word about each is in order.

The first and most important area of the rebuilding plan was Response and Recovery. In light of the great need felt throughout the metro area, CCANO set a goal for itself in which case management and counseling would be provided to 20,000 individuals. As of 2008, this goal was not

only reached, but surpassed, with 54,600 people receiving professional guidance and services. In addition to case management, a related dimension of this first major area was the need to provide direct assistance to those facing financial challenges. Again CCANO set an ambitious goal – to provide as much as $7 million in direct assistance to the most needy of families. Again, CCANO exceeded its goal, doubling the assistance provided, with $15,035,538 of direct aid being distributed.

"As a single person on Social Security disability, I had no flood insurance, only homeowners'. I had no one to help me. I don't know what I would have done without the blessing of Catholic Charities helping me. This was a blessing from Jesus Christ to send a 14-member crew to clean and gut my home ... Without your organization, people like me could not afford to get the work done." (Jocelyn M.)

Catholic Charities targeted housing as the second major area of the rebuilding project. Once again, CCANO's vision was bold – it needed to be. Hurricane Katrina and the subsequent flooding caused severe damage to many homes. This housing destruction and shortage was keenly felt, not surprisingly, among the poor, the elderly, and those in the

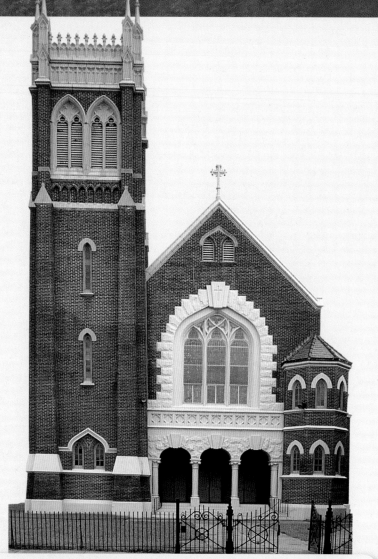

• The Shirley Landry Benson PACE Center at St. Cecilia.
Photo courtesy of Catholic Charities Archdiocese of New Orleans.

A Catholic Charities' Louisiana Spirit crisis counselor shares resources with a man rebuilding his home in 2006. Louisiana Spirit provided crisis counselors who went door-to-door in the community to help people in need and was a Catholic Charities program through 2007. Photo courtesy of Catholic Charities USA.

region who could least afford to repair and rebuild. The goal for housing was set for the repair and rebuilding of 2,400 homes and apartments. Besides the repairing and rebuilding of existing dwellings, CCANO was committed to developing and building 1,200 new homes and 3,400 new apartments. Not left out of the CCANO's goal-setting were those who needed both housing and healthcare along with social services. The effects of Katrina were especially hard on those with special needs. A goal of reaching 2,500 people with these needs was set.

The results of this bold goal-setting are impressive: as of 2008, 1,925 homes have been gutted. In terms of rebuilding, CCANO has rebuilt 113 homes, with 717 more houses under construction. Also, there are 1,524 dwellings under development, along with 1,450 homes in a pre-development stage. As to those with special needs, the goal of 2,500 has been reached, and in fact, almost doubled, with 4,198 people requiring medical and support services being cared for.

This special needs' population includes those children with developmental disabilities, the abused, disturbed children who have been neglected and emotionally troubled, battered and homeless women, those in need of family services, children and families who suffer chronic mental illness, and those who are living with AIDS. Once again, Catholic Charities Archdiocese of New Orleans has far surpassed its goal.

The third major area of rebuilding was healthcare, which included the crucial component of sound nutrition. In many ways, sound health practices begin with sound eating habits. Sustaining health also requires proper eating habits and nutritious food. CCANO wanted to provide 177 million

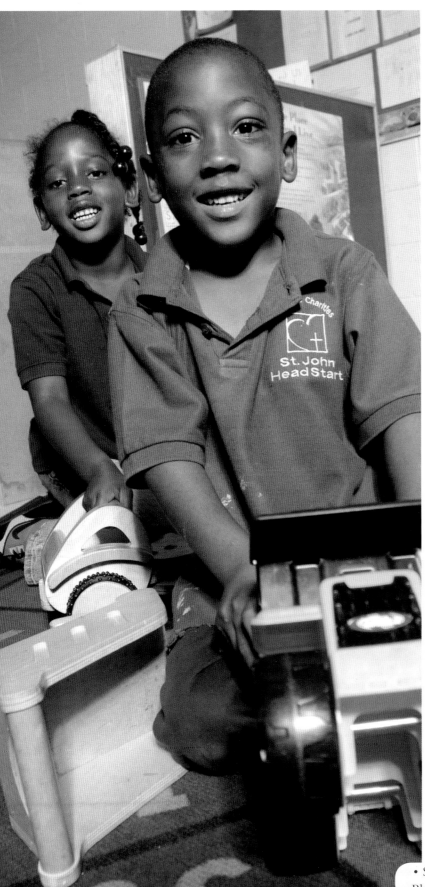

pounds of food to families and agencies that feed the hungry in the metro area and throughout the state. By the end of 2008, CCANO, through Second Harvest Food Bank had distributed more than 156 million pounds of food. While falling slightly short of its three-year goal, the work of food distribution continues.

The goal of food distribution (177 million pounds) cannot be separated from the closely related objective of *providing meals* to the hungry. The goal was to provide a *minimum* of 960,000 meals. As of the end of the fiscal year 2008, CCANO had provided 61,175,858 meals to the hungry! The foundation for sound health, through proper nutrition, had been laid. This foundation became essential in light of the physical and emotional stress caused by Katrina.

Hurricane Katrina not only took its toll on the body but on the emotional well being of people as well. Hence, mental healthcare became a priority for CCANO. As one

Catholic Charities provides much-needed help for working mothers

• Students at St. John the Baptist Head Start Center learn and play. Photo courtesy of Catholic Charities Archdiocese of New Orleans.

might expect, crisis intervention and counseling were the services most needed and provided by CCANO. A goal of 200,000 recipients was set for providing crisis intervention and counseling. The response was staggering. As of the end of fiscal year 2008, CCANO's professional staff provided these mental healthcare services to 864,547 people (extraordinary even when taking into account that there may be some duplicate counting due to the same person availing themselves of related services offered by Catholic Charities). In addition to crisis intervention and subsequent counseling, CCANO sought to expand its counseling services to include clinical counseling. While a target of 6,000 was set, CCANO provided clinical counseling for 6,491 individuals.

Hurricane Katrina caused special stress for children (which spilled over to stressful relationships between children and parents, children and their peers within the school community). Catholic Charities Archdiocese of New Orleans was prepared to offer counseling to 20,000 children, parents, and faculty. As of 2008, 4,787 children, parents, and faculty had taken advantage of these services. Since these services were for Catholic schools, one could reasonably speculate that Catholic schools might have their own counseling resources and develop their own programs for parents and faculty. Parents with economic means may have sought private counseling services.

Healthcare involves more than the psychological dimensions of the human person. Effective healthcare requires a holistic approach. CCANO sought to provide medical care to 20,780. Medical services as of fiscal year 2008 reached 4,483 persons. While the gap between the goal and the actual delivery may seem disappointing, several factors should be kept in mind. After Katrina, the metro area experienced a severe shortage of qualified medical personnel. Those in need of medical care may have sought help from other agencies or were able to secure needed services in the private sector. The metro area did not repopulate as rapidly or as extensively as was expected. Hence, the actual need was below the projected need. It should be kept in mind that the willingness and ability to provide medical services is ongoing.

• One of CCANO's foster grandparents helps a student with his homework

Catholic Charities' Operation Helping Hands volunteers remove a mattress from a home that had been sitting in flood waters from Hurricane Katrina for weeks

• Catholic Charities volunteers organized
relief efforts to distribute food to the needy

The fourth major area of CCANO's rebuilding plan centered on education. While not directly linked to the archdiocesan school system, CCANO does conduct educational programs outside of, and in addition to, those offered by the various traditional school settings. Educational opportunities offered by CCANO include programs for early childhood, afterschool and summer. The report card for Catholic Charities in terms of goal and actual service is quite good. The goal for early childhood education was for 1,800 children to receive instruction. The figures for the 2008 report indicated that 1,063 children had been served. In terms of afterschool and summer educational opportunities, the goal was 4,600 children with a realization of 3,691 youth involved in some type of program (as in previous reports this is through the end of fiscal 2008). Teens and young adults were not left out. CCANO was prepared to educate 1,700 individuals. In nearly reaching its goal, CCANO has provided educational services for 1,560 teens and young adults. As with some medical goals not reached (school counseling, medical care, and early childhood education), it should be remembered that economic hardships may have forced parents to sacrifice educational plans. Many adults had to find additional work to

supplement their primary employment. Young people also looked to gain employment so as to provide for extra family income. Some young people took employment as a means for future educational opportunities (college, technical, or career schooling). As with other medical areas of CCANO's overall educational program, the work of Catholic Charities Archdiocese of New Orleans is ongoing.

"I was a convicted felon at age 15, and I came out of prison a grown man. There aren't many opportunities in the city for people like me. This program was a blessing." (Joseph Jordan on Cornerstone Builders of CCANO)

The final area of CCANO's three-year rebuilding plan was economic development. Not surprisingly, the focus was on jobs. The need to develop a highly skilled and productive workforce is always a crucial concern. This issue became more acute due to the scope and magnitude of Katrina. The task of rebuilding after the storm posed a particular challenge, namely, to find both highly skilled and unskilled workers from a general population that was severely depleted. Before significant rebuilding of structures and the infrastructure could proceed, the enormous task of cleaning up had to be accomplished. In addition to the local population,

Catholic Charities
Archdiocese of New Orleans
and program partners
who collaborated during
Hurricane Katrina recovery.

economic development, set a goal for itself of providing job training, placement and development for 3,000 individuals. Since Katrina 3,842 people have received these job-related services. CCANO continues to provide these opportunities as the work of rebuilding and the need for economic development continues. The challenges left from Katrina and the downturn in the national economy (the global recession has also hurt the local economy) only magnified the importance of CCANO's comprehensive job training, placement and development programs.

the metro area witnessed a large influx of workers, many of whom were Hispanic and Latinos. This influx of the Spanish-speaking individuals gave rise to a number of new challenges ranging from food and housing to medical care and education. The Hispanic Apostolate Community Services, a part of CCANO, worked in collaboration with other community service agencies to provide the resources to meet these needs. These workers, along with those drawn from the metro area, made a significant contribution to the rebuilding of the region. This contribution extended beyond the general clean-up of the area. Many family members secured employment in the service industry which had reopened for business and helped other establishments to open, while skilled workers provided much-needed basic services, and, in general, helped to jump start the economy and repopulate the area.

Not only short-term workers would be needed, but if rebuilding was to be truly effective, a workforce would be needed which could fill a wide array of needs. Catholic Charities Archdiocese of New Orleans, committed to

• Food for Families completes its first distribution in St. Bernard Parish.

Each of the major areas of CCANO's three-year rebuilding plan, in order to be effective, required a number of essential and creative programs. While not providing a comprehensive list of all Catholic Charities' services the following deserve mention. Several *Community Centers* provided direct assistance to Katrina victims in the immediate aftermath of the storm. This assistance included providing cash for food, rent, medicine, and utilities. Also included was extensive counseling for those experiencing trauma in the wake of the storm. This early response has been extended into a

A worker cleans out the flooded basement of the archdiocesan office building at 1000 Howard Avenue

long-term program involving case management. In addition to financial assistance, case management included an analysis of needs, a detailed plan for meeting those needs and goals through self-sufficiency and empowerment, and an offer of training so employment could be secured. A related program was *Katrina Aid Today* (KAT), which targeted the needs of the elderly, disabled, mentally ill or anyone who was left especially at risk after Katrina. KAT also helped to place children in school, obtain needed medical care for those in need, and assisted with the crucial task of rebuilding housing. As for housing, another program of CCANO, *Operation Helping Hands*, sustained by thousands of volunteers who came from all parts of the country, has gutted well over a 1,000 homes. These "pilgrims of love" proved to be a special blessing to the elderly, the disabled, and those who lacked the financial resources to clean and rebuild.

In addition to emergency relief and the need for housing, healthcare proved to be the most pressing challenge. Hurricane Katrina was devastating to the metro area's medical delivery system. As noted previously, not only was the brick and mortar infrastructure severely damaged, but professionally trained healthcare personnel also were in short supply. CCANO provided a number of basic medical services, a mobile medical van (operated from September 2005 through April 2006) along with the standard CCANO medical care that had been provided before Katrina. The *Shirley Landry Benson PACE Center* provided basic adult healthcare and promoted on-going wellness for seniors. The *Padua* program offers residential and community-based healthcare programs for people with development disabilities.

The need for healthcare in terms of mental and emotional well being was keenly felt after Katrina. The psychological stress and fatigue resulting from the storm increased tensions within many families. CCANO historically has offered a number of special programs to meet these needs: *Therapeutic Family Services,* for foster families with a special emphasis on the challenges faced by the children; and *Family Preservation,* a 24-hour emergency on-call program that provides crisis intervention, child protection, and family therapy. Two other programs, *Foster Grandparents* and *Adoption Services,* bring together those in need with volunteers.

Volunteers from Catholic Charities' Operation Helping Hands pull out the walls of a home that flooded so that the home can be rebuilt. Photo courtesy of Catholic Charities Archdiocese of New Orleans.

Hurricane Katrina severely affected the lives of children in the metro area, especially in terms of education. Katrina arrived just as the school year had begun. The school setting holds a number of crucial components for the development of the whole child. In addition to the obvious benefits of a sound formal education, school is a place of order, security, and loving discipline, all of which are fundamental for human development. Within the school setting, children and adolescents are encouraged to mature socially, spiritually, and morally. Through the ongoing web of social interactions with peers and faculty, the child learns those mores, manners, values, and empathies necessary for living, competing, and cooperating with others. The young person learns to respect authority while maturing in the responsible exercise of freedom. In a Catholic school setting, the importance of faith for authentic education is front and center. Katrina caused a profound rupture in this most basic dimension of a child's development.

CCANO already had an array of creative programs and counseling services to help fill existing educational gaps in the metro area: *Head Start* continues to provide crucial early education along with much-needed medical services for toddlers and pre-school children; *El Yo Yo* offers bilingual Head Start programs and educational childcare which frees parents to find and keep employment; *Independent Living Skills Program* cares for young adults (ages 14–21) who can transition from foster or state care to independent living; and *Catholic Charities School-Based Counseling,* which is placed directly within the Catholic school setting and offers a multi-dimensional approach for addressing the stress caused by many factors, including Katrina.

From the beginning CCANO was sensitive to the challenges that particular segments of the area might experience because of Katrina-related stress. A number

• Gumbo, the official mascot for the New Orleans Saints, visited a celebration at PACE (Program of All-Inclusive Care for the Elderly) Greater New Orleans and asked one participant for a dance

of existing programs were offered by CCANO that were perfectly suited to address the increase in domestic violence after Katrina. Several CCANO programs confront this issue – *Crescent House Healing Center* for battered women and children; *Project SAVE,* wich provides free, emergency legal representation to survivors of domestic violence in Orleans Parish; and the *Sexual Assault Program,* which is a counseling program for men, women and children experiencing abuse.

Among the many blessings of living in the metro area is the rich diversity of races, ethnicities, nationalities, gifts, and faiths. Katrina presented different groups with special challenges.

The Spanish-speaking and Vietnamese communities have grown in size, not only in the metro area but throughout the archdiocese as well. Due to financial challenges faced by many within the Vietnamese community, only made more challenging after Katrina, parents and guardians found it necessary to spend more time outside the home in order to meet financial obligations. This economic necessity can leave children without parental or adult supervision for a significant period of time during the day and even at night.

As for the Hispanic/Latino community, post-Katrina metro New Orleans witnessed a large influx of Spanish-speaking workers. Along with making a significant contribution to rebuilding the area, Hispanics and Latinos were in need of many of the programs offered to others, but through the lenses of the Hispanic/Latino culture. For a percentage of

• Housing was a critical need for the rebuilding of the area, and Our Lady of Guadalupe set up a temporary shelter in the St. Jude Community Center on Rampart Street

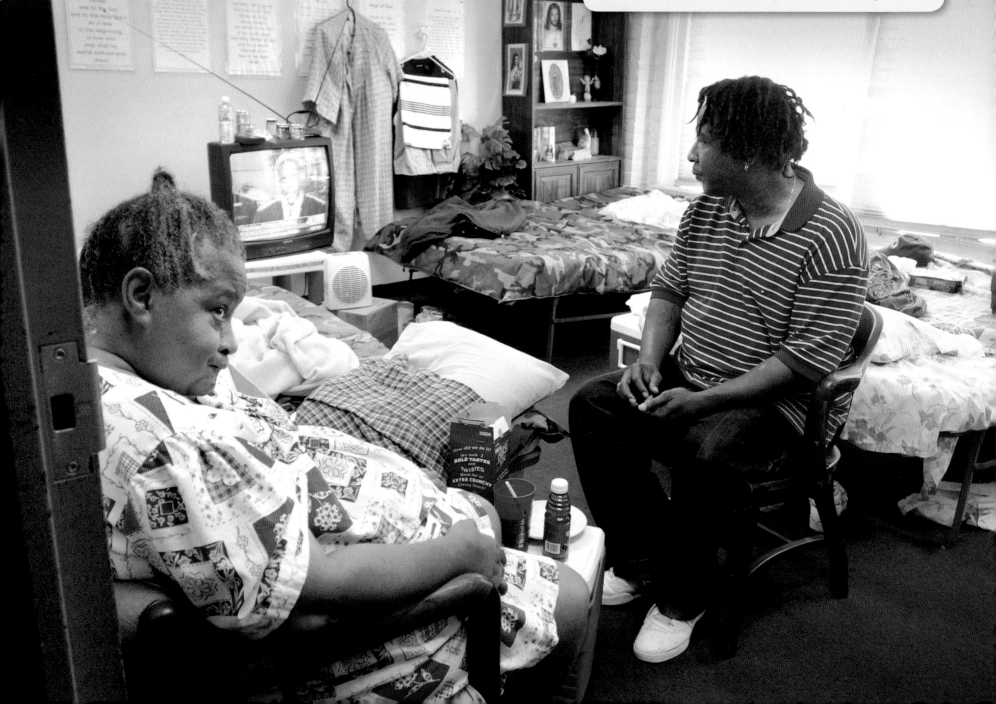

these new arrivals, a number of programs from CCANO were designed to meet their needs. *Immigration and Refugee Services* and *Hispanic Apostolate Community Services* is a multi-layered program providing employment counseling and placement; ESL (English as a Secondary Language) literacy classes; and specific counseling services for the newly arrived, in order to help them become familiar with local customs, mores, and social networks. Of special concern to and for the Hispanic community is the issue of immigration and the law. Two CCANO programs bear mentioning: *Legal Resettlement Services* provides low-cost immigration-related legal services to those who are new to the area. A second program, *Asylum Services*, provides for those in need of legal services, and seeks out those who might benefit from the other CCANO or community programs.

Hurricane Katrina seriously affected several already at-risk groups in the community. Three such segments of the community for whom CCANO offers help, a help which became more necessary after Katrina, are the deaf, those in the grip of substance abuse, and individuals suffering from AIDS.

Anyone with a hearing and/or sight impediment faces significant challenges. These challenges were greatly compounded after Katrina. When information was crucial, especially in the early days after the storm, the Deaf Action Center proved invaluable in providing signing services to public officials who were disseminating essential safety and social services information.

Substance abuse levels increased after Katrina. The loss, stress, and challenges of rebuilding after the storm proved overwhelming for many. Alcohol and drugs became attractive ways of coping with day-to-day demands. *Counseling Solutions* is a multi-layered service provider which offers a number of counseling options, including the *Men's No-Abuse Group*. For women 40 years or older who suffer from substance abuse and related mental problems, *Voyage House* provides a residential facility with therapeutic counseling tailored to the particular needs of the individual.

In normal times, those with AIDS face severe challenges. The need to provide adequate housing after Katrina was among the most pressing concerns facing community leaders. This need for adequate housing was crucial for those in need of medical care. CCANO responded to the need for housing for those with AIDS through the establishment of the *AIDS Housing & Shelter Program*. Along with housing, this emergency outreach provided rental and utility assistance to those who qualified. During its first year of operation after Katrina, the AH&S program ministered to 81 people.

Partners for Hope

The vastness and depth of destruction delivered by Katrina could not be handled by any one organization, no matter how well motivated or deeply funded. Over the years, CCANO has developed a number of working relationships with like-missioned groups (Catholic and non-Catholic), along with various secular entities. This network of relationships proved indispensible in responding to the massive needs involved in emergency relief, recovery, and rebuilding.

Through networking with governmental agencies at the local, state, and national levels, CCANO has also formed fruitful alliances with other non-profits and social service organizations. As mentioned throughout, housing was a critical need after Katrina. Catholic Charities Archdiocese of New Orleans joined with a number of group agencies, including Christopher Homes, to develop *Providence Community Housing.* This housing program provides affordable mixed-income housing using a blueprint that establishes residential communities characterized by diversity. Coming together to provide the much-needed financing and capital investment were diverse groups such as Enterprise Community Partners, the Order of Malta, Fannie Mae, Chase Bank, and the AFL-CIO Investment Trust.

Catholic Relief Services (CRS) provided much-needed support to CCANO so its essential work would continue. As was stated earlier in the chapter, the storm made it impossible for CCANO to operate out of its main headquarters in the New Orleans area. CRS provided CCANO with funding, general support, and solidarity in prayer as members of the Body of Christ.

Catholic Charities Archdiocese of New Orleans received vital support from its national association, Catholic Charities USA, in terms of funding, counseling, and workers of every sort. At the administrative level, CCUSA provided invaluable support and guidance in the planning and delivery of life-saving services.

Along with housing, the need to provide food was essential. CCANO and its affiliated ministry, *Second Harvest Food Bank of Greater New Orleans and Acadiana* partnered with

America's Second Harvest to provide food, water and trucks before and after the storm. This vital work was ongoing as survivors were still in need of these basic services through 2007.

• An elderly survivor displays a saved treasure

No matter how well-planned a program, and no matter how well-intentioned and determined those on the frontline, financial support is crucial. CCANO joined with a long-term, valued partner, *United Way,* so many of its hurricane responses could commence and continue. *United Way* provided essential funding for hurricane-related services, as well as direct support for victims.

Throughout CCANO's comprehensive plan for recovery and rebuilding from Katrina, schools occupied a place of great importance. CCANO launched an innovative program, *Project Fleur-de-Lis*, which sought out the youngest and most vulnerable victims of Katrina. Among the services provided the following were primary: long-term care and recovery, specialized training for school counselors, professional support to those who work with students, healing workshops for those students who suffered acute trauma; and "wrap-around" services – food, clothes, and financial assistance. The project was open to students, faculty, and families of Catholic school students. That program was the genesis of the current *Catholic Charities School-Based Counseling*.

The above listing of CCANO's partnerships is not exhaustive. The ones mentioned played a significant role in the three-fold response of Catholic Charities to Katrina – Emergency Relief, Recovery, and Rebuilding. There is one other collaboration mentioned earlier that deserves special mention and elaboration: the Army of Hope.

An Army of Hope

The noted 19th-century sociologist, Alex de Tocqueville, in his classic work on American society, *Democracy in America*, was impressed by many characteristics of the American national character. One such quality bears directly on our topic. Namely, de Tocqueville saw that Americans loved to form associations or clubs around common interests or values. These associations were essential for liberty, since for the most part, they were not promoted or regulated by government. They were the creation of like-minded individuals. At the same time, Americans took it as their right, indeed their duty, to actively participate in all levels of public life. Freedom of association and civic virtue deeply impressed Tocqueville.

To many today, the notion of individuals banding together for some civic good, the common good, seems a thing of the past. Contemporary, conventional wisdom holds that Americans are materialistic, pleasure-seeking, sex-driven and individualistic consumers who live only for the moment. While not denying these elements are present, this characterization, more like a caricature, is certainly not the whole of the American character. Katrina also revealed those, to use the words of Lincoln, "finer angels" that were present in those who came to do what they could.

Archbishop Hughes offers support as military personnel look on

In the days, weeks and months after Katrina, the nation and world was flooded with images of devastation and enormous human need. It was clear there were not enough financial resources, supplies, and people to meet the challenge. From across the country and around the world, thousands of people came to the metro area, motivated by the desire to help, to make a difference, and to bring comfort to the broken-hearted. They came – young and old, people of all races, individuals of means and meager resources, those of faith and no faith to speak of, all united in a common work – to witness to hope.

Many of the thousands who came did so at great personal and family sacrifice. Countless men and women left homes and jobs. They came, this Army of Hope, because there was a great need. They came to a place many did not know and did not want to experience. They came not looking for reward or recognition, save to bring hope to those without hope. They came as strangers and left as a beloved community of friends, members of newly formed extended families. The work was hard and hours long: passing out basic supplies, gutting homes, offering gestures of compassion, and at times simply keeping company with the broken-hearted in holy silence. Throughout, CCANO organized, mobilized, and directed thousands of volunteers, as well as fed and housed those who came. If indeed it is in giving that we receive,

this Army of Hope received an outpouring of love and gratitude, as well as an enduring example of what is possible when people band together for the common good. It is fashionable today to proclaim that the "Greatest Generation" appeared in some long ago period of our history. Today's young people, we are told, think of themselves and live only for the moment. Such is not true of the countless young people who came to make a difference. If the young who came are not of the Greatest Generation, they certainly were among the "Most Needed Generation." These young people put their education, careers, and family plans on hold for a greater good – the needs of others.

A question keeps intruding: Where do we get such people? Where does this Army of Hope come from? Clearly it is not from human willing or planning. Faith must provide guidance on the occasion of great selflessness. Simply put – they are raised up by God's grace. For everything there is an appointed time under God's providential care. In the time of destruction, there followed a time of rebuilding. God's grace is for every season, bright days *and* dark nights. God writes straight with crooked lines and raises up those after his own heart and will. Whether conscious or not, this Army of Hope made God's work their own.

The day before Archbishop Gregory Aymond's installation as Archbishop of New Orleans in 2009, Archbishop Aymond and former Archbishop Alfred Hughes took time to visit the Catholic Charities staff. They both gave blessings to the staff and the work done in the building. They are pictured here with employees from Catholic Charities' Finance Office.

In Their Own Words

The vast majority of this chapter on Catholic Charities Archdiocese of New Orleans has been taken up with various programs, plans, and a series of statistics highlighting the breadth and depth of the services offered. As important as all this is, it pales in power to the simple voices of those who have been served. What follows is a small sample of those who were touched by the work of Catholic Charities Archdiocese of New Orleans.

Evelyn is a 31-year-old, single mother with two small children. She was not able to get out of the city due to lack of transportation. She and her two children rode out Katrina at home. She and her children were finally rescued after almost two days. She was brought to a Catholic Charities emergency distribution center. "I never thought we'd make it. I kept praying and thinking of my kids. I couldn't let them see me afraid. At the center, we were given food, water, and a safe place. I just kept thanking God, hugging my kids, and just being so glad to be safe. It was not just the food and water, but those who were helping were so nice. They kept saying things would be OK. I felt like I, and my kids, were in my church."

Steve is a 40-year-old electrician, with one daughter and a wife who works part-time to supplement the family income. Steve lost his house to the winds and waters of Katrina. Steve stayed in New Orleans for work, while devoting all his spare time to the challenges of starting all over. His wife and daughter relocated temporarily in Georgia. After the family was able to reunite, Steve noticed the stress, hard work, and financial pressures were taking their toll. Anger, depression, and increased alcohol use were becoming more pronounced. Steve turned to CCANO for counseling. "I felt things were just out of control, crashing in on me. The more I did, the more I felt I was falling further behind. I was yelling at my wife and daughter. I knew I needed help. A priest friend of mine suggested counseling through CCANO. Thank God I followed his advice. The counselors were very professional and caring. Things are not perfect, but they are a whole lot better. The atmosphere at home is not so tense. I've cut back a great deal with the drinking. It made a big difference."

George and Margaret have been married for over 60 years. They are cradle Catholics. Both are retired; however, Margaret assures us that as a housewife and homemaker she is "still on duty." They saved their money, lived modestly within modest means, and expected to live out their remaining years enjoying one another. Katrina dealt a different hand of cards. Their home was severely damaged by flooding. Their three grown children live in other parts of the country. For George and Margaret, living anywhere but New Orleans was out of the question. What to do? "We were born, raised, and expect to stay here until the good Lord punches our tickets," offers George, a retired railroad man. "We saw our house after the storm and wondered if we could ever rebuild," adds Margaret. "I was told about a program by Catholic Charities where volunteers come in to clean and gut your flooded house. I couldn't believe the energy and kindness of the volunteers, especially the young people," said George, his voice breaking. "We're back in our home because of them. We're so grateful. We'll never forget."

Rob is a 20-year-old college student from a Catholic university outside of Louisiana. He is majoring in political science with an eye on a career in teaching or public service. "From my parents and my Catholic education I've learned the importance of giving and not just taking. I don't claim to be a 'Super Catholic,' but I go to Mass and believe our faith calls us to help those in need. I saw all the pictures on TV and just knew I couldn't resume my plans as if nothing happened." After a long pause Rob added, "I don't regret my decision. I got a lot more than I gave. The courage and faith of so many people hurt by the storm gave me a perspective I didn't have before. I also met so many other young volunteers. I left New Orleans very hopeful and proud of my generation."

Sandra is a 29-year-old native New Orleanian. Before the storm she lived by herself in a rental unit. She did not complete high school. Unfortunately, Sandra has bounced from service job to service job. Nothing much ever came of her plans to obtain her GED and go on to further her education or obtain vocational training. But then Katrina came. "I know you're going to think I'm crazy, but Katrina helped me to do something I just couldn't seem to do before. After Katrina I had time to think. I didn't like myself very much, and I didn't like where my life was headed – nowhere. If I got the chance I was going to get more education." Sandra is getting the "more education" she needs, but never seemed to be able to make the crucial first step. Through CCANO, she earned her GED and is now in the process of obtaining an associate bachelor's degree. "So many people helped me to help myself. It was not really Katrina that turned me around, but my going back to school. Without Catholic Charities, I wouldn't be where I am today." At last report, Sandra was about to earn her degree. She hopes to work in home healthcare. "I received so much, now I want to help others." With a big smile she adds, "Now I can."

Jorge is a 44-year-old skilled carpenter. He learned his trade working with his father in Colombia, and continued working with his father when the family came to America. Unfortunately, his English language skills were very under-developed. Even after Katrina, work was spotty since he had to help his now-sick father. In addition, Jorge and his own family (a wife and two children) experienced a great deal of loss after the storm. Jorge, a devout Catholic, was directed to CCANO. Through its *Immigration and Refugee Services* and *Hispanic Apostolate Community Services*, Jorge was able to receive counseling and enroll in the ESL program. "I knew I had to learn to get better at speaking English. My family speaks little English. Always having a job with my father, I didn't work on my English. The language classes have made a big difference. One day I want to have my own business. I must be able to speak English. Also I was able to talk to some people at Catholic Charities about my father and the stress I was feeling. It helped very much."

Dominic is a 15-year-old "at risk" young man. But it wasn't always so. Dominic's family had to evacuate for Katrina. They had relatives in Houston. Because of the damage to their house, and lack of resources to start rebuilding, the family remained in Houston. There was work for his parents and Dominic could continue his education. Dominic enrolled in one of the public schools. Unfortunately, the experience was not a good one. After his family was able to return, a definite change had taken place. Dominic, the good student and respectful son, seemed to give up on school and became more defiant at home. Grades declined and disobedience at home increased. Most troubling, Dominic was mad a good deal of the time and isolated from old friends and family members. Something had to be done. Through family friends, Dominic's parents were directed to *Vietnamese Youth Services*. "It was not good for me at first," reflects Dominic. "I didn't want to talk to anybody. I just wanted to be left alone. The people I talked to took a lot of time with me. I felt they cared about me. I was angry, but that didn't seem to matter. They continued to want to help me. I felt I could trust them." Asked why he was so angry and withdrawn, Dominic offered the following: "After Katrina, we had to leave. I had to start a new school without any friends. My parents were both working and had me do more stuff at home. When we did return, it was like starting all over. I had to go to a new school. Many of my old friends were gone or in a different school. It all seemed so unfair. I'm able to see now that I was just thinking of myself. It was selfish. I'm trying to make up for the things that I did." Dominic is "making up" for the past. His parents report vast improvement in his behavior at home, as well as a return to a high standard of academic achievement. Dominic's father observed, "We have the old Dominic back."

The Work Goes On

No one chapter – indeed no one book – could do justice to the extraordinary witness of Catholic Charities Archdiocese of New Orleans before, during, and after Katrina. The storm affected thousands of lives. Countless hearts and homes were broken. For many, especially those who have made new lives for themselves in other places, life will never be the same. In the midst of all the destruction, one thing remains clear: within the human spirit there lives an invincible summer, a will to live, and the need for a hope stronger than a menacing despair. This "strong hope" is an essential grace which drives CCANO's mission. Archbishop Alfred Hughes put it this way, "Our challenges are many, but we have learned that death and destruction do not utter the last word. Here in New Orleans there is much hope, optimism, and spiritual prosperity."

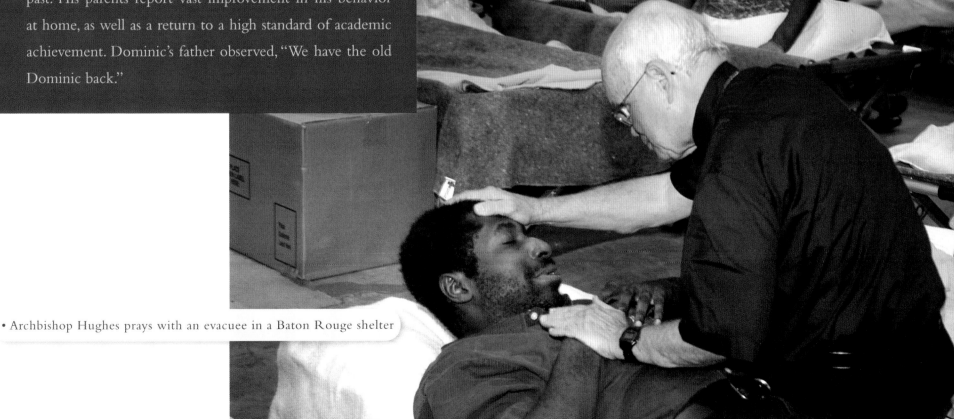

• Archbishop Hughes prays with an evacuee in a Baton Rouge shelter

Chapter 4 ——————————

CLERGY AND RELIGIOUS:
AN UNCOMMON VALOR, A FAITHFUL PRESENCE

Throughout the history of Louisiana, and the New Orleans metro area in particular, the work of Catholic priests, along with men and women religious, has played a vital role. One example is illustrative of the heroic witness of priests and religious during times of crisis.

During the seasonal Yellow Fever epidemics of the 18th and 19th centuries, many residents who had the means would leave the city until the danger subsided. Over the years, thousands died excruciating deaths, while a countless number who recovered were affected for the rest of their lives. At the time, it was standard practice to burn the bodies of the dead in order to keep the fever from spreading. Rather than leaving the deadly fever, priests and religious

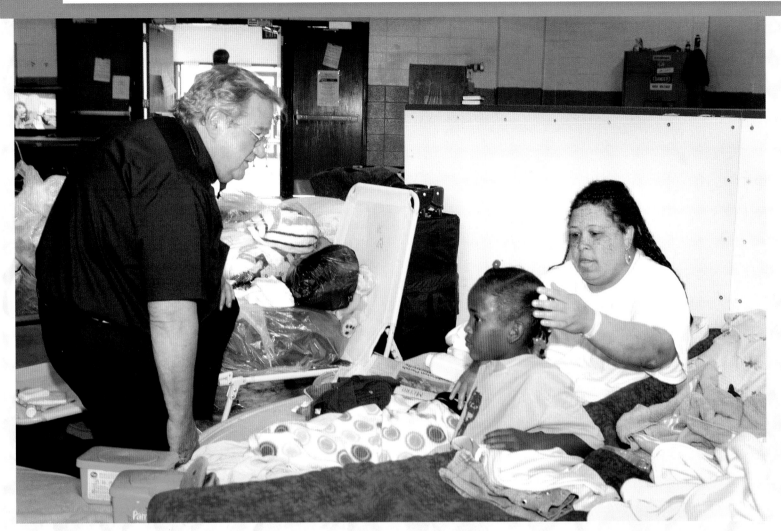

New Orleans Auxiliary Bishop Roger Morin, who lost most of his priestly belongings when his house burned down after Katrina, ministers to evacuees in a shelter

held fast in order to care for the sick, comfort the sorrowing, administer the sacraments, and bury the dead. Many priests and religious imitated Christ in laying down their lives in fidelity to the Gospel and the command of Jesus to love one another. This heroic example of Christ-like, sacrificial love did not go unappreciated by a grateful citizenry. One example of the admiration accorded to Catholic clergy and religious for their witness in the face of Yellow Fever was the practice of allowing women religious to ride public transportation for free. This practice continued well into the 20th century.

The legacy of heroic priestly and religious ministry gained a new chapter with Hurricane Katrina. Like their ancestors,

this present generation of disciples answered the call to love God by loving and serving those in need. This response of faith took many forms and manifested itself in untraditional places. Priests and religious found themselves in evacuation shelters, basic-needs distribution centers, airports, makeshift medical facilities and a variety of transportation locations.

The lower parts of Plaquemines Parish, both east and west banks of the Mississippi River, suffered severe wind and water damage. Father Gerard Stapleton provided extraordinary priestly witness and service at both St. Patrick Church in Port Sulphur (West Bank) and St. Thomas in Pointe a la Hache. Father Stapleton not only was a spiritual leader, but his priestly presence was valued by the larger community, especially in the early days and weeks after Katrina. St. Thomas Church was still undergoing renovations in 2009.

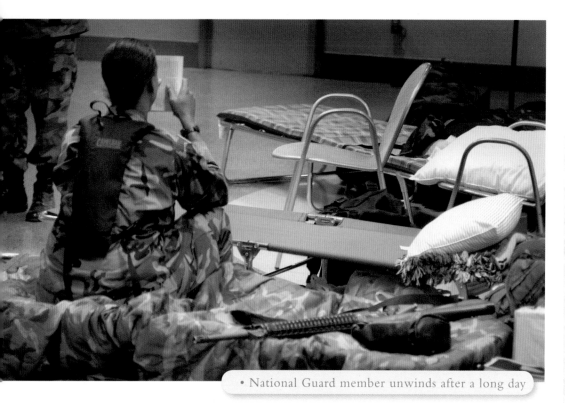
• National Guard member unwinds after a long day

volunteers some water, the priest joined the group in prayer. "I'm ashamed to say I can't remember the priest's name, but as tired as I was, I could have cleaned another 10 blocks," offered Tony with a smile.

Our Lady of Lourdes Church in Violet

Clergy used these new settings, new "chapels" if you will, to offer Mass, administer the sacraments, and provide on-site pastoral counseling to those who were helping as well as to those who were hurting. Regardless of the setting or ministry, the focus was the same – fidelity to Jesus through being with and for those most in need. It is often in times of crisis that the taken-for-granted, the familiar and routine take on special value. Those "ordinary" things that priests and religious do every day were viewed as "extraordinary." Consider the example of Tony, a college student from the northeast who took a semester off in order to help with the Katrina cleanup. After one exceptionally exhausting day he and some of his fellow volunteers were sitting on the ground trying to muster the energy to get up. As Tony was about to stand, he felt a hand on his shoulder. "I sure admire you all," said the unknown priest. "I think I'm looking at a new greatest generation." After offering Tony and his fellow

Along with priests and religious, permanent deacons provided a splendid example of Christ-like service. Even before Katrina, ordained permanent deacons were providing valuable ministry throughout the archdiocese. Permanent deacons provide sacramental ministry (baptism and marriage), often read the Gospel at Mass, preach, lead parishes and various communities in a variety of prayer settings (for example holy Communion services), and take part in a significant way in a multitude of archdiocesan ministries.

Permanent deacons, their wives and families play a significant role in the pastoral work of the archdiocese. On October 25, 2005, Deacon Jim Swiler indicated in a memorandum that 43 deacons (23 percent of the archdiocesan total) suffered a total loss of their homes, businesses or both. An additional 15 percent of the deacons' homes or businesses experienced a significant degree of damage.

● Father Ed Brienz, a priest of the Diocese of Youngstown, Ohio, administers ashes to a college student volunteer

The ministry of permanent deacons after Katrina took on a new urgency and an added challenge for them and their families. The needs were great after Katrina, but so were the opportunities to serve. Permanent deacons were present in shelters and food distribution centers. Even those deacons who had to relocate sought out those from the metro area and provided ministry. In those churches and makeshift locations where the Eucharist was offered, deacons continued their ministry of sacrament and Word. In many ways, when a man answers the call to serve as an ordained deacon, it is in the context of his family. Permanent deacons, in addition to their clerical responsibilities, had the added obligations associated with caring for their own families. The wives and children

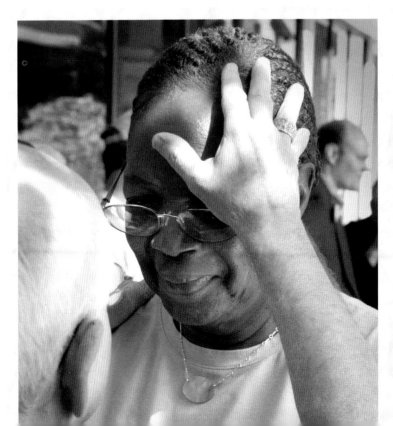

Katrina, like the sacramental ashes, reminds us to value what is really important

of permanent deacons are very much a part of a deacon's vocation and the numerous sacrifices required of one in the clerical state. This family dimension to the vocation of permanent deacon, while adding additional responsibilities, brings an abundance of extra graces and support in doing God's work.

The Archdiocese: Then and Now

In an age when most things are being "super-sized," Hurricane Katrina forced the archdiocese to "down-size." In place of expansion, the operative words became "cut back and reduce." Not only was there a general reduction in the scope of goods and services offered in the region, but the overall quality of life underwent dramatic change. Such was the case not only for the metro area, but for the archdiocese as well. Every aspect of archdiocesan life was altered by Katrina.

The Administrative Council of the United States Conference of Catholic Bishops, which includes about 50 bishops, formulated plans for a nationwide program in which parishes and schools would be urged to adopt or "twin" with parishes and schools in the Archdiocese of New Orleans.

The life-altering impact of Katrina on the archdiocese is evidenced when one views the clergy and religious. In 2005, just before Katrina struck, there were 343 priests engaged in various forms of ministry within the archdiocese: 148 diocesan priests and 195 religious order priests. As of 2009, the breakdown of priests serving in the archdiocese is as follows: 134 diocesan priests and 155 religious order priests, for a total of 289 priests supplying ministry within the archdiocese. If the number of sick, retired, absent, and those serving outside the archdiocese is included, the total number of diocesan priests is 360. In 2005, there were 186 permanent deacons in parish ministry; by 2009, the number of deacons serving in the archdiocese actually rose to 197. Katrina's effect on the number of archdiocesan clergy could be termed a mixed bag: There was a decline in the number of priests, while the number of permanent deacons rose by 11.

Hurricane Katrina could not silence the Gospel at Mary, Queen of Vietnam, where a generator powered an electric lamp to illuminate the Gospel

Throughout the history of the archdiocese – even before there was an archdiocese and before Louisiana was purchased by the United States – the presence of religious brothers and sisters has been a vital and vibrant dimension of church ministry. The various congregations of brothers and sisters offer a wide variety of ministries ranging from education, to health care, to an extensive institutional presence addressing a number of social concerns. The aftermath of Katrina affected this valued presence. Right before Katrina, there were 103 religious brothers and 695 sisters providing a wide variety of ministries. By the year 2009, the number of sisters serving in the archdiocese had declined to 487. The acute medical needs of a number of sisters accounted for the reduction. By contrast, the number of brothers actually increased after Katrina. Many religious communities assigned additional brothers to the region in order to help with the ever-rising demand for ministry. The fact that so many brothers and sisters were able to return and desired to return is a powerful testimony of their dedication to the people they serve. Many religious communities suffered extensive damage to their properties, yet their communities continued to support their work in the archdiocese, both financially and with additional personnel, where and when needed.

Recognizing the importance of religious men and women (priests, brothers, and sisters) in the archdiocese, Archbishop Hughes convened a meeting for all the major religious superiors with communities serving in the archdiocese. In addition to this initial meeting, the archbishop was kept abreast of the needs of religious men and women through the archdiocesan Department of Religious. During the formulation of the archdiocesan pastoral plan in response to Katrina, the on-going input of religious played an important role in the plan's final edition.

Catholics: People of a Place

Catholics are a people committed to a place, specifically, their parish. So much of life and death, and all points in between, are connected to the parish church. It is there that one is born into the church through baptism, experiences the initial sacramental healing through penance, receives that first feeding at the Lord's table, gains strength in the Holy Spirit at confirmation, celebrates the joy of marriage or offers a first Mass after ordination, and is passed into the hands of the Lord when one's earthly pilgrimage ends. Much of the anguish associated with Katrina resulted from the damage and destruction done to our homes, our place of everyday residence, as well as our spiritual residence, the parish church.

Archbishop Hughes offered the first Mass since Katrina at St. Louis Cathedral on October 2, 2005

• Archbishop Hughes, with Louisiana Gov. Kathleen Blanco and Archbishop Paul Josef Cordes of the Vatican to his left, meet in Baton Rouge in September 2005

Before Katrina, the parish and related settings yielded the following picture: there were 142 parishes and 8 missions. Clearly this picture was going to undergo a significant change in response to Katrina. Archbishop Hughes, after extensive consultation with numerous advisors and a number of listening sessions with parishioners, devised a pastoral plan for parishes. In February 2006, the archdiocese permanently closed six parishes and did not reopen two dozen others. At that time, $45.9 million was received in donations, of which $32.9 million was distributed to parishes for restoration and rebuilding. The re-establishing of various ministries within the parishes was included. This completed Phase I of a two-phase pastoral plan.

In April 2008, Phase II of the pastoral plan went into effect. This phase called for 27 parishes to merge with neighboring parishes and for four parishes to become missions. The remaining $13 million of the initial $45.9 million was allocated for the implementation of this second phase of the plan. This remaining money was used, as in Phase I, for repair and restoration of buildings, as well for as the re-establishing of parish ministries. At the completion of both phases of the pastoral plan in 2009, the following emerged: The archdiocese now consisted of 108 parishes, nine missions, two campus ministry centers and a pastoral center. The Archdiocese of New Orleans post-Katrina was downsized to 83 parishes with a resident pastor, 21 parishes with a resident religious priest as pastor, and four parishes shared a pastor, who resided in one of the parishes. Plans were being formulated to establish seven newly named parishes from those which had to merge due to population and financial considerations. The newly named parishes would emerge after an extensive process of consultation among all the relevant parties.

Our Lady of Good Harbor Church, Buras, has not reopened

The contraction of the archdiocese was not only due to the vastness of the destruction, the severe strain on economic resources, and the decline in archdiocesan personnel, both lay and clerical. An important additional factor was demographic. As noted in Chapter Two, in 2005, there were 490,898 Catholics out of a total population of 1,361,488 within the boundaries of the archdiocese. By 2009, that number shrank to 387,101 Catholics out of a total population of 1,075,283. Of course, these factors for reduction fed into each other: a decreased Catholic population, extensive destruction with a severe cost for repair and rebuilding made it necessary to delay reopening parishes and in some cases, necessitated the decision not to reopen at all.

The decision not to open parishes was reached only after extensive meetings, consultations, and a prudent evaluation as to the best use of resources in light of Katrina realities. The reaction of clergy and parishioners to the decision not to reopen a parish was predictable – sadness, a deep sense of loss, a determination not to let this happen, frustration, and in some instances, deep anger. However, under the pastoral leadership of Archbishop Hughes, along with the prayerful guidance of parish clergy, the acceptance of hard realities, in most instances, was achieved. The overwhelming majority of laity affected by parish closings found new parish communities for worship. The long love affair between individual parish and parishioners would be changed, not ended, strained but not broken. Those parishes which remained open would make special efforts to welcome the newly arrived. While much about one's former parish abides in heart and memory, overall new memories and strong bonds of faith are being forged. A new chapter in parish life is being written, not because of Katrina, but through the Holy Spirit, "the Lord and Giver of Life."

• Father John Asare-Dankwah in front of Blessed Trinity Parish, formed through the merger of St. Matthias, St. Monica and Our Lady of Lourdes parishes.

A related situation that affected parishes, namely, the need to join neighboring parishes into one faith community, posed a new set of challenges. As parishes merged, each community wanted to retain the familiar, as well as the distinctive. The need for a creative synthesis called for imaginative sacrifice, mutual respect, and fraternal charity. The parish clergy would play a key role in this demanding process. Parishioners from the parish being absorbed had to deal with profound feelings of loss, sadness, and anger. Parishioners of the parish that would remain had to wonder what this merger would mean for existing ministries, services, schedules, and what effect the influx of new parishioners would have on the parish culture. Real feelings. Real concerns.

The establishment of Blessed Trinity Parish, by merging St. Matthias, Our Lady of Lourdes, and St. Monica, exhibited all the key elements necessary for a fruitful merger. Priestly and lay leadership and communication at every level sustained welcome and outreach for the newly arrived, respect for the closing parishes, and a deep call to faith in order to witness the work of the Spirit in bringing forth something new.

From the first, Father John Asare-Dankwah, the first pastor of Blessed Trinity, made sure all were welcomed. At the entrance of the church (the former St. Matthias) was placed a large red welcome mat containing the following words of Scripture: "Behold, I make all things new." Father Asare went on to establish a number of ministries, from a youth group to a ministry for the bereaved, and was careful to include and blend members of former parishes (as well as those who entered the parish family for the first time) into a unified whole. As parishioners from various parishes merged, Father Asare was most sensitive to the stories, symbols and traditions

• The charred remains of Bishop Roger Morin's chalice and paten (see page 42 for the "resurrected" chalice)

of each church. During the offering of Mass, Father Asare would utilize various symbols and sacred vessels in order to remind the congregation that the church is a community of memory and hope. Such a reminder embodies the Memorial Acclamation, "Christ has died, Christ is risen, Christ will come again." Throughout the entire merger process, Father Asare met with the various congregations in order to obtain their input and keep them updated as events unfolded.

Finally, the indispensable element for Father Asare was the need to guide the merger process through the lens of faith. Time and time again he told the people, "God is always making something new in our lives." This is not easy in such situations. But Father Asare compared the situation to that of the early church. "People from different parishes come together to form something new. They know we are not alone."

• Archbishop Hughes celebrates Mass at Mary, Queen of Vietnam in New Orleans East.

• The first Mass celebrated in New Orleans East offered great hope

Eucharist: Hope and Heart

For Catholics, the central focus of place is the parish. The central act for Catholics is the Eucharist. Hurricane Katrina scattered so many to every part of Louisiana and the nation. In God's providential wisdom it was only fitting that the Eucharist would be that which gathered the community of faith. Each time, Catholics felt a "real homecoming," a "real presence," once their parish threw open its doors to proclaim the Gospel and offer the Eucharist. Alice, a life-long resident of New Orleans and a "forever Catholic," summed up the sentiments of so many: "I returned to my home in New Orleans about a month after the storm," she said fighting back tears, "but I knew I was home when finally my church announced the first Mass after Katrina." This feeling of "homecoming" was not only important for parishioners of individual parishes; but these "first Eucharist" celebrations also carried implications for the metro area as a whole. Two such offerings of the Mass carried special significance.

On Sunday, October 23, 2005, Archbishop Hughes celebrated Mass at Mary Queen of Vietnam in New Orleans East, one of the area's most devastated sections. The Mass had for its theme, "Resurrection Mass for New Orleans East." While the church building still lacked water, sewerage, and electricity, there was no shortage of Holy Spirit energy flowing through the more than 1,000 worshippers who had gathered. The archbishop began the Mass in Vietnamese from note cards that he removed from his vestments. This episcopal effort was warmly received by the congregation.

The strong Catholic faith of the Vietnamese was evident after Katrina

The theme of the archbishop's homily was the reality of misfortune in light of the deeper reality of faith. In Vietnamese, the archbishop told the people, "God has seen the suffering from the hurricane, and he is with you." Archbishop Hughes went on to relate the experience of the Vietnamese people as they fled the communists to their experience in fleeing the waters of Katrina: "You know what it is, in the midst of all this, to have faith." The archbishop invited those in attendance to open themselves to God's grace by examining American culture and their own values. He challenged worshippers to seek after the things of God and not the material things that can so quickly be lost. Katrina presents all of us, the archbishop went on to say, with the opportunity to be less self-indulgent and more self-sacrificing.

• Young Vietnamese Catholics gather for worship

Father Warren Cooper, pastor of Immaculate Conception Church in Marrero, displays a profound symbol of the crucifixion resulting from Katrina

The importance and spiritual strength of culture was noted by Archbishop Hughes. Music for the Mass was offered by various church choirs in different languages. Choir members came from different racial and ethnic backgrounds. "Who can say there is no hope for New Orleans East? God is our hope…What a magnificent expression of the church: Different cultures, different races, one faith," observed the archbishop. The importance of ethnic and racial harmony was not a new theme for Archbishop Hughes. This challenge had been addressed in various columns, homilies, and a pastoral letter devoted to the topic. The need for cooperation across racial and ethnic lines became more urgent after Katrina.

A previous offering of the Eucharist, one with metro-wide implications, occurred on October 2, 2005. Archbishop Hughes offered the first Mass since Katrina at the historic St. Louis Cathedral. The cathedral, shadowing Jackson Square, serves as the heart of the city, and on that day, served as a witness to hope.

The heart of New Orleans was left broken after Katrina. There was so much death and destruction that many were left to wonder if New Orleans would rise. So many people had moved away to build new lives. Many more were not able to return, though every fiber of their beings longed for home. This broken heart was in need of the medicine of hope. It came as the venerable bells of the cathedral beckoned all to come and be renewed and recommitted. And come they did. More than 1,000 worshippers of every race, creed, ethnicity, and socio-economic background filled the church. Police, firefighters, and soldiers stood along the back walls since all the pews were full. The vision of Isaiah – all peoples will be drawn to the holy dwelling of the Lord – was realized on this Sunday of hope.

Archbishop Hughes began this special Eucharist with these words: "This is indeed an historic moment in the life not only in the Church of New Orleans, but in the whole city. The structure which harbors the soul of our city has come back to life…Thanks be to God." During the liturgy, a delicate balance was maintained between the recognition of loss and destruction and the need to celebrate a greater hope being celebrated through the Eucharist. In his homily Archbishop Hughes explored a theme that was presented many times over the weeks and months after Katrina. He said: "God tolerates evil in order that we may ultimately realize a greater good." That greater good could manifest itself in the rebuilding of communities with a stronger moral commitment, racial tensions being replaced by a spirit of solidarity, a dedication to the common good, and the fostering of lifestyles exhibiting simplicity and concern for the poor.

As Mass was being offered, relief workers continued the daunting task of cleanup and recovery outside the walls of the cathedral. One relief worker on the way to finish a detail in another part of the city offered this statement, "There are many times you get so tired, frustrated, and just plain overwhelmed. I was going to finish a job and all I wanted to do was go rest. I heard the bells from the cathedral. I'm not a religious guy, but those bells gave me chills. All I wanted to do was finish my work." These words could have been echoed by many. Bread and wine, bells, hymns, and people gathered all these together made visible the words of the Communion hymn, "I am hope for all who are hopeless. …I will bring you home." This hope gave comfort to the heart of New Orleans.

A Greater Love

A favorite question posed by history professors to college freshmen goes something like this: Do events give rise to historic figures or do those with certain personality or character traits bend events for their purposes? This version of the "chicken or egg" debate usually ends in a stalemate with both sides offering good examples to bolster their position. Hurricane Katrina was an historic event that gave rise to a wide spectrum of responses. For some, the storm proved overwhelming and led to a decision not to rebuild or return to the Crescent City. Others suffered various emotional and physical setbacks ranging from mild depression to the need for supervised therapy, from the aggravation of existing medical infirmities to the causing of death, especially among the elderly. Then there were others who responded in a completely different manner. For these individuals, the greater the destruction, the more intense became the determination to rebuild and follow the road home. It was as if the very challenges of the situation drew on energy held in reserve for such occasions. No matter the distance, the thoughts of coming home shrank the miles. Like General MacArthur, they would return.

Young Catholic school students at St. Michael's Special School are glad to be together again

As the Letter to the Hebrews in the New Testament reminds us all, every high priest is chosen from among men, human beings. And the very weakness of the human condition provides the medium through which God's grace is revealed. Once more, those chosen by God to serve as priests, brothers and sisters were afflicted in every way by Katrina, but prevailed by grace. In the spirit of St. Joseph, clergy and religious went uncelebrated, little noticed, and with quiet integrity in the work of cleaning up, recovery, preservation, and restoration. There were countless examples of clergy and religious going about doing good. Away from the glare of the spotlight, these men and women spent countless hours cleaning classrooms and churches, gathering and preserving school and parish records, restoring sacred vessels and symbols that make schools and churches places of grace, opening doors for learning and worship, and visiting parishioners in shelters near to home and around the country. In these activities, as well as the sacramental and prayer ministries we associate with priests and religious, the men and women raised up by God's grace were being true to their call – being Christ to those in need.

As just mentioned, the contributions of priests and religious remained unknown to the world, except, of course, to those who were blessed by their ministries and the One who writes names in the Book of Life. At the same time, there were instances of extraordinary dedication that came to the attention of the wider community. The number of such heroic examples exceeds the limits of the scope of this book; however, three examples can serve as disclosure models for the uncommon valor and faithful presence of numerous clergy and religious.

We begin in Baton Rouge, which is not so surprising since so many from the metro area sought shelter there, and much of the early relief from Katrina came through the joint efforts of the Archdiocese of New Orleans and the Diocese of Baton Rouge. Especially hard hit was the Vietnamese community who, over the years, had settled around the coastal areas of Louisiana due to fishing and related business opportunities. The hurricane caused a sizable number of Vietnamese to lose both homes and businesses. Baton Rouge was the nearest place of shelter for many Vietnamese, a significant number of whom were Catholic and who sought aid from the diocese.

Many Vietnamese in need of shelter and aid found their way to St. Anthony Catholic Church in Baton Rouge. At its peak of outreach, the church provided aid to 250 members of the Vietnamese community. The aid offered to them ranged from food, shelter, and clothing to medical care. Enter Father Tam Pham of the Diocese of Baton Rouge, who is also a trained physician. Father Pham not only continued the priestly ministry at his parish but also went to various evacuation shelters to offer pastoral and medical care. This two-fold priestly presence was important for the elderly. In the words of Father Pham, "People are struggling a lot and are very delicate now." He expressed a deep kinship with the victims of Katrina who knew well the feeling of loss and displacement, especially those who fled communism in the 1970s. "They have lost a lot and they feel very concerned about their future." Father Pham was in a unique position to be a doctor of the soul as well as the body. His presence offered the medicine of hope on so many levels.

• An elderly Vietnamese woman communicates with her eyes and face

Along with Father Pham, the ministry of Sister Hong Tran bears notice. Sister Tran found herself an evacuee in a Baton Rouge shelter. Rather than simply riding out the storm and waiting to return to the metro area, Sister Tran began to offer ministry immediately to her fellow evacuees. She went about listening, consoling, trying to contact separated family members, praying, and like Father Pham, offered hope by reminding people of their blessings rather than dwelling on all the loss. "I would tell them, 'Maybe it will be better now; at least you know English…(you) who were single (in Vietnam) now have a family, children who are OK, a wife who is OK.' I helped them to look for the positive," says Sister Tran, who embodies the wisdom of St. Francis of Assisi – it is in giving that we receive.

Closer to home, Mary Queen of Vietnam in New Orleans East garnered national recognition in response to an archdiocesan priest who exhibited extraordinary dedication. Even before Katrina, Father Vien Nguyen made a significant difference in the lives of his parishioners and the larger community. Father Nguyen's prophetic voice was raised against a toxic neighborhood landfill off Chef Menteur Highway. Also of concern was the need for adequate medical care, especially for those who were in need of long-term, critical care. These concerns, and many others, were only made more acute after Katrina.

The New Orleans East area was especially hard hit by the storm. Under the priestly leadership of Father Nguyen, a massive effort was organized to provide a wide range of relief services – food, water, shelter and vital electrical power so residents could return and businesses could start to reopen. However, more than the restoration of basic services would be required if area residents were to be enticed to return. Father Nguyen supplied that "one more" basic requirement: Hope. Hope empowers people to look beyond the immediate and see what is currently beyond reach. His commitment to the Gospel, the Church, and those under his care was clearly the energy that drew the storm-scattered back home. Even though New Orleans East experienced severe destruction, 95 percent of the area's residents returned, the highest rate of return in Orleans Parish. Father Nguyen was instrumental in this crucial phase of the recovery.

Father Nguyen was recognized by Pax Christi USA, not just for his extraordinary efforts during and after Katrina, but also for his priestly witness on behalf of the vulnerable. Upon awarding Father Vien with the Eileen Egan Peacemaker Award in 2008, this international organization for justice and peace cited the following: "Father Nguyen is recognized as an individual who has made a strong and extraordinary prophetic witness for peace in a time or situation of devastating violence or injustice."

As one might expect, Father Nguyen deflected attention and recognition away from himself. In an interview with Catholic News Service, he stated: "It is not for me; it is for the whole community. It is a recognition of what we have endeavored, our accomplishments, and the value that was in our endeavors. No one in the community set out (to do what he or she did) so that we would be recognized." He went on to explain the goal of the work, which involved so many hands. "The goal was to return to how we were before, whatever it took, and we did it. In it, values were identified and acknowledged." Father Nguyen viewed this award as a way of calling attention, beyond the local area, to a wider audience which could help the recovery. "Certainly, coming here and having Pax Christi make connections will make our needs better known," he said.

The third example of heroic service, sadly, comes by way of one who gave the last, full measure. It is to his priestly commitment that we now turn.

Jesus, the night before he died, gathered with his disciples and left them an example of humble service: He washed their feet, and he left them a deep wisdom as to the depth of love – his love. There is no greater expression of love than to lay down one's life for one's friends. Like so many in the metro area, the archdiocese suffered great destruction, loss, and death. Especially painful to the archdiocesan family was the death of Father Arthur J. "Red" Ginart.

Father "Red," as he was affectionately known, died as a direct result of Katrina. Father Ginart served as pastor of St. Nicholas of Myra Parish, a small parish established in 1971 to serve the Chef Menteur community. There are two main groups that comprised the parish: permanent residents of the area and those who had fishing and hunting camps. The church itself was located on the edge of the marsh near Lake Pontchartrain.

Father Arthur "Red" Ginart, pastor of St. Nicholas of Myra, died during the storm. His body was never recovered

• A memorial Mass held for Father Ginart where St. Nicholas of Myra Church once stood

Soon after Katrina, reports were received that Father Ginart was missing. It was initially thought he had evacuated and was not able to communicate his location because of the storm. This hope became increasingly unlikely as time passed and information was received that he chose to stay at the church. An extensive effort was organized to locate Father Ginart, but this search proved to be futile. With each passing hour, the hope of finding him alive dimmed and the hard truth of his death became more apparent. The goal of the massive search by law enforcement, fire personnel, and Wildlife and Fisheries agents turned now to locating his remains. Unfortunately, this search effort proved unsuccessful.

The archdiocese as a whole, and especially the parishioners of St. Nicholas, were in need of closure. If his physical remains could not be located, then the body of believers, those who loved Father Red, would gather around the Lord's Table for Eucharist. A first memorial Mass was offered in Baton Rouge by Archbishop Hughes at Our Lady of Mercy Church. Since Father Ginart's remains had still not been located, uppermost in people's minds was the need for an appropriate resolution. Parishioners also wanted to know what else might be done to find his body. It became clear Father's body was claimed by Katrina after a number of exhaustive searches and the passage of time.

Adding to the parishioners' pain was the decision not to rebuild and reopen St. Nicholas. Once more the faithful requested closure, this time for their parish. In response to this need for closure, a memorial Mass was offered at the actual location of where the church once stood. The Eucharist was offered for both Father Ginart and the St. Nicholas of Myra community. Archbishop Hughes offered the Mass, attended by many who had to travel a great distance since the Chef Menteur Bridge had been washed out in the storm. Katrina had taken a beloved pastor. Its winds and water leveled a church building. However, Katrina was unable to diminish the faith of those present. In face of such loss and pain, the people of St. Nicholas made the words of St. Paul their own: "in every circumstance give thanks."

A question naturally arises – why? Why didn't Father Ginart leave? He, above all, should have known of the potential deadly consequences of such a massive storm. Again, why did he stay? A parishioner who attended both memorial Masses supplied the answer. "I begged Father Ginart to leave," she said while fighting back tears. "He wouldn't leave. I was at church for Mass on the Sunday just before Katrina. I tried once more to get him to leave. It was no use. He told us at Mass his place was in the parish. He wanted to be at the church when people returned and began to clean up and rebuild. I guess God had other plans," she said, her head bowed into her chest and slowly shaking.

Father Ginart stayed because he was a faithful priest of Jesus Christ. He followed the example of Jesus by laying down his life because he loved his parishioners, his friends. He was the good shepherd who knew his own by name. When the storm approached he did not flee; but this good and faithful servant stayed with them to the end. The waters of Katrina took Father Red's life, but the One who is life itself welcomed this good, faithful servant into life eternal.

In Their Own Words

Augie and Angeline are native New Orleanians and residents of the French Quarter. From the first, they attended St. Louis Cathedral, where they were married and their four children were baptized. They remained in their home during Katrina. Looking back, they wished they had decided differently. "Part of living in this area is putting up with hurricanes," said Augie. "So we didn't want to leave. We've done it so many times in the past. This time we weren't going to go - a big mistake." Augie and Angeline soon lost electricity and had to eat canned food that they had stored. That was not the worst of it. "I don't remember ever being so afraid," said Angeline as those memories came rushing back. "We tried to go outside a couple of times, but we knew it wasn't safe. There were gangs of people roaming around looking for trouble. I just prayed no one would break into our house." No one did, and eventually safety returned. One of the happiest days of their lives was the day when the cathedral reopened and the first Mass after Katrina was offered. "I never heard the bells sound so strong," said Augie with a smile. "You could see the people coming from every direction. For me and Augie the sadness was lifted." Angeline smiled in agreement and added, "I couldn't help but think of all the times Augie and I would go to the cathedral. We didn't know if we would ever be back again. I remember crying all the way to the cathedral that day, and Augie telling me to stop. I didn't." As Angeline retells the story, tears are once again falling. Augie grasps her hands.

Alma and her husband **Ray**, are life-long residents of lower Plaquemines Parish. Ray is a commercial fisherman and hunter, just as his father and his grandfather were. Alma stayed at home to raise two sons, both of whom work with Ray in his fishing business, and she "helps where needed in the business." Ray and Alma were faithful parishioners of St. Nicholas who had a deep respect and love for Father Red. "I hate to think of Father Red dying like that," said Ray. "When I saw all the destruction, I knew deep down he couldn't have made it…too much water." Alma had a special reason for her devotion to Father Ginart. "Because of Father Red, Ray had come back to the church. For a number of years he stayed away. Father Red was able to win Ray over." What was so special about Father Red? According to Ray, "Father was a man you could talk to and he would understand the problems we faced in this place. He didn't give you a lot of talk, just words. I just felt he understood. He was a man of God."

Alice moved from Orleans Parish about 15 years ago and settled in St. Bernard Parish. At the time of Katrina she was employed by an area realty agency performing administrative and general office tasks. Alice attended Mass "on a regular basis." She was in attendance when Archbishop Hughes offered Mass for the residents of St. Bernard Parish at Our Lady of Prompt Succor in Chalmette. The Mass drew a large gathering of worshippers. The offering of the Eucharist by Archbishop Hughes served as a sign of God's faithful love, as well as the commitment of the archdiocese to the people of St. Bernard. "After I came back to St. Bernard for the first time since the storm, I couldn't speak; all I could do was cry. It was as if an atomic bomb had been dropped. There was also a lot of talk about St. Bernard never being rebuilt. There was a lot of despair. We needed, I needed, to know that we weren't going to be forgotten, abandoned. I heard about a Mass the archbishop was going to say. I can't tell you what that meant to me and those who went to the Mass. Having that Mass with the archbishop was like a message you see written in the sky. It said to us that we weren't alone."

Hank was a long-time resident of the Lower Ninth Ward in New Orleans. He was a laborer and took "various jobs… work was work…you need money to live." Over the years Hank managed to save enough to buy "a little house…it was good for me since I live by myself." As the storm approached, Hank managed to get to the Convention Center, where he was then evacuated to Houston. Once in Houston, he was sent to a huge shelter filled with evacuees from the metro area. "For some time I was afraid. Even though there were a lot of people from New Orleans in the shelter, I didn't know too many of them. After I heard about all the damage, I was more afraid. I didn't know if I could go back home, if I even had a house. I didn't know what I would do if I had to stay in Houston. One day in the shelter, all these fears were really pressing on me. A lady, she was a Catholic sister, came over to me to see if I needed anything. I told her I wasn't Catholic, but that didn't matter to her. She got me a bottle of water. We sat and talked. She offered to pray for me and with me. I felt tears in my eyes. We spent a few minutes just praying. I will never forget that lady. After she left to see other people, I didn't feel so scared. I even went around the shelter seeing if I could help. Now I wasn't just thinking about myself."

Lester is a resident of New Orleans East, an area especially hard hit by Katrina. Before the hurricane, he was a parishioner of St. Simon Peter Parish. Lester evacuated to northern Louisiana during and after the storm. In the years since the storm, he has returned to New Orleans East, but now rents since his small house was destroyed. Lester currently attends St. Maria Goretti Church which now serves as the parish of worship for former parishioners of St. Simon Peter and Immaculate Heart of Mary parishes. Those two parishes were closed after Katrina. "I lost my little house and my parish church," says Lester as he slowly shakes his head. "I go to St. Maria now. The priest and the people there have been very nice and made new people feel welcome. But you know everybody wants their own parish. St. Simon Peter was my spiritual home. This might sound strange, but I'm still trying to adjust to things after Katrina. I don't know if I ever will. I learned as a boy that when one door is closed, God opens another, even better door. We just have to walk through it. Look, I've lost a lot, but so have many others. Others lost more than me. I am alive. I have a place to live. I have a job. I have a church. I'm blessed. I'm blessed. Thank God, I'm blessed."

Worship:
In All Things Give Thanks

The attitude of Lester, reflected in his words of gratitude and blessing, touches the very heart of worship. Regardless of the circumstances one faces, the grace is offered to lift one's mind and will to the God who cares and sustains. The grace of gratitude in the midst of destruction and loss is enacted and embodied through worship, especially through the offering of the Eucharist. The celebration of Mass, as well as other sacramental expressions of liturgy, involves the use of sacred objects, vestments and designated places for worship. The Office of Worship is entrusted with the responsibility of providing for the reverent use of and care for all sacred and blessed objects, liturgical vestments and consecrated places for worship. The destructive effects of Katrina posed a significant challenge to the Office of Worship in honoring its responsibilities.

• The vibrant faith of the African – American community was evident after Katrina

The Office of Worship was able to reopen along with other archdiocesan offices on October 1, 2005, in Baton Rouge. After a week of organizational meetings and a series of sessions dealing with future needs of the archdiocese in light of Katrina, the Office of Worship was able to be re-established at St. Rita Parish in Harahan. The Office of Worship set for itself five essential tasks in order to meet archdiocesan needs.

The initial task of the Office of Worship was both obvious and necessary: the collection of sacred objects and related artifacts from flooded and destroyed churches. Closely related to the first task was the need to catalogue the objects recovered, and to collect and distribute donations from around the state and country so parishes could purchase sacred vessels, vestments, statues, and various books and hymnals for liturgy.

The third aspect of the Office of Worship's work was planning and assisting at the Masses celebrated by Archbishop Hughes at St. Louis Cathedral, as well as liturgies offered at various other locations throughout the metro area. These eucharistic celebrations were attended not only by the Catholic community, but many people from other faiths also attended and found much comfort and spiritual support.

The Office of Worship assisted many institutions and parishes in the restoration and renovation of chapels and churches in order to assure that the requirements of canon law as it relates to liturgical practice were properly observed. Finally, as churches, and other sacred places for worship were renovated and reopened, the Office of Worship assisted in the planning and celebration of the blessings and dedications of these holy places.

In the aftermath of Katrina, many needs became evident, none more important than the need for people to come together and worship. There was a deep desire to thank God and pray for those graces necessary to persevere. There was not only the need to preserve, reverently care for, and distribute sacred objects, but also to recognize the archdiocese as a source of records and documents for parishes and for civic life in general. The need to preserve, restore, and catalogue these records became a major priority of the archdiocese after Katrina. It is to that important work that we now turn our attention.

• The saving of sacred vessels was crucial for ongoing parish worship. Father MichaelJoseph Nguyen of Resurrection of Our Lord Parish, right, examines a monstrance

Preservation Amid Destruction

Damaged sacred objects

Church records damaged by water and mold

A major theme, if not *the* major theme, of this book is hope. (The concluding chapter of this book addresses this theological virtue in some detail.) Hope is often associated with the future and what might come to be. However, if hope is to be realistic and not degenerate into unfounded optimism or wishful thinking, hope must be joined with memory. This union of past and future is fundamental to the Catholic mind. The past – memory – is not the recalling of long-ago events. The church's memory is preserved and kept alive in the present through tradition – the living faith of the dead and not the dead faith of the living. The memory of what God has done serves to strengthen the Church in the present and guide her pilgrimage into God's future. The present, devoid of memory, yields a rootless wandering about, and a future without direction.

• This church safe could not protect important records and sacred objects

The Archives of the Archdiocese of New Orleans is charged with collecting, cataloguing, and preserving the historical experiences of the archdiocese. The Old Ursuline Convent, the Howard Avenue building, and the archdiocesan building on Walmsley Avenue were used as housing facilities. Hurricane Katrina delivered severe damage to church parishes, schools, archdiocesan facilities, and the three archival sites. The archives office faced two initial challenges: the transportation of archival holdings to a safe storage location in Baton Rouge, and locating and assessing the condition and availability of records within archdiocesan parishes. The damage was so severe in some parishes that records were completely lost.

As with most things Katrina-related, Dr. Charles Nolan and Dr. Emilie Leumas, archdiocesan archivists, had to develop through trial and error, new techniques for the recovery, restoration, and preservation of severely damaged artifacts and documents. Upon receiving damaged documents, they were appraised, recorded, processed, and then sent to a sub-zero freezer at Hill Memorial Library at Louisiana State University. The freezer was crucial for killing mold and inhibiting any future growth. A special conservation room, kept at an average temperature of 72 degrees and humidity of 40 percent, was set up in the Catholic Life Center in Baton Rouge.

Invaluable assistance was provided by LSU Graduate School of Library and Information Science volunteers and students. Elaine Smyth, special collections curator at LSU, visited with archives staff and provided guidance in setting up the conservation room. Since Katrina, archdiocesan archivists have made major national and international group presentations on their work. The work and ministry of the archives staff is ongoing, and because of Katrina has expanded in new and innovative ways.

Lectionary at Immaculate Conception, Marrero

• Removing church registers from St. Philip the Apostle, New Orleans

Dr. Charles Nolan, archivist for the Archdiocese of New Orleans

In times of destruction and dislocation, the need to preserve and honor in memory all that has gone before is essential for hope. The Archives of the Archdiocese of New Orleans is entrusted with the crucial task of recording and preserving sacramental records and sacred objects. After Katrina, this work became more critical, and time was of the essence. With so much destruction and water, along with exposure to heat and humidity, recovery had to be done quickly, but with great care. Through the efforts of Dr. Charles Nolan and Dr. Emilie Leumas, the Office of the Archives was able to retrieve and document an astonishing 5,311 sacred objects, 3,761 sacramental records, and 2,500 images. This monumental task was completed according to a sacred patrimonial, that is, an archdiocesan wide policy, which established guidelines for the proper removal, documentation, restoration and reuse of sacred and temporal objects (those not used in worship). The sacred patrimonial was prepared by Deacon David Warriner, vice chancellor for the archdiocese. There was also the need to formulate policy for the proper retrieving and preserving of sacramental records which canon law requires each parish to maintain. Dr. Leumas was

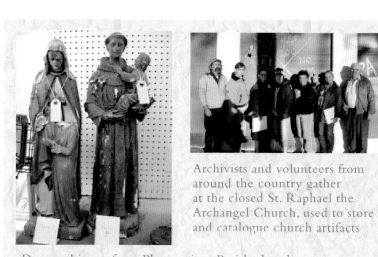

Archivists and volunteers from around the country gather at the closed St. Raphael the Archangel Church, used to store and catalogue church artifacts

Damaged items from Plaquemines Parish churches

responsible for preparing this policy for the Office of the Archives. The work of the archivist is important for several additional reasons. Because of the long historical reach of the Catholic Church in the metro area and throughout the

• Toppled pews at St. Frances Xavier Cabrini Church

state, the preservation of records is crucial if researchers are to obtain a glimpse into the past. Churches, convents, and chapels kept records of important events in the life of the individual and community. From birth to death, churches were the depository of the key events associated with a community. More often than not, the administering of various sacraments – baptism, first Communion, weddings – were community occasions that blended faith and culture. Since the Catholic Church performed the vast majority of funerals, the recordings of death by the churches proved to be a vital asset to civil authorities, especially in terms of listing the cause of death.

Dr. Emilie Leumas, left, with members of the Association of Catholic Diocesan Archivists

Volunteers help clean and restore artifacts

The extraordinary work of Drs. Nolan and Leumas in recovering, restoring and preserving sacred vessels greatly exceeded the basic requirements of canon law. They took on the added work of helping churches that were able to reopen, but found their sacred vessels badly damaged, destroyed, or simply washed away in the waters of Katrina. Parishes that were unable to reopen, as well as those with surplus vessels, were in the position to donate their vessels and objects for worship to those parishes in need. While worship may not continue in one church, through the passing on of sacred

• Archival recovery begins on church sacramental registers

• Chadron State College volunteer catalogues artifacts at St. Raphael the Archangel Church

The Legacy Endures

It may strike one as odd that a chapter on Katrina, a still fresh wound, should open with a view to the past historic sacrifices of priests and religious men and women. Yet, if the notion of legacy is rightly understood, then to look into a distant mirror is most appropriate. For a legacy is not something static or frozen in time. An authentic legacy endures and continues its power to inspire through the centuries. As Sir Isaac Newton so wisely observed, if we see further than others, it is because we stand on the shoulders of giants. These giants in faith, this great "cloud of witnesses," provide the shoulders upon which we stand to confront and overcome our present challenges. A living legacy is a gift of grace which reminds us that we are not alone. In bright days and starlit nights, there is an unconquerable power for good, a Light which shines and is not overcome, a Love which drives out all fear, a Hope which draws us beyond every reason to despair.

When future generations look back on the destruction of Katrina, may they, with the eyes of faith, see a people tested, but not overcome. May they see a cloud of witnesses to life and hope, and draw strength, as we do, from previous generations who answered the call to serve. May they see, as they face their own time of testing, what good can be brought forth through the Holy Spirit who renews earth and heart through love. May that same Holy Spirit raise up giants in faith for every time and season; and may God raise up priests, brothers and sisters after his own heart.

• Biloxi Bishop Thomas Rodi, left, reviews damage to a church in Biloxi. He was joined by Baton Rouge Bishop Robert Muench and Archbishop Paul Josef Cordes of the Vatican.

vessels, the Lord continued to be praised. And this "passing on" of sacred vessels was not limited to churches under archdiocesan auspices. For example, the Belle Chasse Naval Air Base Chapel had to be rebuilt after the storm. The Archives office was able to supply the base with a tabernacle, altar, candle holders, and most surprisingly, with stained glass as the result of a donation from Holy Cross Parish in New Jersey.

The work of the Archives office proved invaluable to the archdiocese as a whole and individual parishes in particular. The wind and water of Katrina washed away so many structures and changed so many lives. The need to preserve sacred vessels and church records grew in importance with the passage of time. The heroic work of those in the Archives office in honoring the past, keeping alive sacred memories, and reverently caring for sacred vessels provided hope in a time of destruction.

The preserving and cataloguing of church documents was a vital and challenging undertaking for the Archives staff. Dr. Charles Nolan reviews documents temporarily stored at the Catholic Life Center in Baton Rouge

St. Frances Cabrini
Church, two weeks
after Katrina

Chapter 5 _____

COMMUNICATIONS: THE MILK OF EMERGENCY MANAGEMENT

A distinguishing feature of much of the contemporary world is the pervasiveness of technological communications. From the Internet to the cell phone and all matter of gadgets in between, we find ourselves tied to an artificial umbilical cord.

It's hard, and for some impossible, to remember a time when we were not surfing the Internet, text messaging, or answering the cell phone that seems to be our constant companion. Not only can we be in touch with important persons and events, but we also can connect instantly. Information races as never before. Events, effects and reactions all mesh with dizzying speed. We find ourselves in a wired world.

The efficiency and economy of telecommunications have become self-evident even to the most resistant among us. To hold on to one's No. 2 pencil and writing tablet instead of logging on and e-mailing reveals a refusal to be a passenger on the superhighway into the future. Yet we know that while everything has its value, we also know that everything comes at a price.

The new information technologies open up a number of dangers. Many people store vital, personal information in their computers. Hackers find ways to access this information for financial gain, as well as a desire to cause embarrassment. Many computer users have had their personal identities stolen, causing great damage. Those who study the human brain are finding the extended use of computers affects the development and function of the brain. This is especially true for the very young. Brain centers that control such things as thinking, producing and coping with emotions, the processing and evaluation of external reality, and the ability to form face-to-face relationships, have been physiologically and chemically altered in recent generations. The overwhelming presence of information technologies has affected the learning process and the school setting itself. Due to the powerful and pervasive presence of new learning technologies, which are visual and interactive, the traditional book as the medium for learning is being replaced. The ability of students to concentrate for extended periods of time without visual stimulation has been diminished.

A seafood truck caught in a tree in Empire, La.

All of the concerns associated with the new information technologies, not to mention the real dangers of sexual exploitation on the under-regulated Internet, have not slowed our appetite for newer and faster gadgets. "Slow start-ups and dropped calls" are drawbacks that just come with the territory. We have hitched our wagons to the technological stars of these new and constantly changing modes of telecommunications. With each passing day, we become more and more drawn into and dependent upon the web of our creation. Such dependency carries its own dangers. Hurricane Katrina revealed just how dangerous our addiction to technology can be. And in no area were the effects of the breakdown in information technology so keenly felt as that of communications.

Technology vs. Katrina: Katrina Won!

The story of the Tower of Babel is as old as the Scriptures and as current as our newspapers. Throughout history man has sought to go it alone without any reference to a transcendental reality. Belief in the power of our intelligence and its application through technology has given rise to an arrogance that acknowledges no limits and seeks total power and control. From the latest computer to the marvels of the "new biology," we celebrate the work of our hands, too often uncritically.

• The fourth floor Clarion Herald office at the Howard Avenue location experienced severe damage

No one would reasonably deny the contributions of modern technology to the quality of life we enjoy. Perhaps the greatest impact of our technological culture is in the area of telecommunications. The computer and cell phone are pervasive. We are "wired" as no culture before. Cell phones are part of our everyday world and wardrobe. Everywhere we go we stay in touch and informed. The portable nature of these devices makes them convenient and ever present. With every passing day we become more dependent on our technology.

Just how dependent we are became clear during and after Katrina. The winds and waters of Katrina rendered inoperable the means of communications that have become part of our taken-for-granted world. Numerous cell phone towers were knocked down. For weeks cell phones with a 504 area code would not work. Large areas of metro New Orleans were without electricity. Everything from telephones to computers to ordinary televisions were not functioning. The major local television stations were severely damaged and had to partner with sister stations in the area, or re-route signals to transmitters in other states. Even radio stations experienced a rough go since the radio towers were either severely damaged or completely put out of service. The only major daily newspaper in the metro area suffered extensive damage to its facilities. Publishing had to be suspended while a new operations center was found. All of the familiar forms of communication, personal and public, came to a sudden and protracted halt.

Armed members of the Louisiana Wildlife and Fisheries Department escort Notre Dame seminarians from flooded buildings

Not only were profound shocks delivered to our technological systems and infrastructure, Katrina landed a traumatic blow to our psyche. As with the sinking of the Titanic, the massive disruption and destruction of our technological power to communicate was impossible to comprehend. The Titanic was unsinkable and our telecommunications could not fail on such a grand scale. Yet both did occur. The storm not only toppled buildings and towers, something deeper and more lasting occurred, namely, the belief in the absolute power of technology to render us secure was called into question. We were trapped in a silent nightmare. Our calls, texts, and e-mails for help, rescue, and deliverance could not be heard by the outside world. We were alone. The very means of our comforts and efficiencies had become the source of many frustrations and even torments. Our eyes had been opened. We would never again look at what we had built and come to depend on it in the same way. Katrina left its scars on the land and the terrain within.

The Inside Job

All of the destructive effects from Katrina on the metro area were experienced by the archdiocese. The vastness and organizational complexity of the archdiocese (the archdiocese reaches into eight civil parishes) only added to the challenges. The contributions and work of the archdiocese are not restricted to Catholics only. Many non-Catholics avail themselves of the numerous services and programs offered. The Catholic archdiocese affects large segments of society, and this civic dimension adds greatly to the common good and the quality of life which many enjoy. It became imperative, despite the many challenges, for the archdiocese to be up and operational as quickly as possible.

The communication problems had to be confronted head on if the mission of the archdiocese was to continue. When it became clear that the storm was not going to veer away

The "Grand Old Flag" still proudly waves after Katrina

from the metro area, meetings and plans were already being formulated. This initial pre-emptive approach proved crucial. Archbishop Hughes, even before the storm struck, was having conversations with public officials and members of his Administrative Council. As we said in the previous chapter, Catholic Charities Archdiocese of New Orleans would play a key role, especially immediately after the storm passed. In fact, members of CCANO were making preparations to care for the displaced even *before* the storm arrived.

offered and gratefully accepted as a temporary headquarters. This was an indispensable asset in gathering personnel, planning tactics and strategy, evaluating approaches, and gauging progress. This temporary headquarters became the center from which all communications, both internal and those directed to the general public, would be formulated and then disseminated.

Bishop Robert Muench of the Diocese of Baton Rouge provided invaluable support by opening the Catholic Life Center as a temporary headquarters for the archdiocese. This temporary headquarters became the center from which all communications were prepared and disseminated.

• The city sat in flood waters for two weeks before the waters receded. The green roofs of buildings at Xavier University are easy to spot.

After the storm passed and the subsequent flooding occurred, Archbishop Hughes and Baton Rouge Bishop Robert Muench joined together to pool resources so a coordinated response could be put into action. Bishop Muench provided invaluable support. The Catholic Life Center, the administration offices of the Baton Rouge Diocese, was

Within a few days after Katrina, Archbishop Hughes was holding daily meetings with his Administrative Council and other archdiocesan officials. These meetings were held daily, usually two hours in duration. Each Administrative Council member would present a daily report as to plans, activities, progress, frustrations and any new proposals for service.

These afternoon sessions proved invaluable: the archbishop was kept updated and offered his own guidance on various issues and proposals. Individual council members were kept informed about the work of other departments. These exchanges were crucial, for they invited feedback that was essential in going forward. In addition, the perspective of participants was enlarged beyond the responsibilities of their own departments. Session participants received a sense of the whole picture and how a particular department blended with other projects and perspectives. This holistic approach proved quite effective in terms of avoiding duplication and working at cross purposes. These daily meetings facilitated the work of the archdiocese in responding to the manifold needs of people.

Besides these planned briefings, there were small meetings among members within the same department throughout the day, as well as unscheduled meetings among members of other archdiocesan departments. The fact that the archdiocese was housed in a single location made these informal and unscheduled meetings more likely and more productive. The Catholic Life Center's telecommunications infrastructure was sound. After several weeks, a portion of the cell phone network was operational from the 504 area code. This development greatly aided the archdiocese's ability to conduct its ministries. A number of new cell phones, with area codes outside of 504, were secured, which increased communications. Computers, fax and copy machines allowed for more extensive contact and greater coordination. This increased contact through meetings,

Standing in Jackson Square, Archbishop Hughes speaks at press conference accepting a $1 million show of support from the National Catholic Educational Association.

conversations, and telecommunications was most important for creating an atmosphere of cooperation and collaboration between the two dioceses. Employees of the archdiocese were the invited guests of the Baton Rouge Diocese, and as such, a prime objective was to respect and learn from the practices and information resources of the host diocese. While the two dioceses worked together in close quarters, which easily could have caused tension, Archbishop Hughes and Bishop Muench placed a high value on cooperation, collaboration, and sensitivity to the needs of others. Through their positive daily working relationship, what could have become contentious remained hospitable and harmonious throughout.

• Baton Rouge Bishop Robert Muench, center, explains some post-Katrina strategy to Archbishop Hughes, far left, Gov. Blanco, Archbishop Cordes, Father Larry Snyder of Catholic Charities USA and U.S. Rep. Bobby Jindal.

"We Were Moving Men..."

The Archdiocese of New Orleans, like any major, modern organization, is very dependent on technology, especially information technology. Katrina inflicted severe damage to telecommunications equipment and infrastructure. The need to address this damage was essential from the very beginning. The lion's share of the work fell, naturally, to the Internet Technology Office (IT). It was to that office that the work of recovering equipment, restoring services, and rebuilding the infrastructure was assigned.

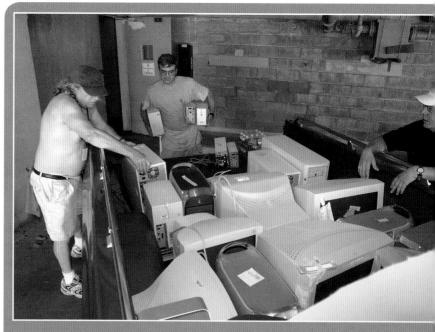

One of the great challenges and most pressing needs confronting the archdiocese immediately after Katrina was re-establishing communications. Charles Wayne Hunter, a 32-year AT&T employee, worked tirelessly to restore telephone service to the archdiocesan building on Howard Avenue, home to Catholic Charities Archdiocese of New Orleans and other offices. Hunter, along with Xavier University and Louisiana State Baptist laymen, was also responsible for bringing thousands of volunteers to New Orleans to gut over 200 houses and repair over 75 homes in the New Orleans area.

The battered remains of Prince of Peace Church in Arabi

Leaving aside for a moment the immense technical challenges and sheer volume of work, several other factors complicated the recovery. Although the archdiocesan administration building at Walmsley Avenue and the archdiocesan office building at Howard Avenue were severely damaged, there were still important and undamaged equipment and records that needed to be retrieved. In order to accomplish this task, members of the IT Department made numerous trips from Baton Rouge to these sites in New Orleans. Due to the limited presence of law enforcement personnel, these trips were dangerous. At times, military escorts were needed. In spite of the danger, staff members from IT were able to obtain almost all the computer systems for staff from each location.

In the face of personal danger, IT staffers were a kind of "advance party" in search of temporary facilities in the metro area. Technical supplies were hard to come by. Yet IT personnel were able, in an amazingly short period of time, to obtain computers, files, and technical supplies that enabled archdiocesan personnel still in Baton Rouge to go forward with some sense of normalcy. Members of the IT Department were, in the words of Justin Gibson, IT director, "moving men; we scrounged for supplies; we worked outside of the normal IT box to provide support to the needs of the archdiocese."

Not only day-to-day challenges had to be met, but the long-term rebuilding of the archdiocese's telecommunications system and infrastructure also had to be addressed. A significant step in this work was accomplished when the archdiocese reopened a temporary administration office in Orleans Parish at Incarnate Word Parish. This was achieved at the beginning of 2006. The next major step was the outfitting of both the Walmsley and Howard Avenue locations. This infrastructure rebuilding was completed over the next *four months*! It was an amazing feat.

Katrina has taught all of us a great deal. Perhaps the major lesson to be learned as it relates to telecommunications was this: the best practices and standards in the telecommunications industry were followed, but they *didn't* work in the face of Katrina. The traditional best practices for IT in responding to a weather event made a fatal assumption: that servers could be quickly recovered after a storm. Not so with Katrina. It took several weeks for these essential pieces of equipment to be retrieved. In order to ensure this doesn't happen in the future, all archdiocesan disaster recovery responses are now placed in automated and push-button formats. This new structure allows for technical operations to be completely restored from a facility in Monroe, La., within eight hours.

Communications is not just an "in-house" task. The archdiocese is a significant presence throughout the region. Hurricane Katrina left many challenges for the dissemination of crucial information to wider audiences. The archdiocese took advantage of the availability of both religious and secular media to accomplish this important task. It is to this dimension of communications that we now turn.

Public Voice of the Archdiocese

Thousands of individuals and families are touched daily through the multiple ministries offered by the archdiocese. It was only natural that the public voice of the archdiocese would be both important and eagerly awaited. In addition to those who had previously been aided by archdiocesan programs and services, in the aftermath of Katrina thousands more turned to the archdiocese for aid and comfort. Public information was a crucial challenge and a serious responsibility in service of the common good.

promoting recovery is information. Factual information presented in a prudent, responsible manner – not rumors, gossip, or unfounded speculation – is expected from those in positions of authority. With the prevalence of personal forms of telecommunications, the challenge to provide factual information, correct rumors, and supply important details to stories is a demanding, ongoing responsibility. In the early days and weeks after Katrina there was enormous pressure for information concerning everything from anxious parents worried about schools, to parishioners wanting to know about their parish churches, to employees seeking information about their futures with the archdiocese. These major areas of inquiry and numerous others made it imperative that the public voice of the archdiocese be clear, consistent, factual, prudent, and in service of the public good.

Frank J. Methe, Clarion Herald photographer, took post-Katrina photographs to record historical events for the Clarion Herald.

• Bishop Muench welcomed Archbishop Hughes in Baton Rouge and provided invaluable support to the New Orleans Archdiocese

During times of emergency and crisis, one of the most important elements of securing good public order and

As was mentioned previously, during the first week after Katrina, Archbishop Hughes and his administrative council had gathered in Baton Rouge, emerging from the initial meeting with a number of important operational principles to guide the work going forward. As these principles related to communications, the directive was simple and imperative: in light of the People First Principle, all public communications must be such that the well-being of those who look to the Church for material and spiritual support are truly served. Specifically, all communications from the archdiocese must be accurate, not speculative, so as to avoid raising false hopes which could produce unrealistic expectations. A corollary to the Accuracy Principle was the Timely Principle. Simply put, it was more important that information be presented, not quickly, but within a timeframe that ensured accuracy, completeness, and allowed those affected by the information to make prudent decisions. In the days and weeks after Katrina, the general public was starving for any bit of information. Also the secular news outlets – local, national, and international – were under enormous pressure to "get the story" and "get it first." It was decided early on that while maintaining cordial and cooperative relations with the media, the archdiocese would resist those pressures seeking public statements before they could be prudently offered. This was not always easy to accomplish, but in the long run the public was better served and less time was spent having to correct or clarify statements.

• Archbishop Hughes speaks at a news conference with an interfaith group

The Daily Plan

A delicate balance had to be struck when it came to public statements. While the need to refrain from speculation or wishful statements was in order, there was an equally important need for the archdiocese to keep the public informed about its plans and the services offered. How to accomplish this Solomonic task?

"The proper exercise of this right (society's right to information) demands that the content of the communication be true and – within the limits set by justice and charity – complete. Further, it should be communicated honestly and properly. This means that in the gathering and in the publication of news, the moral law and the legitimate rights and dignity of man should be upheld." – *Inter mirifica, No. 5, on the Means of Social Communications, Second Vatican Council*

The following approach was formulated: Archbishop Hughes would offer a daily briefing to the media concerning present and future plans of the archdiocese. The Archbishop would make known his schedule for the day and the week as a whole. Also, this daily briefing offered the opportunity to answer questions, clarify statements and correct any stories making the rounds. Along with the briefings, the Archbishop would make a daily video of the briefing and include any message he wished to share with the people of the archdiocese and the wider public. These videos were sent to local media outlets. Once again, the assistance of the Diocese of Baton Rouge proved invaluable. Not only did the diocese make its media facilities available, but the communications office produced and distributed the videos to the local media sources.

Along with the daily briefings and video presentations, Archbishop Hughes wrote a number of letters to the people of the archdiocese. In those areas where churches were operational, the letters were read. Even where churches would not open because of storm damage, temporary locations were established so Mass could be offered, parishioners could reconnect for mutual support, and information such as any communiqué from the archbishop could be shared. Beside these archdiocesan-generated communications, the archbishop made himself more available for interviews with various media outlets. Just as effective, if not more so, were the numerous visits by the archbishop to such sites as shelters, food banks, hospitals, and homes for the elderly. Of great importance were the numerous meetings and presentations to various political and faith-based organizations. On many occasions, the archbishop and members of the archdiocese led visitors on tours of devastated areas. To see the damage caused by Katrina on television was one thing, but an onsite inspection often left those who came speechless, heart-broken, and committed to providing assistance.

While the archbishop was tending to his many pastoral and administrative duties, in addition to reporting on the state of the archdiocese through various forms of media, the archdiocesan Office of Communications was given a role to play. The archdiocesan spokesman was to be readily available to all media in order to present information and clarify and answer questions that could arise. Over the years leading up to Katrina, the archdiocese had established a good, professional working relationship with local media. This proved to be quite important after Katrina. For while the media (local, national and international) can often rightly be accused of sensationalism and an uncritical rush to be first with a story, the media after Katrina was highly professional and responsible. The archdiocese was able to freely access media – print and electronic, local, national, and international – in order to inform both Catholics and the general public about events and programs. Of special value was the availability of radio in those early days and weeks after Katrina. Specifically, WWL-870 AM radio was most cooperative in informing the public about the work of the archdiocese. Also, WWL Channel 4 television, operating temporarily out of Baton Rouge, went to extraordinary lengths to provide air time for the archdiocese. The same can be said for the other television stations as they began rebroadcasting. The working relationship between media and the archdiocese was one of mutual respect and trust.

Archdiocesan Media

The major instrument used by the archdiocese to address Katrina-related issues was its own newspaper, the Clarion Herald. Before Katrina, the newspaper was published on a biweekly basis with a circulation of 69,000 and a working staff of 12 full-time employees and one part-time employee. The usual method of delivery was through the U.S. Postal Service at a cost of $250,000 per year (the cost of mailing is one of the most expensive aspects of publishing).

When television station WLAE-CH32 resumed broadcasts, the archdiocese was able to provide viewers with comprehensive summaries of activities and future plans concerning schools, parishes, and the overall condition of the archdiocese.

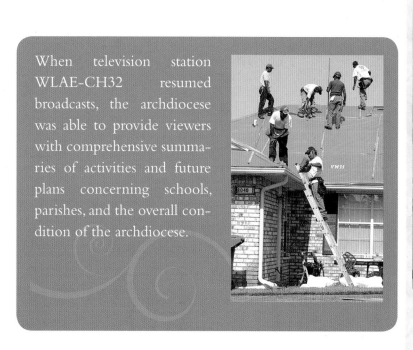

Clarion Herald staff members working out of the Catholic Life Center in Baton Rouge prepare the first post-Katrina issue on October 1, 2005

Pre-Katrina, the offices of the Clarion Herald were located at the Howard Avenue site of the archdiocese in downtown New Orleans. The office experienced severe damage and was unable to publish. Like other archdiocesan offices, the newspaper staff assembled in Baton Rouge and operated out of the Catholic Life Center. It was a high priority to restart publishing as soon as possible. The need for information from the official newspaper of the archdiocese became more urgent with each passing day. As the Clarion staff worked feverishly to publish, they also filed numerous stories with the Catholic News Service (CNS) in Washington, D.C. The stories filed with CNS played a crucial role in connecting the archdiocese with those who were displaced around the country. The Clarion also set up a Web site that served as the official outlet for news concerning the archdiocese. The Web site proved to be a vital link between the archdiocese, the Catholic population, and the general public. The Web site also was an effective way of informing those who could provide assistance in meeting the needs of the archdiocese.

• Prince of Peace Church, Arabi

Through determination and effective leadership, in a little over one month after Katrina (October 1, 2005), the Clarion Herald published its first post-Katrina issue. The first issue consisted of eight pages with a 35,000 issue run. The newspaper had to be printed in Lafayette due to the lack of availability of undamaged equipment and facilities. Granted a first issue was in hand, but an obvious and challenging question arose – how would delivery of the newspaper be accomplished? Mail delivery in the metro area was non-existent. Committed to fulfilling its mission as the official newspaper of the archdiocese, along with an unflinching resolve to serve the church and the common good, the decision was made to have staff members drop bundles of newspapers at every large church parish in the Diocese of Baton Rouge, Lafayette and Houma-Thibodaux. These dioceses were selected because of the large concentration of evacuees who had sought refuge from the storm. In a show of splendid cooperation, these large churches not only served the spiritual needs of the newly arrived, but they became points of reconnection with home for evacuees. Also, neighboring churches would pick up copies of the Clarion Herald and provide them to the displaced who attended Mass.

Through determination and effective leadership, in a little over one month after Katrina, the Clarion Herald published its first post-Katrina issue. That initial publication consisted of eight pages with a 35,000 run.

The rush of important news events prompted the Clarion Herald to grow in size and publish more frequently. The newspaper grew in size from the initial eight pages to 12 pages. The Clarion would now publish on a weekly basis. The size and frequency of publishing continued from the temporary Baton Rouge offices through Thanksgiving 2005. Just after Thanksgiving, the Clarion Herald was able to set up publishing offices in New Orleans at the Old Ursuline

Convent. It was not until March 2006 that the CH would be able to return to its pre-Katrina offices at Howard Avenue.

Doing Good And Doing Well

Conventional wisdom holds that doing well while doing good is mutually exclusive. As with a great deal of conventional wisdom, the above view is wrong and unsubstantiated by the work of the Clarion Herald after Katrina. This is especially the case when we are called to confront unconventional times and events. And Katrina certainly qualifies as an unconventional event which ushered in unconventional times. The ability to "think outside the box" became imperative after the storm.

Peter Finney Jr., executive editor of the Clarion Herald

Under the leadership of Peter Finney Jr., executive editor of the Clarion Herald, a number of prudent and responsible practices were undertaken. A prime example of doing both good and well was the decision that, as the newspaper grew in size and, with it, advertising, the Clarion Herald would cut its advertising rates in half! This decision was good for advertisers who faced challenging economic circumstances. As one might expect the volume of advertising increased, which helped newspaper's bottom line – a clear case of doing good and well at the same time. Just as important as bolstering the financial picture, the amount of good will generated was enormous.

In the early days and weeks after Katrina, the general situation in and around Baton Rouge was stressful with new tensions arising from an influx of displaced persons, which increased frustrations from having to make significant adjustments in daily routines such as driving, shopping, and related activities. The Clarion wanted to make the newspaper available with as little difficulty as possible. Through distribution efforts, the Clarion reached its readership and no doubt increased the number of readers. As with the decision to discount advertising rates, distributing the newspaper in Baton Rouge, Lafayette and Houma-Thibodaux engendered a swell of good will. The practice of fostering good will was not done in a manipulative manner, but it was enacted out of a deep commitment to the overall mission of the archdiocese to be of service, especially at this time.

The decision to deliver the Clarion in bulk by courier proved to be crucial for the bottom line and the very survival of publishing operations. Prior to Katrina, it cost approximately $250,000 a year to mail 26 issues to the 68,000 subscribers. Post-Katrina, the cost to deliver 45 issues to a circulation of 58,000 was estimated to be $50,000 a year. This amounted to a yearly savings of $200,000 based on the cost of issues produced, and with this savings the Clarion would continue to publish. Once again, we see a splendid example of doing good and doing well.

Across the country, newspaper publishing is facing serious financial challenges. This is especially true for dioceses with newspapers. After Katrina, the desire to continue a crucial medium for information and evangelization had to confront hard economic realities. The Clarion Herald received two large grants from the Catholic Communication Campaign ($225,000 a year for two years totaling $450,000), which allowed the newspaper to continue to be published and distributed. Also, these grants provided the much-needed time for the rebuilding and strengthening of the Clarion's advertising base while continuing to publish. As important as these grants proved to be, the long-term survival of the Clarion had to be faced.

Before Katrina, the operating budget for the Clarion Herald was derived from two main sources – circulation (70 percent) and advertising (30 percent). The vast majority of circulation income was obtained by billing the individual parishes based on the number of subscribers within each local parish. Every family with a child in a Catholic elementary school receives the Clarion and pays a fee at the beginning of the school year. In the post-Katrina world, significant adjustments had to be made, adjustments that would allow the Clarion to continue publication while taking into account the new economic realities affecting parishes, schools, and families.

Once again following the "doing good and doing well" principle, the decision was made to chart the following course: with the grants from the Catholic Communication Campaign and Our Sunday Visitor ($25,000), along with an improving advertising base, the Clarion decided not to charge parishioners for the newspapers. This practice was kept in place for 11 months! In addition to the above-mentioned grants and increased advertising revenue, prudent stewardship in the years before Katrina had allowed the Clarion to build up financial reserves in case of an economic slump or emergency. Well, Katrina certainly qualified as an emergency. The willingness of the Clarion to offer the newspaper without charge by drawing on its own reserves evoked an abundance of good will throughout the archdiocese. And good will should never be undervalued as a critical resource.

• Few houses remained standing on the Mississippi Gulf Coast

• Vehicles resting on houses were a common sight

After Katrina's waters left Notre Dame Seminary, brown grass and sheep remained

At the end of this 11-month grace period, August 2006, the Clarion was granted permission to resume billing church parishes for the newspaper. In consideration of post-Katrina realities, the Clarion would charge 80 percent of what a parish was paying pre-Katrina. While this represented a 20 percent reduction in cost to each parish, it was decided that parishes still experiencing financial difficulties would pay what they could reasonably afford. If a parish simply could not pay for the newspaper, that parish would continue to receive the newspaper at reduced or no cost.

As more and more aspects of normalcy returned, the Clarion began to reevaluate some of its pre-Katrina practices. The 80 percent billing to parishes has continued into 2009. Further financial decisions would be made as circumstances prudently indicated. As to advertising rates, it was decided that the 50 percent discount rate offered the first year after Katrina would be adjusted (a 40 percent reduction in rates was offered the second year after Katrina, a 25 percent reduction during the third year, and 15 percent in 2009). The $15 dollar per family fee from Catholic elementary schools has continued. Overall, there has been a dramatic shift in the percentages of contributions from the standard sources of the Clarion's operational budget. Pre-Katrina, approximately 70 percent of income was derived from circulation and 30 percent from advertising sales. Post-Katrina, about 50 percent of income was realized through circulation and 50 percent of revenue was obtained through advertising. This shift could be accounted for in light of the smaller population in the metro area, hence, circulation would decline along with revenue percentages. As to the increase in advertising revenue, the decision to deliver the Clarion in bulk to local parish churches has struck a responsive chord with both parishioners and advertisers. The fact that the newspaper is readily available enhances the visibility of the advertisers' messages. Parishioners in the course of attending Mass are able to take home both the church bulletin and the newspaper.

The example of the Clarion Herald gives clear evidence that doing good and doing well are possible, and even desirable. Through fidelity to its own mission, prudent stewardship of resources, and an extraordinary commitment to serve its readership, the Clarion Herald has not only survived Katrina, but in many ways, has emerged even stronger.

In Their Own Words

The following stories are a cross section of those individuals who were affected in various ways by Katrina, and what archdiocesan communications meant for them, their families, and loved ones.

Albert and his family evacuated to Memphis as Katrina approached. He is a young professional who lives in the Uptown section of New Orleans. "I guess I waited too late to make arrangements for my family. I was hoping the storm would turn. When it became obvious it was coming here, the closest place I could find a room was Memphis. I expected to be away a couple of days. When the levees broke, and I saw the pictures on TV, I knew we would be away for awhile. In addition to national coverage, I became a regular visitor to the archdiocesan Web site. My wife and I are active in our parish and my daughter attends a pre-kindergarten program in a Catholic school. Through the daily updates, I felt I had the information I needed that things were being done. This gave me and my wife confidence and a determination to come back to New Orleans."

Ethel is a retired and "dedicated" Catholic. She lives alone since her husband died several years ago. She evacuated to Baton Rouge and lived with her daughter. Ethel stayed in Baton Rouge for almost a year until she could "get enough money to get the house back up." "My parish church has always been important to me, more so after my husband died. Ever since we've been married, we always went to Mass together. I had been worrying that I'd never get back to New Orleans and my church. It was such a comfort to keep seeing and reading about the archdiocese. I was so proud of the archbishop and seeing all the things he was doing. I went to a Catholic church in Baton Rouge and messages from the archbishop would be read. This would give me hope that I would go back to my house and my church."

An archdiocesan priest, who asked that his name not be used, offered the following. "I always thought of the Clarion Herald as part of the furniture, nothing special, and very familiar. Not anymore. It was not just the excellent way they handled Katrina, but I was very impressed with the understanding shown to parishes. For a number of months there was no charge for the paper. When payment was resumed, it was at a reduced rate. Consideration was given to the parishes facing difficult financial problems. I'll never think of the Clarion in the same way. There was a lot of loss after Katrina. There was also a good deal of grace."

Louis is a 38-year-old medical technician who stayed in New Orleans "to help people who were worse off than me." He sent his wife and two children to Arizona to stay with relatives. "To see them go away, even for a short time, was the hardest thing for me. I knew it was for the best. They'd be safe." Reflecting on those days and early weeks after Katrina, Louis said, "Along with all the police, military, and aid workers, there were priests among us. This was so important. I felt proud to be a Catholic. The priests would hear confession, give words of support and comfort, and they were able to bring us news. We were so busy and communications were so bad, the priest would often try to contact our loved ones. We didn't feel so isolated. A priest was able to make contact with my family. I can't tell you what that meant to me."

Notre Dame Seminary had to move its operations to St. Joseph Abbey in St. Benedict, La.

Communications Is Evangelization

For the Catholic Church, evangelization and communication cannot be separated. The commission to evangelize to the ends of the earth, until the close of the ages, comes from Jesus just before the Ascension. The primary means of evangelization is through preaching, that is, communication through the preached word. Under the guidance of the Holy Spirit, communication is not just the sharing of news, but good news – the Gospel. Each period employs its own method, from the time of St. Paul to the electronic circuits of modern media, but what remains constant is fidelity to preaching the Gospel. From the catacombs of the early

church to the shelters after Katrina, the Good News was shared by clergy and lay people. From the first rush of the Spirit at Pentecost to the winds of Katrina, people of faith were people who were hungry and thirsty for the living word of God.

For the archdiocese, communications after Katrina was more than providing information, as important as that was to the community. Communications, like the entire archdiocesan response to the storm, was directed by the "People First Principle." This translated into an unflinching commitment to serve the people of the archdiocese and the larger community as well. This commitment to serve meant the prudent, factual,

- 122 -

and timely dissemination of information. Over time it became clear to many within and outside the archdiocesan family that the church could be trusted with its statements and relied upon in working for the common good.

The commitment to serve through communications was more than a pledge to follow recognized professional practices. The archdiocese was not engaged in public relations, but was guided by the mission given by Jesus to his church: proclaim the Good News to the whole world. The overall archdiocesan response to Katrina gave clear evidence that there are many fruitful ways to communicate the Gospel and provide information crucial to the region as a whole. Once again, it was shown there were many responsible ways to communicate critical information. From the initial meetings convened by Archbishop Hughes to his visits to the displaced, along with his almost daily

communiqués and various public announcements, a high priority was placed on providing and receiving information. There were other ways to communicate, as witnessed by the priests who cared for aid workers and those seeking refuge in shelters, and the creative efforts of the Clarion Herald. Hope was being offered by personal witness and the printed word. Each of the above, along with countless other examples, gave witness to truth in love. In so doing, the archdiocese remained faithful to the mission of the Church given by the Lord to that first community of believers as he was taken from their sight.

• The Louisiana Superdome had its layered roof peeled away by Katrina

CATHOLIC SCHOOLS: OPEN THEM AND THEY WILL COME

In the cult baseball movie, *Field of Dreams*, Kevin Costner receives a message, a kind of revelation that advises him "to build it and they will come." The "it" is a baseball field, and the "they" are legendary stars of the game he so passionately loves.

These greats of yesteryear can only return if there is a place to play. And not just any field will do. The legends will return only to a diamond formed by one who is passionately in love with *the* game.

"Build it and they will come" proved to be, with a slight variation, the guiding principle behind the Office of Catholic Schools' approach to education after Katrina.

Within a week after the storm, various members of the Office of Catholic Schools (OCS) gathered in Baton Rouge at the Catholic Life Center. From those early meetings of OCS staff members there emerged two basic approaches to Catholic education after Katrina: the "big tent" approach or the "magnet" approach.

The "big tent" model advanced the idea that schools should only open when a sufficient number of students would be able to attend. There would be no reason to open a school without students. Without the required number of students the financial burdens would be too great to prudently assume. In other words, the school – the "tent" – must be filled to such an extent that education – or the "show" – could commence. This approach gained a great deal of traction with public school officials and government leaders in Orleans Parish.

The second approach, the "magnet" model, offered a different tactic while hoping to achieve the same goal – a sufficient student population so education could continue as quickly as possible. By reopening schools, families with children in need of schooling would have a reason to return. There would also be the added benefit of revitalizing the community. If the tent was going to be filled, there must be a reason for people to come inside.

From the beginning, OCS was committed to the "magnet" approach. The wisdom and necessity of the "magnet" model strategy became evident on both empirical and social policy grounds. As mentioned above, public school officials,

The issue of vouchers for students displaced by Katrina heated up. As usual, the teachers' union was opposed. However, officials from the archdiocesan Office of Catholic Schools worked with members of Congress to obtain "Restart money." These funds could be used for repairs and materials that did not advance religion. The use of vouchers for students in Katrina-affected areas was rejected by Louisiana lawmakers. Again, public school unions and Governor Kathleen Blanco joined forces to defeat this much-needed and socially just legislation. However, with the election of a new governor, Bobby Jindal, a limited student voucher program was enacted. Before being elected governor, Jindal, as a member of the U.S. Congress, was instrumental in the passage of three bills to protect the educational opportunities of impacted students.

• A religious education classroom at San Pedro Pescador Church in Florissant

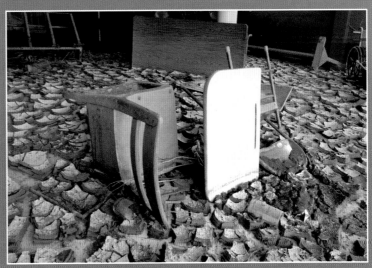

along with elected political officials, early on indicated that education in Orleans Parish would not take place during the 2005-06 school year. The community was told there simply were not enough students in Orleans Parish and it was too costly to repair the damaged properties.

After Katrina many Catholic schools such as St. Joan of Arc in LaPlace welcomed evacuees into their ranks

To OCS, this public policy regarding education was just another reason for families and businesses to stay away. The road home was not made easier with the canceling of public education. OCS became more determined to reopen Catholic schools. OCS approached the issue of post-Katrina education as a way of serving the local church, as well as the wider community. OCS looked at past disaster recovery reports, in particular that of Hurricane Andrew. Those who read the after-storm report on Hurricane Andrew found that along with energy and sanitation, the reopening of schools was a critical factor in people's decision to return and rebuild. This lesson was not lost on OCS. Nor was this approach lost on parents with children who had been enrolled in Catholic or public schools before Katrina. By the hundreds, and then thousands, students were returning. The magnet was exhibiting its power to attract. The big tent was being filled. Families had a reason to return. Businesses had an incentive to reopen. Slowly, but without a doubt, signs of life were returning. Each day more and more people would come home.

Clearly OCS's commitment to the "magnet" approach involved a risk and faced many challenges. Obviously, the biggest risk was that families and students would not come even if schools were reopened. By God's grace, working through the extraordinary efforts of countless principals, administrators, teachers, parents, communities, and students themselves, schools were reopened, and they did come. Those families and students who attended early in a school's reopening drew other families and students. It was as if these early returnees became magnets attracting those in far-away places to come home. The early arrivals were saying to those looking for encouragement, "Come home.

Come home, education is taking place. Come home, things are not perfect, but safe. Come home, we welcome you, we need you." We know in those early days after Katrina how quickly rumors and misinformation spread. Even faster than rumors was the news of a school reopening. Parents and students made sure other families and friends knew school was open. At one elementary school's reopening, administrators, faculty, students, and parents gathered for a morning prayer service. As the parents were leaving, the father of one of the students sought out a member of OCS and, with tears in his eyes, said, "My wife and I are so grateful that the school is open. I returned to New Orleans while my wife and son had to remain in Houston. They're back home now. We're all together again. The opening of school gave me back my family." Time and again with each new reopening this sentiment was expressed. The reopening of schools reunited families.

Destroyed religious education classroom at San Pedro Church

Besides the major risk that enough students would not be present to conduct classes, there were a number of other challenges faced by those schools which reopened. The most obvious challenge, in light of the extensive damage, was the sheer task of reopening the school itself. Reopening schools after Katrina involved much more than turning a key and flipping a switch. The first order of business was a thorough cleanup and assessment of the facility. Health and safety issues abounded. From the need to abate mold, to checking the infrastructure, to ensuring gas and electrical safety, it was essential that priority be given to protecting all who would enter and work in a building. There were many hands at work in the process: dedicated school personnel, concerned parents, enthusiastic students, involved members of the wider community, and, in a special way, civil authorities and members of the military who not only took on the exhausting task of cleanup, but who also provided electrical, plumbing, carpentry, and general construction skills to the work at hand. Direct stakeholders in the schools, members of the broader community, and volunteers from other states were drawn to schools. Everyone seemed to sense how important it was to make sure education would continue.

A second major challenge that confronted newly reopened schools was the influx of new students who had once attended public or private schools and were now in need of schooling. How was the archdiocese to respond? Simply put, as it has done from the first since the Ursuline nuns initially set foot on Louisiana soil in the early decades of the 18th century, the archdiocese would meet the educational needs of all, regardless of status, religion, race, or prior affiliation. Individual schools that had reopened would accept any child seeking an education. It did not matter if that child had previously attended a Catholic school. The child and the region needed education to go forward. In being true to its mission, education would be provided not because the student was Catholic or had attended a Catholic school before Katrina. Being Catholic, the school would open wide

• Teachers and parents listen intently to news about school reopenings

its doors to all who wanted to attend. This approach was especially important in Orleans Parish, where the ability of public schools to reopen was very much in doubt.

This policy of "open admissions" would raise a number of challenges, not the least of which was financial – 95 percent of a Catholic school's operational budget is tuition-funded. How would the newly arrived be processed, especially since the vast majority could not afford tuition? Each school faced this fundamental tension, which has been part of the story of Catholic education from the beginning, namely, the responsibility to be faithful to its mission given by Jesus to teach and at the same time to be prudent stewards of its limited resources. While material resources were limited,

• Classroom damag at Our Lady of Lourdes, Slidell

A longtime supporter of school choice, State Representative Austin Badon called on fellow lawmakers to provide state funds to private schools that were providing education to displaced students. "The Catholic schools don't care if you're Catholic, Baptist, whatever; they want to make sure that every child has the opportunity for an education."

Rummel Transition School Principal Nancy Hernandez speaks to her new students on their first day of school.

God's grace is not. If faith was to be more than words or ideas, then schools would welcome all who came and confront financial responsibilities at some later hour. This "foolishness according to the world" proved to be the "wisdom of God." To be sure, a financial strain was placed on schools, especially those located in inner-city areas which had limited resources before Katrina. Also, inner-city schools were likely to attract students who had previously attended public schools and had not been formed in a Catholic school culture. Yet, as we shall see later in this chapter, resources came forth from an unexpected source. Once more, God provided. The common good was to be served.

In some quarters, concerns were raised that the influx of public school students would change the culture of Catholic schools. These concerns, voiced by parents and administrators of Catholic schools, were serious and needed to be addressed. While it was true that the cultures of Catholic and public schools are quite different, there is no "iron law" that mandates that the presence of public school students will fundamentally alter a Catholic school culture. The fear was that this influx of public school students would cause an erosion of Catholic values, which are essential for Catholic education.

Leaving aside the question of Catholic education's mission, history teaches a lesson that should allay fears. The experience of previous generations of Catholic educators indicates that the Catholic model of education works across religious, racial, ethnic, and various socio-economic categories. The research of noted University of Chicago sociologist James Coleman clearly reveals that inner-city and minority students do well, if not flourish, in a Catholic school setting.

The development and achievement by these students did not come at the expense of the existing Catholic culture. There are some indications that students from diverse backgrounds *enriched* the pre-existing culture.

Before proceeding with the story of Catholic education after Katrina, it would be helpful to offer a word about Catholic education within the archdiocese before the hurricane. Secondly, archdiocesan Catholic education, soon after Katrina, was greatly assisted by Catholic schools within the Diocese of Baton Rouge. The Office of Catholic Schools for the Baton Rouge Diocese provided indispensable access to those schools which could accept displaced students. In addition, OCS-BR did a splendid job of coordinating the students with the appropriate school (such issues as travel and course of studies were but two of the many educational and administrative considerations that went into student-school placement).

Catholic Education: Tradition of Excellence

The Catholic presence in Louisiana involves a commitment to education from the beginning. The Ursuline nuns, who arrived in the first quarter of the 18th century to what would become Louisiana, established a school in 1727 as one of their first apostolates. Down through the decades and centuries, various religious communities of men and women have built on this Ursuline tradition of providing education. The archdiocese has developed an extensive network of parish or parochial elementary schools and a number of secondary schools to prepare the area's young for higher education and meaningful participation in business and civic life.

Catholic education has also exhibited, indeed is grounded in, a core set of beliefs and values about the dignity of each human person. Human dignity is derived from each person being created in the Divine Image and called to grow into the very likeness of God. Essential to human dignity is the capacity to learn. God created us for truth, for God is Truth itself. This Catholic pedagogy fosters an educational culture characterized by respect between students and teachers, high standards of achievement, a willingness to conduct oneself in a moral manner, an acceptance of loving discipline as essential for human maturity, and the welcoming of parental involvement in the life of the school.

As a result of heavy flood damage from Katrina, Xavier University's Institute for Black Catholic Studies had to relocate temporarily. The university received several invitations to relocate the Institute until Xavier could reopen. The decision was made to select the University of Notre Dame from the nine offers. Among the reasons for selecting Notre Dame was the university's close proximity to the large black Catholic community of the Archdiocese of Chicago.

In addition to Xavier University, two other Catholic institutions of higher learning serve within the archdiocese – Our Lady of Holy Cross College and Loyola University. OLHCC was able to reopen for the spring 2006 semester. The college conducted off-campus courses before the spring semester so students scheduled to graduate in December could complete their requirements. Enrollment at OLHCC has since risen above pre-Katrina levels. Loyola University was able to reopen in the spring 2006 semester as well. The campus experienced slight structural damage from Katrina. Its current enrollment is also above pre-Katrina levels, although several programms had to be cut or scaled back.

• Dominican Sister of St. Cecilia Mary Rose Bingham, Cathedral Academy principal, rings the bell of hope to signal the first reopening of a school in Orleans Parish

Over the years, Catholic education has proven to be an indispensable blessing for the Church and the wider civic community. Countless graduates, Catholic and non-Catholic, have benefited from Catholic school education. Graduates have made significant contributions to their parish churches, schools, and the wider community. Catholic and non-Catholic families have indicated their support by entrusting their children to a Catholic school. In many cases, their support has been multi-generational. Parents wanted for their children what they had found so valuable, namely, to be educated and morally formed by a Catholic education. Nationwide, statistics indicate that Louisiana has the highest percentage of school-age students attending faith-based or private schools (19 percent). A significant portion of this 19 percent is found in Catholic schools.

• Mt. Carmel Academy students at an assembly with their principal, Sister of Mt. Carmel Camille Ann Campbell.

Catholic education extends far beyond academic performance. The foundation of Catholic schools, its very reason for existing, is the moral and spiritual formation of the student's character through Catholic teaching and participation in the sacramental life of the Church. This education and formation for both the present and the world to come would provide an indispensable source for the spiritual strength needed to face the challenges posed by Katrina. Time and again, principals and teachers heard stories from their students and the parents of students about their Katrina experiences and the role faith played in their personal recovery. Parents were vocal in their praise of Catholic education for the spiritual strength it provided their children. In the words of one family, "My family was among the thousands that had to evacuate. It was a terrible time. I was afraid for my family. I didn't know what to expect. I didn't know when, or even if, we would return." Alex, father of a Catholic school student, went on to share his daughter's advice after one especially stressful day. "I returned to the apartment we managed to rent. The stress and worry must have shown on my face because my daughter took my hand and said, 'Dad, why don't we all say a prayer?' She had never said anything like that before. We did pray. I felt such peace. I believe this idea of turning to God was learned in school. At that moment, I knew every dollar of tuition was worth it."

Baton Rouge:
Time Toward Home

Like other components of the archdiocese, the Office of Catholic Schools set up temporary operations in the Catholic Life Center. The Office of Catholic Schools for the Diocese of Baton Rouge not only provided office space but also was most generous in sharing resources in terms of various supplies and making available support personnel for the numerous clerical and administrative tasks that faced both offices.

The most pressing concerns of parents and students who had evacuated were two-fold: Would Catholic schools reopen in the archdiocese, especially since public education officials had indicated public schools in Orleans Parish would probably not reopen for the academic year 2005-06? Also, how would education be provided for students in

Baton Rouge until they could return home? As indicated previously, the archdiocese was determined to reopen schools as quickly and safely as was prudent. This resolve to reopen schools in the archdiocese was strengthened by the real possibility that public education in Orleans Parish would not occur. It is the second part of parents' and students' concerns – the ways in which education would be provided until families would return home – that posed the greatest challenge to both diocesan school offices and the individual Baton Rouge Catholic schools. It is to the meeting of this set of challenges that we now turn our attention.

Father William Maestri, superintendent of Catholic Schools, coordinated a well-attended meeting with displaced parents in Baton Rouge

One of the first challenges faced by both schools offices, and one which would persist, was the issue of the highly fluid nature of the student population. Just how many students were in need of school placement? This difficult question would have to be answered before any thought could be given to school assignment. Compounding the challenges was the inherent imprecision in determining the evacuated student population. It seemed at times that Baton Rouge was just one huge revolving door. Each day new families and students were arriving, especially in the early days and weeks after the storm, as well as leaving Baton Rouge in order to return home or take up residence elsewhere. This highly fluid population would pose significant challenges to those

schools that welcomed the "Katrina students," as they came to be called. It was next to impossible for schools to develop any long-range plans when the size of a school was in such flux. In some schools, the population would fluctuate by as many as one hundred students or more within a week's time! The operative values were adaptability and creativity, and a good-sized dose of the patience of Job.

Along with this unprecedented situation of student population ebb and flow, there were other challenges. Many students who needed to continue their education did not have the basic documentation for entrance into the host school. For example, past grades, standardized test scores,

• Sister of the Holy Family Leona Bruner, Edmundite Father Michael Jacques and Father William Maestri greet returning students to St. Peter Claver School

medical and sacramental records, and learning and behavioral reports for those students with particular needs were not able to be presented to school officials. Often the new school was asked to extend admission to a student without the most fundamental information. What was paramount to Baton Rouge Catholic schools was this – because of Katrina these students were no longer able to attend their former schools. Catholic schools in Baton Rouge were being asked to help, and help they did.

In addition to a highly fluid student population and lack of basic school records, a third significant issue arose: the financial burden faced by those Catholic schools that made space for the newly arrived students. Not only had Katrina destroyed or made inaccessible the retrieving of records, but many who came to Baton Rouge took only enough money for a few days or a week at most. The damage to the metro area severely hampered, if not made impossible, the obtaining of cash through banks and ATMs. Cash was frozen. It was commonplace to have parents with little if any money and a big need – a child or children requiring schooling. No doubt common sense advised caution and a hesitation for assuming too large a burden. Yet faith counseled the taking of a different path.

Under the leadership of Sister Mary Michaeline, Superintendent of Catholic Schools for the Diocese of Baton Rouge, area Catholic schools threw open their doors and hearts to those displaced by Katrina. To be sure, the administrative, financial and planning strains were real and called for sacrifice. And while classes grew larger in size, so did the understanding of what it meant to be Church, members of the Mystical Body of Christ. Not only did diocesan officials

work tirelessly to make families and students welcomed, but parents, teachers, and students in Baton Rouge-area Catholic schools also went to extraordinary efforts to supply "Katrina students" with school supplies and uniforms. Baton Rouge parents and sympathetic people offered their residences to those who could not secure housing. Through this heroic witness to hospitality, students would experience a stable environment and the stress on parents would be eased. "I'm a Vietnam War veteran," said Ken, "and I remember all the people fleeing from the communists. They had to leave everything but what they could carry. A lot of people lost everything in the storm. I live by myself. I have the extra room. I just had to open my house to those in need." Ken opened his home to a young couple with a child who was attending Sacred Heart Catholic Elementary School. The family stayed with Ken for six weeks. Ken's generosity was duplicated many times over by Baton Rouge residents, Catholic and non-Catholic.

The need to provide Catholic education for those displaced in Baton Rouge was a pressing concern for high school students, especially graduating seniors. In an extraordinary witness to Christian hospitality, St. Michael the Archangel High School opened its facilities to more than 1,000 "Katrina students"! Instead of ending the school day at its regular time, St. Michael's would remain open until 9:30 p.m. each school day. After the normal school day was completed, the campus would be turned over for the beginning of a new school session, which commenced at 3:45 p.m. and concluded at 9:30 p.m. This evening high school was administered and staffed by archdiocesan personnel whose schools could not reopen because of the extensive damage to their buildings following Katrina. The platooning of two student bodies posed great challenges involving issues of facility maintenance, traffic engineering, and the crucial need for student and faculty safety. In addition to the evening school at St. Michael, Catholic High School in Baton Rouge also began an evening program which catered mostly to students who had been attending Brother Martin in New Orleans. Both Catholic High and Brother Martin are schools sponsored by the Brothers of the Sacred Heart. In spite of enormous challenges and the need for many individual and institutional sacrifices, the overall outcome proved to be a blessing for many parents and students. Brittany, a high school senior who attended a Catholic school in Metairie and was forced to evacuate to Baton Rouge, voiced the sentiments of many. "Once the shock of Katrina wore off, my parents started worrying about school. How would all that happened affect my plans for college? I was nervous when I started St. Michael's for the afternoon program. I can truly say, not only did I learn, but everyone was so nice and helpful. I also made new friends. I never want to go through anything like that again, but St. Michael's made it easier."

Pilgrims for Education

As the days in Baton Rouge turned into weeks and it became clear the archdiocese as a whole was going to remain displaced until the end of 2005, it became equally clear that the archdiocesan Office of Catholic Schools needed to embark on a different strategy. It was decided that OCS would move and set up temporary offices in those areas where schools were reopening. The final goal was to return to Orleans Parish as soon as possible. Before this final goal could be realized, a number of steps along the way would be

necessary. No matter the delay OCS was as relentless as the wind and waters of Katrina.

Great Britain's Prince Charles visits with Cathedral Academy students and supports Katrina rebuilding in Louisiana and the Gulf Coast.

As schools were reopened, beginning in the western parts of the archdiocese because the damage was not as severe, the possibility of OCS moving to one of these sites became more probable. Serious thought was given to seeking office space in one of the reopened schools, such as at St. Charles Catholic High School in Saint Charles civil parish. However, this did not become necessary. OCS was notified that two archdiocesan high schools – Archbishop Chapelle and Archbishop Rummel – were planning to reopen in early October. Both schools are located in Metairie (more will be said about each school in this chapter). School officials at Archbishop Rummel made the generous offer to set up a complete office so members of OCS could be near Orleans Parish. This offer was quickly accepted and would prove to be crucial for OCS's return to the city and the reopening of numerous schools.

Operating out of Archbishop Rummel, OCS was able to focus attention and resources on reopening other Catholic schools, especially in Orleans Parish. The need to reopen city schools, especially inner-city schools, was imperative. The archdiocese has a history of commitment to inner-city schools. For many families, both Catholic and non-Catholic (pre-Katrina, 60 percent of inner-city students who attended Catholic schools were not Catholic), Catholic schools offered an important way out of poverty and into a better life. That witness to hope could not be allowed to die. It was vital that inner-city schools be reopened. The reopening of these schools sent a clear message: the archdiocese's commitment to inner-city Catholic education was not washed away with the waters of Katrina. The archdiocese wanted families to come home, and the Church wanted to give them a reason to return. The school doors, the way into hope, were once again open providing the opportunity for a better tomorrow.

• Holy Cross School in the Ninth Ward was severely damaged but was relocated to the Gentilly area to revitalize the rebuilding effort there

The operational philosophy of OCS in reopening schools was simple: OCS is a resource to empower and assist the individual school with its own recovery. Following the fundamental Catholic principle of subsidiarity (never impose a higher or more complex level of organization upon a level which is smaller, more intimate, and more knowledgeable of the local situation), OCS was present to assist principals, faculties, staff, parents, and community leaders in reopening schools. Individual schools possessed the "human capital" through the creativity, dedication, and energy of those who were committed to their schools being reopened. Time and again, as OCS members visited schools about to reopen, there was a pride and resolve to meet the challenges at hand. This determination did not come from a central office directive, but from the faith-in-action of those in love with their school. Power from above (God's grace) working through power from below (constructive people) joined in proclaiming a defiant "Yes we can!" to the destruction by Katrina.

As God's providence blessed OCS with a base of operation at Archbishop Rummel, once again God's grace provided a new location for OCS, this time in Orleans Parish. The president of De La Salle High School, Kenneth Tedesco, and principal Gina Hall offered OCS office space to conduct its work. At last OCS would be able to establish its base of operations within Orleans Parish. This was important for both a practical and symbolic reason. Practically, OCS would be geographically proximate to where the greatest number of schools were reopening; hence, OCS would be in a better position to provide resources in a more effective and timely manner. Symbolically, the re-entry of OCS into Orleans Parish gave visible expression to the archdiocese's commitment to education in Orleans Parish. There would be a further move for OCS before its final return to the original headquarters at Walmsley Avenue. Nonetheless, the return to Orleans Parish was cause for great joy and hope.

The feelings of joy and hope were tempered by a realism born from the massive destruction in St. Bernard Parish. Prior to Katrina, the Archdiocese of New Orleans operated four elementary schools and one high school in the parish. At one of the elementary schools, an innovative pilot program for children with autism was about to commence just weeks before Katrina struck. Unfortunately, the damage in St. Bernard was so extensive that the program could not continue. The school, St. Louise de Marillac, which was to set to house the program, was destroyed, and with its destruction the hopes of many were dashed. All Catholic schools in St. Bernard experienced damage so severe that it was thought none would reopen, certainly not for the 2005-06 school year. Just as the archdiocese strongly desired to provide Catholic education in Orleans Parish, likewise the archdiocese was equally determined to provide Catholic education in St. Bernard Parish. Parish residents and leaders were as welcoming of this desire as the archdiocese was committed to its being achieved.

• Our Lady of Lourdes School in Slidell experienced devastation

St. Bernard Parish, as a whole, was more devastated than Orleans Parish. From elected officials to civic leaders to ordinary citizens, everyone was looking for signs of recovery, signs of hope. Parish leaders were especially eager for churches and schools to reopen. The archdiocese felt a special urgency to reestablish a Catholic presence in St. Bernard. All of the archdiocesan properties were damaged, many beyond repair. The challenge was to find, if possible, one that could be restored. After a careful survey of all properties, it was determined that a site could be realistically and safely reopened – Our Lady of Prompt Succor (OLPS) Elementary School in Chalmette.

Many challenges had to be addressed before OLPS could be reopened. These challenges clustered around three major areas: facilities, finances, and population. While OLPS did not sustain the degree of damage inflicted on the other schools, the work of cleanup and repair would be a major undertaking. In addition to the structural compromise, extensive damage was done by standing water to the materials and furnishings inside. Serious health issues were present due to the significant presence of mold. Through a massive joint effort by the archdiocesan Building Office and the Department of Finance, the support and encouragement of civil authorities, the untiring effort of OLPS parish and school personnel, and the generous efforts of parents and volunteers, the facilities of OLPS were ready for reopening.

The cleanup and rebuilding posed a heavy financial burden to the church parish and the overall financial resources of the archdiocese. However, Archbishop Hughes had made a clear public commitment to the Church's presence in St. Bernard. The last thing anyone wanted was to send a signal that the archdiocese was not fully committed to being a part of St. Bernard's recovery. Even though OLPS had few resources and its ability to generate funds was quite limited, the archdiocese proceeded with the cleanup and repair so both the church and school could reopen. The archdiocesan Department of Financial and Administrative Services had been working with FEMA authorities from the beginning in order to secure funds for purposes of recovery and rebuilding. OLPS would begin receiving insurance money, which could be used for the reopening project. Also, by this time, significant donations were starting to be received which could be applied toward the reopening of OLPS.

Storm damage at Our Lady of Lourdes School in Slidell led to the rebuilding of a new campus

Even with the cleaning up and repair to OLPS, the issue of population loomed large. As with the reopening of schools in Orleans Parish the question arose — would students attend OLPS? The issues of safety, severe limitations on basic services, a heavily damaged infrastructure, and concerns over emergency medical services were not small issues to parents making decisions that seriously affected their children. Again, as with Orleans Parish, the great unknown regarding the number of students who would return could not be answered in advance. This would be another example of reopening a school so parents would have a reason to return. The decision to reopen OLPS was more an act of faith than one based on statistical analysis.

Under the leadership of Sharon Coll, who was serving as principal at another Catholic elementary school in St. Bernard just prior to Katrina, and a dedicated faculty supported by determined parents, OLPS was reopened before the end of the 2005 school year. That first day, 24 students with their parents, were present for the first bell and the offering of a Mass of Thanksgiving in the parish church. The long road back to St. Bernard had been achieved. The longer road to recovery had become more hopeful. The news media were in attendance that first day. One reporter asked the superintendent of Catholic Schools if he was "disappointed at the small number who had returned." He replied, "Not at all. Remember Jesus began with 12 disciples. God has sent us twice as many to begin our

• Teachers comfort each other as they gather in Baton Rouge

work." Just as the interview was being completed, all 24 students, along with faculty and families, gathered in front of the church. Each adult and child tightly held a string with a balloon attached. In unison they released the balloons skyward. The wind carried them high and far. The same can be said for God's grace. This day, a day of hope and recovery, God's grace carried those present and all of St. Bernard, higher and farther than once thought possible.

The story in St. Bernard was being repeated in St. Tammany civil parish. The Covington area, and to a greater degree the Slidell area of the northshore had experienced significant damage. Some Catholic schools in the eastern and western sides of St. Tammany were not able to be occupied after Katrina. As in St. Bernard, archdiocesan and community personnel came together to reopen schools. Throughout the reopening process, an excellent spirit of cooperation and the willingness to share resources made the many burdens lighter. For example, St. Margaret Mary Elementary School in Slidell was able to reopen more quickly than its nearby Catholic school, Our Lady of Lourdes. In the spirit of true Christian community, St. Margaret Mary offered to share its facilities with Our Lady of Lourdes. This decision lessened the disruption for students and families. Education could continue and parental anxiety was greatly eased. Parents could focus on work and recovery knowing that their children were safely in school. Both church parishes and schools clearly demonstrated what leadership, cooperation, sacrifice, and Christian love can accomplish. These two schools gave Slidell a reason to hope.

On the northshore, St. Scholastica Academy in Covington and Pope John Paul II High School in Slidell experienced severe damage from wind, water, and falling pine trees. Through the efforts of the school communities, both schools reopened, made room for displaced students, and were able to complete the academic year.

De La Salle High School students collect food items for Second Harvest Food Bank

Home at Last

While the Office of Catholic Schools (OCS) did not remain in Baton Rouge, the major components of the archdiocesan administration did so until the end of 2005. With the coming of the new year, and the archdiocesan Administration Building on Walmsley Avenue still months away from being ready for reoccupation, a suitable facility needed to be located. One was found a few blocks from the Walmsley building. Incarnate Word Parish was selected because of its proximity, its space, and because the archdiocese would not have to meet the financial burden of a lease or rental fee. Grateful to De La Salle for its hospitality, OCS left to join the rest of the archdiocese at the Incarnate Word site. This move made sense since it was becoming increasingly necessary for OCS to interface with other archdiocesan offices, especially the Finance Department and Building Office. With more and

more schools reopened or about to reopen, it was essential for all three offices to be in daily contact. OCS needed to be present at these reopening events in order to acknowledge the achievement and to assess the ongoing financial and material needs of individual schools. The issue of federal aid for recovery in devastated areas became increasingly important. Throughout the early period of recovery, schools played a major role. If this contribution by schools was to continue and expand, OCS needed to be a major voice in the conversation. It became increasingly clear that OCS would need to turn to Washington, D.C., for assistance and open up those lines of communication with the appropriate officials for facilitating such funding. (Much more will be detailed about OCS's work with governmental leaders and agencies at the local, state, and national levels in Chapter Nine.)

De La Salle
students enjoy
getting back
to their school
routine

• Empty school playground at Our Lady of Lourdes in Slidell added to the feelings of sadness

The months spent at the Incarnate Word facility went quickly. Time was taken up mainly with administrative duties and acknowledging the achievements of schools as they reopened. Finally, in April 2006, the archdiocesan administrative building at Walmsley was reopened. The long pilgrimage from Baton Rouge to Archbishop Rummel High School in Metairie, to De La Salle in New Orleans, to Incarnate Word, and now finally to Walmsley was completed. A profound sense of gratitude, along with a humble satisfaction with all that had been accomplished, pervaded OCS personnel. At the same time there was an awareness of and a commitment to the miles yet to travel in the odyssey that was education after Katrina. If anything, the

return to Walmsley only strengthened the resolve of OCS to complete the ongoing work of recovery.

In looking back over those first eight months after Katrina, from evacuation to Baton Rouge, through the return to Walmsley, OCS employed three key tactics that significantly contributed to the reopening of schools. First, and perhaps the most important of these, was the decision from the beginning to keep moving closer to New Orleans as schools reopened in order to be present and provide assistance. Effective aid and guidance would have been seriously hampered had OCS remained in Baton Rouge. Secondly, and related to the first tactic, was the application of the Catholic principle of subsidiarity. OCS held to the belief that each individual school was in the best position to direct its own reopening. The central office would offer aid, advice and encouragement but not try to micro-manage each school's recovery and reopening plan. This approach had the effect of empowering each school to take responsibility for its reopening. Such empowerment would instill a sense of accomplishment and deep investment in the outcome. Finally, the decision was made to welcome any child who was in need of schooling. This called for a willingness to take a huge risk, especially in light of hard economic realities. But what is faith if not a risk? God would not be outdone in generosity. Furthermore, is not the welcoming of children in need an essential part of the mission of Catholic education? Faith in God and fidelity to mission yielded an abundant harvest in the lives of those families and children whom the schools welcomed. This was one of the Catholic schools' finest hours.

Among the Notables

Throughout the long ordeal that was Katrina, each school in its own way made a lasting contribution to the recovery and the road home by reopening wide its doors. None of this was easy and no reopening was without sacrifice. However, there were some schools whose circumstances and response transcended their individual school and local community. There were schools whose response had implications for the whole city, the state, nation, and even reached far away parts of the world. It is to these transcendental examples that we now turn our attention.

It is fitting that our presentation commence in Orleans Parish. As previously indicated, the archdiocese placed a high priority on providing an educational presence in the city. This goal was realized with the reopening of St. Louis Cathedral Academy on October 17, 2005. The school's reopening marked the return of education to the east bank of Orleans Parish. Under the leadership of Dominican Sister of St. Cecilia Mary Rose Bingham, school principal, the opening bell greeted about 90 students eager for routine, order, safety, and education. As with the first Mass offered at St. Louis Cathedral after Katrina, the sound of the school bell sent forth a clear message of hope. A city hungry for signs of life, recovery, and normalcy welcomed the sounds of children talking, singing and laughing. In the words of one parent, "I haven't seen or heard Jasmine laugh since the storm. Look at her now." Many parents echoed similar experiences.

So significant was the school's reopening that Britain's royal couple, Prince Charles and his wife Camilla, visited Cathedral Academy on their tour of Katrina-damaged areas of the Gulf Coast. The Prince said it best, "Where there's life, there's hope." One Cathedral school administrator built on the words of Prince Charles: "They wanted to be here as a symbol of hope. Their being here said, 'We're here to let you know that the world knows what you're going through.'"

The reopening of Catholic schools was not all ringing bells, happy children, and royal visits. As is often the case in complex situations, there is a mixture of sadness and joy. One such example concerns St. Frances Xavier Cabrini Elementary School, Redeemer-Seton High School, and Holy Cross middle and secondary schools. First, let's address the sadness. The damage inflicted on Redeemer-Seton and St. Frances Xavier Cabrini was so extensive that the schools could not be reopened. In addition to the pain experienced because of the loss of the facilities, several other factors came into play. Redeemer-Seton served a critical educational need in Orleans Parish, offering a Catholic education to those of modest financial

Archbishop Rummel's morning assembly of students

means. Secondly, the loss of Redeemer-Seton meant that the archdiocese no longer had a sponsored secondary school in Orleans Parish (all other high schools in Orleans Parish are sponsored by various religious communities).

The loss of the Redeemer-Seton/Cabrini presence did not mean the schools would stop continuing to serve Catholic education. Holy Cross, long a fixture on the New Orleans

educational landscape, found itself in much the same devastated condition as Redeemer-Seton and Cabrini after Katrina. Was there a way to bring forth something new out of this seemingly hopeless situation?

If Katrina taught us anything, it was not to be too hasty in setting limits as to what was possible. In a splendid example of cooperation between the archdiocese and the Holy Cross religious community, the following suggestion was proposed and accepted. The archdiocese and Redeemer-Seton did not have the financial resources to rebuild the school. Even before Katrina, enrollment at Redeemer-Seton had been a concern. After Katrina, this concern was only magnified. Holy Cross had the financial resources to rebuild through insurance, endowment funds, and support from the Holy Cross priests and brothers. Enrollment would not be an issue. Hence, a plan was formulated in which Holy Cross would purchase the Redeemer-Seton/Cabrini property in order to relocate and rebuild its campus. This creative endeavor would keep Holy Cross in Orleans Parish and allow the school to play a major role in the Gentilly area's revitalization. Though they were gone, Redeemer-Seton and St. Frances Xavier Cabrini would continue to serve Catholic education through their campuses now used by another school. This initiative would not have been possible without the self-sacrificing decision by Cabrini parishioners to allow their church and school property to be sold to Holy Cross.

In another part of the Gentilly area, a story of determination and courage was unfolding. The Sisters of the Holy Family have established over the years a treasured footprint of service to the Church and wider community. Of special importance is the contribution of the sisters to the education of children of color. The specific focus of the sisters' apostolate is to young women in need of a secondary education. Long a part of the educational landscape in New Orleans East is St. Mary's Academy. Hurricane Katrina inflicted severe damage on the lower Ninth Ward and eastern parts of the metro area. St. Mary's experienced significant flood and wind damage. There was some doubt as to whether the school would reopen.

There was no doubt in the mind and will of the school's principal, Sister of the Holy Family Greta Jupiter, and her fellow sisters and St. Mary's dedicated faculty. Katrina was not to be the end of a school that had proved to be so vital for so many for so long. Once again, reality had to be faced – how? How could St. Mary's continue in light of the massive damage to grounds and property?

The archdiocese did not want to lose this very important educational institution and ministry. At one point, St. James Major Church operated an elementary and secondary school in the Gentilly area. However, because of declining enrollment and shifting population patterns, the decision was made to close both schools. The buildings had been used on and off by parish organizations and outside groups on a short-term rental basis. After Katrina, the buildings went unoccupied, though they had experienced relatively minor damage. After consultation with the relevant parties, the decision was made to offer the facilities to Sister Greta and the Holy Family community until St. Mary's could reopen.

The offer was accepted, and thus St. Mary's was not ended but reopened at a new location. The news was greeted with great joy by all. A public announcement was made on the steps of the new location at St. James Major, covered by the news media, and welcomed by civic leaders and the entire St. Mary's family. The Holy Family Sisters made an additional commitment to the archdiocese and the Gentilly community. Namely, because of the great need for education, the sisters would welcome elementary school-aged boys and girls. This was a significant departure from their traditional ministry to educate high school girls exclusively.

• The temporary MAX School on Magazine Street opened after the storm with a blend of former Xavier University Prep, St. Augustine, and St. Mary students.

God is never outdone in generosity. With the coming of the new school year in 2006, St. Mary's Academy was able to return to its original home in New Orleans East. God's providential care, building on the faith-filled determination of the entire St. Mary's family, did not prove fruitless. Katrina's interruption could not end the good work that endures.

An important ministry of the archdiocese is the education, training and formation of candidates to the priesthood. This vital service for the Church extends beyond the geographical boundaries of the archdiocese, since other dioceses send their candidates to New Orleans for studies. Notre Dame Seminary (NDS) has been entrusted with the essential task of priestly formation.

Located in the Carrollton section of New Orleans, NDS experienced extensive damage from the winds and water of Katrina to its two major facilities – Archbishop Shaw and St. Joseph halls. Due to the extensive damage, the seminary was unable to reopen. Some seminarians, at crucial stages of their priestly formation, would have their ordinations to the diaconate and priesthood put on hold. This interruption could cause hardships for those dioceses that are experiencing shortages as to the number of priests available for service. How would this urgent situation be addressed?

St. Michael the Archangel High School in Baton Rouge opened its doors to more than 1,000 Katrina students

In another example of Christian cooperation, St. Joseph Seminary College offered its facilities to Notre Dame until it could return to operational status. The hospitality of the Benedictine monks was in keeping with the Rule of St. Benedict and continued the Abbey's long tradition of service. St. Joseph Abbey operates the college seminary, which educates and forms candidates for the priesthood. The college seminary serves the New Orleans Province (the state of Louisiana), as well as other dioceses around the nation seeking a Benedictine formation for their priestly candidates. The Abbey's generous offer allowed the educational and priestly formation of Notre Dame's seminarians to continue without major disruption. The sharing of facilities, which included providing room and board, continued until Notre Dame reopened in January 2006.

Prior to Katrina, the archdiocese offered comprehensive programs of religious education and youth ministries. These educational and youth ministry programs ranged from sacramental preparation, to adult education, to courses for religion teacher certification, and an array of opportunities for young people to participate in activities as varied as being in service to the needy and taking part in numerous sports activities. As with so many aspects of church and civic life, Katrina greatly affected the Office of Religious Education (ORE) and the Catholic Youth Organization (CYO).

The Office of Religious Education, under the direction of Carole Obrokta, met the challenges posed by Katrina with determination and creativity. ORE set as its top priorities providing religious education and conducting the business of the office "as if everything were normal." A key tactic was the establishment of parish satellite offices using donated textbooks and materials to provide certification courses and retreats and meet the needs of the parishes that were in operation. Obrokta used her own apartment as the administrative center so ORE could continue its work. In order to keep operational and not be a financial burden to the archdiocese, ORE devoted a great deal of time seeking funds through grants and contributions. The multiple tasks of ORE continued even in the face of the diminished number of staff workers. Prior to Katrina, ORE had 13 staff members; after the storm, the office's size shrank to seven. Finally, ORE creatively made use of multiple forms of telecommunications media to keep abreast of parish needs and keep parishes informed of ORE courses and programs. Along with this ongoing contact through technology, staff members of ORE made it a high priority to attend parish deanery meetings and visit sites where courses were being offered.

Student drawing reflects acceptance of new school students after the storm

The CYO/Youth and Young Adult Ministry Office (YAM) is a vital part of the archdiocese's overall mission and ministry. This office, under the direction of John Smestad Jr., is charged with nurturing the Catholic faith among youth and young adults. The CYO/YAM office works closely with schools and parishes in sponsoring workshops, retreats, days of prayer, service projects, and opportunities for young people to meet, pray, and share their stories of faith. These opportunities for fellowship involve youth on the local, state, national, and international levels. A strong presence of volunteer youth ministries is indispensable for the ongoing work of the CYO/YAM offices.

While Katrina seriously disrupted the various ministries of CYO/YAM, it did not destroy the resolve of office personnel to continue the archdiocese's commitment to area youth. The Youth Office mirrored the strategy of ORE, establishing satellite offices to be close to the needs of young people. The youth office made a significant commitment to information technology. One of the major challenges posed by Katrina was the ability of friends, families, and associates to communicate with one another. With so many families scattered throughout the state and across the country, there was a great need to locate and reestablish contact. The youth office expanded its use of computer technology and held ongoing meetings with parish youth ministers to assess needs and provide resources.

Youth ministry in parishes is to a large extent volunteer-driven. Katrina greatly reduced the number of volunteers because many youth ministers had to care for their families and restore their own homes. A significant number of youth ministers did not return to the metro area. Parishes often found themselves without the adult leadership that is so crucial for youth ministry. The CYO/YAM worked tirelessly to develop new adult leaders to work with young people in parishes. Many adults who had never been involved in parish ministry or worked with young people before came forward to meet the needs of parish youth.

Through God's grace, an abiding commitment to serve the needs of young people, a cooperative working spirit between CYO/YAM and individual parishes, and the continued support of archdiocesan leadership, the needs of metro area youth were served. In fact, as of July 2009, all major youth office events and programs were operating at pre-Katrina levels and, in many instances, at higher levels.

In concluding this section on notable examples of recovery, we turn to three schools which exhibited extraordinary faith, courage, creativity, and service to the common good.

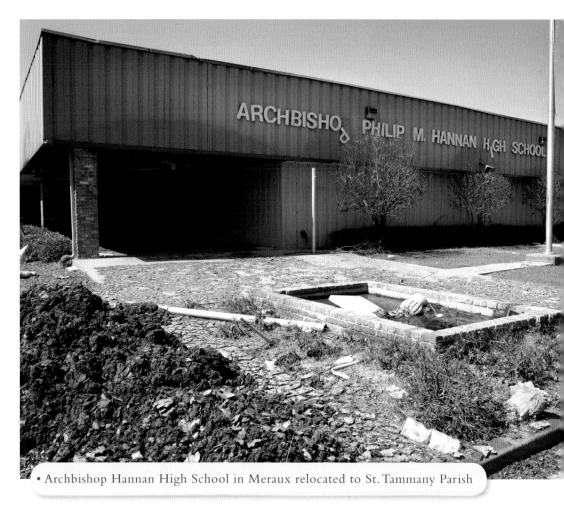

• Archbishop Hannan High School in Meraux relocated to St. Tammany Parish

Archbishop Hannan High School served the educational needs of secondary students in St. Bernard parish. The school was a source of pride to the archdiocese and to the St. Bernard

Parish community as a whole. Through the leadership of its founding principal, John Serio, a dedicated faculty and involved parental base, Archbishop Hannan High School achieved a distinguished record in academics, athletics, and various modes of artistic expression. Unfortunately, like much of St. Bernard, the school experienced a degree of damage that made it impossible to rebuild and reopen at its original site. (Public officials expressed serious reservations about rebuilding due to environmental concerns following oil and chemical contamination.) Was this to be the final chapter of Archbishop Hannan High School?

Hardly. Through belief in God's providential care and a "will do" spirit born from adversity, Archbishop Hannan High would continue its educational ministry. While, sadly, Archbishop Hannan would not continue in St. Bernard, it would continue nonetheless – but where?

Once again the hospitality of the monks of St. Joseph Abbey would play a key role. As the Abbey had made welcome the Notre Dame Seminary community, the Abbey would serve as the temporary home for Archbishop Hannan High. In the words of Benedictine Abbot Justin Brown, "If the Abbey can be of service to the archdiocese and the wider community, then we want to play our part." Naturally, questions arose as to the reaction of the Abbey's neighbors, the other Catholic high schools on the northshore, and governmental officials who would have to approve such an arrangement.

Not surprisingly, all who in any way were affected by this arrangement were not only welcoming of Hannan High but also went to great lengths to extend their hospitality and support. The universal sentiment expressed went something like this: while all of us have experienced the ravages of Katrina, St. Bernard residents have suffered in an especially acute way. We cannot begin to know what those from St. Bernard went through. We find ourselves in a position to help. We couldn't imagine doing anything but responding to our fellow citizens. The need to make welcome our neighbors from St. Bernard became only more urgent when the education of children is involved.

The decision to temporarily relocate was not only motivated by the generous response of the St. Joseph Abbey monks but also because of the relocation patterns of Hannan High families. A significant number of Hannan High families resettled on a specific corridor on the northshore (the Lacombe-Slidell area, westward toward the Hammond area). This concentration of families made it essential to relocate Hannan High on the northshore so families could continue the educational experience so valued by alumni, current

Archbishop Hannan High School, Meraux, had eight feet of water

students and their families. The temporary relocation site at the Abbey was truly providential in reconnecting members of the Hannan High family. A permanent location for the school was selected in the western part of St. Tammany Parish, near Interstate 12.

As with the Redeemer-Seton High School and St. Frances Xavier Cabrini site, the former campus of Hannan High continued to be of service to the wider community. Katrina inflicted heavy damage on the Murphy Oil Refinery. Environmental pollution was extensive, it posed serious health issues for residents and recovery workers. The archdiocese, in response to a request by refinery and government officials, agreed to let the Hannan campus be used by personnel engaged in clean up and pollution removal. Hence, while Archbishop Hannan High School had moved to its new location, the school's spirit of service endured.

The concluding two examples give evidence to the importance of the willingness to adapt and change in order to respond effectively to a crisis. Such a willingness calls for sacrifice and prudent risk-taking if the common good is to be served. Two archdiocesan high schools located in eastern Jefferson Parish, Archbishop Chapelle and Archbishop Rummel, refused to cling to the safe and comfortable routines of past years. Katrina revealed the folly of trying to live as if nothing changed. Katrina changed everything. Both schools were willing to confront new challenges and opportunities for service far beyond anything encountered in their histories. Simply put: both schools displayed the courage to accept sacrifice as a fundamental aspect of being a Catholic school.

Archbishop Chapelle High School is an archdiocesan Catholic girls' secondary school with an enrollment of more than 1,000 students. The school enjoys a fine

• Wind and water damage inside a classroom at Our Lady of Prompt Succor School, Westwego

reputation throughout the metro area because of its record of achievement. Chapelle suffered moderate damage from Katrina and was able to reopen in a relatively short time. Likewise, Archbishop Rummel High School, an all-boys' institution with an excellent reputation and an enrollment of more than 1,000 students, experienced more storm damage than Chapelle but was also able to reopen in short order. Both schools enjoyed a high rate of student return when classes were resumed in October 2005.

Jefferson Parish, as a whole, did not experience the massive damage and destruction on the order of Orleans and St. Bernard parishes. The basic infrastructure in East Jefferson was able to make steady progress in a relatively short time. As the weeks went by after Katrina, more and more businesses, medical services, and financial institutions were reopening. With this progress, a significant number of families had returned home, and more were coming each day. Families were also beginning to return to Orleans Parish in order to begin the recovery process. With this increased presence of families, the need to find a school, especially a high school, became a major parental objective. However, this would not be easy. De La Salle would remain for some time the only Catholic high school in Orleans Parish to reopen (it was reopened one day after the reopening of Cathedral Academy) before January 2006. The demand for secondary Catholic education was growing in the face of a severe shortage of secondary schools in operation. Would Catholic high school students, who had been enrolled in a Catholic school which now was unable to reopen, simply have to wait? This would cause a serious problem for high school seniors and their plans for college. How would this anxiety-producing situation be addressed?

Catholic high schools sponsored by various religious orders have long made a significant contribution to the archdiocese and the wider community. Religious-sponsored schools experienced Katrina-related damage. All these schools were able to reopen with a spirit of faith, dedicated school officials, and support from both religious orders and the archdiocese. Before reopening, however, these schools employed a number of strategies that allowed education to continue while away from their home campus. For example, Brother Martin and the Academy of Sacred Heart established temporary sites at schools sponsored by their religious orders. Xavier University Preparatory High School, St. Mary's Academy, and St. Augustine combined student bodies at the Xavier Prep campus so education would continue. Jesuit High School relocated to a school campus in Metairie. St. Mary's Dominican, Mount Carmel and Cabrini were able to reopen after extraordinary efforts by their respective stakeholders. Each of the above-mentioned schools was able to complete the 2005-06 academic year. In St. Tammany Parish, St. Paul's was able to reopen after an extensive clean up from downed pine trees.

The battered
schoolyard of
St. Monica
School

The then-principal of Rummel, Michael Begg (who now serves as the school's president), offered a daring and generous proposal: Rummel would become the site for two schools. One would be for students already enrolled, and a second school, or transition school, would be opened for displaced students who would attend until their original school reopened. The transition school, or "T-School," would have its own administration and faculty composed of Catholic school personnel whose schools were not yet able to reopen. Secondary education could continue, and Catholic school personnel would be meaningfully employed. The original Rummel School would retain its boys-only composition and would hold classes from early morning (6 a.m.) until

just after midday. The T-School would be co-ed, drawing both boys and girls from all schools, public and private, unable to reopen.

Meanwhile, Chapelle High School, under the leadership of Mary Beth Drez, school president, and Jane Frosch, school principal, made the decision to open Chapelle to students whose schools had not yet reopened. The decision was also made to admit boys in this traditionally all-girls' school! This departure would present a whole list of new challenges, but the overwhelming need to provide Catholic education was too pressing for Chapelle not to be of service. Several hundred new students were greeted with a warm Chapelle

Archbishop Hughes visits young children at St. John the Baptist Head Start Center

welcome. True to its motto, "God will provide," the Chapelle community reached out to those in need, confident that God would light the way.

Returning to the Archbishop Rummel example, the school's response to families and students in need of an educational setting proved to be truly historic. The Transition School, at the point of maximum enrollment, undertook the largest experiment in providing education to students after a natural disaster in American history. The Transition School, under the principalship of Nancy Hernandez (she served as principal of Ursuline Academy before the storm, to which she returned when the school reopened), greeted more than 1,000 students at its peak. Hernandez assured parents and students that the Transition School would be anything but an easy time of tutorials and just "hanging around." From day one, the Transition School operated as a "college prep" institution with the goal of seeing to it that any time away from a student's former school was not wasted. Besides a rigorous curriculum, students would be able to participate in all individual and team athletic events, according to a ruling by the Louisiana High School Athletic Association. Not only did Transition School teams compete, but there was also a new-found spirit of cooperation that developed among the students. From the classroom, to the cafeteria, to the athletic field, students who were once members of rival schools now found themselves united through a common experience. The old stereotypes and prejudices that once divided students now seemed distant and out of place. Students were able to interact on a daily basis, and in a number of different settings, which led to the forming of new friendships.

As Catholic high schools began to reopen with greater frequency, the great experiment of service to those in need of schooling by Chapelle and Rummel would come to an end. While things returned to "normal," much endured in the memory of those families and students who were brought together out of adversity but forged a new understanding of themselves and others that will last a lifetime. When Transition School students now meet, they are quick to share their memories of a time when love and hope flowered amid the ruins.

• Former President Bill Clinton takes a tour of the Xavier University campus with Dr. Norman Francis, university president

In Their Own Words

Fred and his wife, Gwyn, along with their two children, evacuated from Metairie to Baton Rouge. Steve, 16 years old, attended a Catholic high school in Orleans Parish. Fred and Gwyn's child, Charlie, 12 years old, attended a private school near their house. Along with the usual post-Katrina anxieties – work, home, money, etc., Fred and Gwyn were extremely concerned about their children's education, or worse yet, prospects for a lack of education. "Like a lot of people, we expected to be away a couple of days. Of course it didn't turn out that way. So many worries filled our heads. A big issue was how to continue Steve's and Charlie's education. My wife and I will always remember and be thankful to the people in Baton Rouge. Steve went to St. Michael's, which was set up for the students who had evacuated. Charlie went to a Catholic elementary school. They couldn't have been nicer. The school took Charlie in and made sure he had everything he needed. When I tried to explain about money for tuition, they told me all that would be taken care of later. Money never seemed to be an issue. They wanted what was best for our family."

Debbie is a teacher in one of the archdiocesan elementary schools. She is a relatively new teacher. The opening of the 2005 school year marked her third year of teaching. Debbie is single and evacuated to Baton Rouge with her "little dog." The chaos and uncertainty about so much of life in New Orleans left Debbie with more questions than answers. "Like everybody else, I was scrambling to find a place to stay and trying to get in touch with my family. Lack of the ability to communicate was so frustrating and frightening. Naturally, I was concerned about my school and what was going to happen. By word of mouth I found out that the archdiocese had set up an office in Baton Rouge. Just the idea of knowing there was a place I could go to for information calmed a lot of my fears. After going to the school office, I learned that my school was making plans to reopen, perhaps within a month to six weeks. They gave me a contact number for my principal. The people in the schools' office not only gave me information, but I left with a sense that things were going to be OK."

Calvin, 14, had just begun his high school years when Katrina struck. His goal throughout elementary school was to attend a Catholic high school. His parents had made great sacrifices by doing without and taking on part-time work so Calvin could achieve his dream. With Katrina, it seemed that dreams and hard work had been washed away. "All of us ended up in Arkansas after the hurricane. We didn't know what we were going to do. I couldn't help but think about school; and I wasn't going. We didn't know how long we'd be away, so I didn't go to school. I prayed to God for help. My parents heard that school was taking in students whose school didn't reopen. The school was Rummel. We lived with some of my mother's friends so I could go to school. I was really afraid, you know, being in a new place. I didn't know anybody. I was just glad to be in school. After awhile, everything was all right. I made some new friends. I really learned while I was there. I was really glad when my school reopened. Thanks, Rummel."

Jimmy and Gloria were lifelong residents of St. Bernard. They have two children. One graduated from Hannan High, and the other had entered her sophomore year at Hannan. Jimmy and Gloria, along with their two children, "lost everything in the storm." They relocated to the northshore in St. Tammany Parish. Gloria picks up the story: "I wouldn't trade the experience my son had at Hannan. There was a real family feeling at the school. Mr. Serio (the school principal) and the teachers really cared about each student. My son graduated and is now in college. He is doing well and wants to be a pharmacist. He goes to Mass every Sunday. Hannan played a big part in our family's life. When we drove by the school and saw all the damage, we all cried. Hannan was a special place. I couldn't get it out of my head that my daughter would not be at Hannan. Then, in answer to so many prayers, we heard there would be a Hannan on the northshore around Covington. We couldn't believe it. We were one of the first to sign up when they had registration."

Scott, 17, is very active in his parish's youth group. As soon as the parish became operational, he was busy trying to reorganize the group. While a number of former members had not returned, many did; in fact, the group was able to welcome new members who had moved into the parish. The size of the parish youth group approached pre-Katrina level. From October 27 through October 30 the archdiocesan CYO office led a youth delegation of 75 teens and adult youth ministers to the National Catholic Youth Conference in Atlanta. Scott was among the 75 who took part in this special pilgrimage. "I was excited to be able to go to the national conference in Atlanta. I was looking forward to being with some old friends from previous youth conferences. I was also able to tell my Katrina story. The really cool thing was Archbishop Hughes came with us to Atlanta. Everybody was so shocked and impressed that the archbishop would take time to travel with us. That said a lot. I don't think anyone will forget the trip."

Amber, 11, attends an area Catholic school, and like Scott, she is a leader in her parish's youth group. Unlike Scott, she was not able to participate in the trip to Atlanta. One of the projects of her youth group is helping those still dealing with the effects from Katrina. "For a long time after Katrina I was confused and left with many questions. I've always been taught, and I do believe, that God loves us. I couldn't help but think, why did God let this happen? At first I was afraid to ask this question. I was afraid to question God. I didn't want my teachers or parents to think I had turned against God. When I did start to ask this question, I didn't hear any good answers. The more I saw the damage and listened to people's stories, I came to believe there are no good answers. I decided I needed to do something to help others. I wasn't getting anywhere with all my questions. I realized that so many people lost more than me. I was so glad when my youth group started to look for ways to help people. We did things like clean up streets, collected food and clothes, and when possible, helped people who were still fixing their houses. I still have my questions, but I feel much better now that I'm doing something positive. Maybe that's God's answer to all my questions. Maybe God is saying to me, 'Amber, do something good for somebody. Stop looking at what you lost, and see what you can give.'"

A Future to Hope In

The chapter on Catholic schools must conclude, as the work of schools must continue, on a note of hope. As with most things after Katrina, in the words of the Funeral Mass Preface, "...life is changed, not ended." Beyond the shifting circumstances of this life, in which God is ever present, there is a world we have yet to enter but hope one day to reach. The number and size of Catholic schools has been reduced. At the opening of the 2005 school year, there were 109 elementary and secondary schools providing education within the archdiocese. Post-Katrina, the number of schools has been reduced to 86, and the student population has declined from 50,000 to 40,000 thousand (2009). It should be noted that even before Katrina, declining enrollment in Catholic schools – a national trend not peculiar to the archdiocese – was of concern.

The decrease in the number of schools and overall student population poses a special challenge for inner-city parents and students. Even with all the efforts to keep tuition affordable, many parents make enormous sacrifices to provide their children with a Catholic education. And yet, a growing number of parents simply cannot afford the cost.

In an effort to continue a Catholic educational presence within the inner-city, the archdiocese "clustered" a number of struggling schools into several "central schools" strategically located in Orleans Parish. The central school was intended to draw enough students into one site, allowing for a more effective and efficient use of limited resources. No doubt the archdiocese could have used Katrina as an excuse for withdrawing from the inner city. Such an idea was never considered. This "cluster" strategy, which gave rise to the central school concept, sent a clear message: the archdiocese would not abandon the inner city. The Church is committed to providing quality Catholic education to children who are most at risk and greatly in need.

In 2010 it was decided to return the central schools to their pre-Katrina status as parochial schools.

• Students enjoy their post-Katrina field trip in the French Quarter

• St. Michael High School administration with Bishop Robert Muench

The witness of all associated with Catholic education, during and after Katrina, has left to succeeding generations a lasting testimony to God's grace and the human spirit's will to endure. The reopening of schools was not just a commitment to the inner city, but a commitment to a mission not of its own making, one given by Jesus to teach all people, in every time and place until he comes again. Katrina was our time and the archdiocese our place. To the natural eye it was one of destruction and despair, one of darkness and displacement, one of desertion and death. However, to the eyes of faith, which see not just by sight but by insight, there was a deeper reality guiding events and inspiring hearts. Amid the ruins there was still present a grace, a pure gift, through the Holy Spirit. There was a blessing extended that empowered ordinary people to dare to do extraordinary things. There was a moving of the Spirit, which broke down barriers so new bridges across race, creed, age, and socio-economic categories could be built. There was a blessing from the giver of all blessings that moved a people to rebuild a future to hope in. Out of the crucible of a great cross there emerged a deeper resurrection. The story of Katrina was transcended and transformed by the story of Easter hope and life.

Cathedral Academy opens in the French Quarter in October 2005

Chapter 7 ————————————

FINANCES: THE CHALLENGE OF PRUDENT STEWARDSHIP

Few, if any, archdiocesan departments are as deeply involved in the day-to-day operations of the Archdiocese as is the Department of Financial and Administrative Services.

From Internet Services to School Food Services, from the Building Office to Accounting and Payroll, and numerous other offices, the Department of Financial and Administrative Services exercises fiscal guidance and oversight. The need for budgetary discipline is always of great importance for a large organization (and for individuals and families). The archdiocese is not only a large institution; it is also a church with a mission. The Catholic Church has been empowered to proclaim the Gospel and show God's love, especially to those in need. And after Katrina, there were many in need.

In this chapter dealing with finances, it is easy to get lost in numbers and charts. Katrina can look more like a bookkeeping entry than an event that altered the lives of so many. Granted, any effort to convey the magnitude of Katrina is bound to be inadequate. Yet for ourselves and those who come after us, we have an obligation to chronicle the storm. We have the need and the responsibility to find meaning and truth in what seems to be so devoid of purpose. Without undergoing such a painful and necessary reflection we would be without hope. Only the memory of destruction would remain. Death and destruction, not new life and hope, would be victorious.

The post-Katrina challenge for the archdiocese in general, and the Department of Finance in particular, was two-fold: fidelity to its mission to preach the Gospel and serve those in need; and secondly, to exercise prudent stewardship with the resources available. The regular stream of income – regular parish assessments, donations, and various investments – became severely reduced, as well as unpredictable in being received. Many donors to the archdiocese had to curtail or even eliminate their usual support. This reduction and uncertainty as to financial resources made it difficult for the archdiocese to project levels of aid and to formulate plans for rebuilding projects. It was important not to raise unrealistic expectations lest the community experience more pain due to disappointment and disillusionment. The credibility of the archdiocese could not be compromised by

promising what it could not deliver. People were looking for realism and hope at a time when the everyday seemed to oscillate between false promises and despair. It was more prudent and caring to acknowledge the incompleteness and uncertainty of archdiocesan plans than to raise expectations, only to have them dashed.

The archdiocese is a major employer in the metropolitan area. At any given time in the year, the Catholic Church employs 7,000 to 9,000 workers (the number fluctuates during the school year and summer). In addition to payroll issues, the Office of Human Resources (OHR) is charged with monitoring the employee benefits program, especially the healthcare benefits. The OHR is also responsible for overseeing the 401(k) plan, as well as processing medical claims filed by the clergy. Beth Tinto and Pam Power staff the office, and Tinto offers the following: "Every day I try to see Jesus in each person. In the chaotic time after Katrina, I saw him in every employee who called in desperate need of information or assistance. I don't think any of us could have done our jobs without our faith, because truly it was all we had. The faith of those who had lost so much was inspiring to me and made me want to work harder for all our employees."

Along with the need to be forthright as to what the archdiocese could provide, it was equally important to be candid and transparent regarding archdiocesan resources and the extent of losses due to Katrina. In order to provide this financial information, Archbishop Hughes in cooperation with the appropriate archdiocesan agencies, published a detailed report on the economic impact of the storm. Listed below are the main results of the published financial report that appeared in the Clarion Herald.

Archbishop Hughes' Post-Katrina Report

In July 2008, Archbishop Hughes issued a comprehensive report on the state of the archdiocese after Katrina. The salient features are as follows:

- The first priority of the archdiocese in responding to Katrina was humanitarian and pastoral. This humanitarian response was accomplished through Catholic Charities, which received more than $89 million to be used for providing basic human services (food, clothing, shelter), as well as making resources available for the cleaning and gutting of homes, aid to those living in trailer parks, and general assistance to those seeking to return and establish a normal life.

- The archdiocese experienced $287.8 million in property loss to church-owned facilities. Out of its 1,200 buildings, 1,110 experienced some degree of flood and/or wind damage. As of June 30, 2008, the archdiocese had recovered $183.3 million through insurance, gifts, grants, and FEMA. The receiving of funds for recovery is ongoing.

The early days after the storm were especially disruptive to routine financial transactions. Banks were closed and access to cash was all but frozen. Throughout the region, employees were in a state of high anxiety. The archdiocese was the major private employer in the metropolitan area. The needs of employees were a major concern. The tasks of locating and paying employees along with meeting the financial obligations of the archdiocese were the responsibility of the Accounting Office. Kim Ramsey and Ann Roussel were the only department workers who could return after Katrina. Through their efforts, all storm employees were paid on time, and other financial obligations were honored. The duties of the Accounting Office were expanded to include the processing of insurance payments and requests from parishes and other archdiocesan agencies.

- The issue of insurance coverage needed to be addressed. The archdiocese had received a total of $101.7 million in insurance proceeds. The archdiocese recovered 100 percent of its losses due to wind, fire, theft, and other damage not related to flooding.

- The archdiocese carried $13 million in flood insurance from Catholic Mutual and received $15.9 million from additional policies through the National Flood Insurance Program.

- The question that naturally arises is this: why weren't archdiocesan properties covered at 100 percent against flooding? After careful consultation with insurance professionals, archdiocesan officials were convinced that to fully insure all properties at 100 percent against flooding was cost-prohibitive. Parishes, schools, and ministries simply could not afford the initial premium, or the expense of maintaining the coverage.

- Buying extra coverage through National Flood seemed quite prudent at the time. The archdiocese, like the rest of the region's population, could not have foreseen the extensive destruction wrought by Katrina.

Parishes/Schools: Elementary and Secondary

Of the $287.8 million in property losses, the largest deficit came from damage to churches, related places of worship and schools. FEMA assistance could not be used for repairing buildings whose primary purpose is worship and/ or religious instruction. However, FEMA funds could be used at eligible school properties (an eligible building is one in which the instruction or activity is non-religious in nature). FEMA monies could be used for storm clean-up and for the establishment of temporary facilities.

In addition to the charts corresponding to parishes, elementary and secondary schools, the following points are worth noting:

- Even though FEMA funds could not be used for churches and parishes, a significant amount of money was raised through donations from various sources: gifts from other dioceses across the country, individual gifts and grants, and a most generous gift of $9.5 million from Catholic Charities USA. The total in donated monies totaled $45.9 million.

- In February 2006, the archdiocese closed six parishes and did not reopen two dozen others in Phase I of the Pastoral Plan. Of the $45.9 million received in gifts, $32.9 million was distributed to parishes to rebuild and restore their churches and ministries.

• Coastal storm damage in Biloxi, Miss.

- In April 2008, Phase II was announced, calling for the mergers of 27 parishes and for four parishes to become missions of neighboring parishes. The remaining $13 million in gifts was allocated to parishes to implement Phase II. The monies were used to restore parish buildings, repair storm-damaged facilities, and to restart various parish ministries.

- The Office of Catholic Schools was able to reopen 86 schools with a total enrollment of 40,000 students. A Catholic Central School Consortium was formed by joining together five Catholic schools in Orleans Parish with Our Lady of Prompt Succor in St. Bernard civil parish. This consortium allowed for the sharing of resources, the development of more effective and efficient fund-raising techniques, and the introduction of new learning technologies to improve achievement.

- Archbishop Hannan High School in Meraux was destroyed by Hurricane Katrina. The loss of the school to the archdiocese totaled $19.3 million. Unfortunately, only $7 million was recovered through insurance. However, the archdiocese received $17.3 million from FEMA and an additional $4 million so the school could temporarily relocate to St. Joseph's Abbey in Covington. The school has established a permanent campus at Goodbee in St. Tammany Parish.

- The archdiocese established the School Solidarity Fund. Catholic schools were the beneficiaries of FEMA funding. However, these FEMA monies had to be used within a given time period or the resources would revert back to the federal government. In order not to lose these funds some of the monies were reallocated from those schools that would not reopen or from those schools that would not reopen within the specified time frame. A portion of the fund had been kept in reserve for use by those schools which may reopen in the future. This set-aside of resources served as an important sign of support and hope to schools. This bracketed portion of the fund also provided encouragement for schools to reopen.

Catholic Charities: The Long Reach of Love

The financial challenges faced by Catholic Charities were enormous. The work of Catholic Charities Archdiocese of New Orleans, as we have seen in Chapter Three, is extensive in its scope and vital to the daily lives of thousands of metro area residents, Catholic and non-Catholic. After Katrina, the needs of people became more acute and varied. The following list offers some insight into the challenges, as well as the ways in which Catholic Charities fulfilled its Gospel mission of serving those in need.

- Besides meeting a variety of basic human needs (food, water, clothing, shelter, and medical services), Catholic Charities Archdiocese of New Orleans provided $11,201,371 in direct financial assistance to storm victims.

- In a joint effort between church and state, the Louisiana Department of Health and Hospitals and the Department of Social Services provided funds so that Catholic Charities could continue and expand its work of providing humanitarian aid to those in devastated areas.

Badly damaged statues rest
in the parking lot of the
archdiocesan office building
on Howard Avenue.
They were catalogued
for possible renovation.

People on roof
waiting for
rescue

• Catholic Charities Archdiocese of New Orleans received three humanitarian aid grants from Catholic Charities USA totaling $60.8 million. These grants form a substantial part of the $77.4 million received since March 2008 (gifts and grants continue to be received).

• The monies given to Catholic Charities have been used to continue the service programs of Catholic Charities Archdiocese of New Orleans, as well as the development of new ministries in response to Katrina. Included among the 51 programs and ministries are the following:

• Catholic Charities Archdiocese of New Orleans is a founding member of UNITY of Greater New Orleans, a community coalition formed in 1990 to respond to the urgent needs of the homeless. UNITY worked with those who were living in Duncan Plaza and under the Claiborne Avenue overpass after the storm. Catholic Charities' involvement with UNITY extends beyond the issue of homelessness.

• Case managers in Catholic Charities community centers and participating church parishes have provided more than $11 million in direct financial aid to individuals needing to buy groceries, pay utilities, and replace appliances. Some funds were also used to help those in need of meeting rental payments.

• Catholic Charities grant money was used in rebuilding and operating the Head Start center at Incarnate Word in the heavily damaged Hollygrove area. The center serves children ages 2 to 5 by providing a much-needed early educational experience. The center allows parents to feel less anxious while looking for employment knowing their children are in a safe environment.

• The generosity of Catholic Charities USA and the United States Conference of Catholic Bishops was evident in the large grants to Catholic Charities Archdiocese of New Orleans. A portion of these grants was used to benefit Catholic schools through tuition assistance, and the funding of programs and professional positions to help students with the post-traumatic stress of living in post-Katrina New Orleans.

• Another grant from Catholic Charities USA was used to establish the Office of Emergency Management (OEM). This office was established to coordinate relief efforts and plan for future crises in the region. OEM works with a vast number of archdiocesan entities ranging from parishes and schools to the various ministries of Catholic Charities Archdiocese of New Orleans.

One of the great needs after Katrina was housing. Christopher Homes, Inc. (CHI), played a key role in meeting this need. Almost immediately after Katrina, CHI was operating a number of units throughout the archdiocese. By October 2005, CHI had set up offices at Metairie Manor. Progress in reopening units was rapid, and by December 2005, 50 percent of CHI's 2,400 units were reopened. The tasks of clean up, repair, and rebuilding were enormous. Dennis Adams, executive director of CHI, attributed the accomplishment to "the graces of the Holy Spirit and the prayers and financial support of the Church throughout the U.S., the United States Conference of Catholic Bishops' Recovery Committee and the American Association of Homes and Services of the Aged." CHI was not only concerned about repairing buildings; its primary concern was for the spiritual, pastoral, and human needs of the residents. Numerous Catholic and non-Catholic volunteers, along with secular social service agencies, joined together in caring for the residents in a truly holistic manner. Throughout the entire process of recovery, CHI enjoyed an excellent working relationship with governmental agencies and the support of private groups.

More Damage, A Greater Hope

At this point, we offer a brief word highlighting some of the other archdiocesan facilities. These properties experienced a degree of damage, which required them to close for a time. Each of the ministries that operated out of these buildings, now renovated, has resumed providing its services to the needy.

• No one area or ministry of the archdiocese sustained as much damage and loss resulting from Katrina as Christopher Homes. This ministry of the archdiocese provides affordable apartments to low-income seniors and the disabled. Christopher Homes suffered $36.5 million in property damage and initially lost 70 percent of its apartment units. Archdiocesan representatives have managed to recover $9.2 million from FEMA (as of 2008).

Efforts to receive more federal funds are ongoing. One important sign of hope is the reconstruction of Nazareth Inn in New Orleans East. This project is in partnership with Providence Community Housing and Enterprise Community Partners, Inc. A large number of volunteer groups have aided with cleanup and repairs.

• The archdiocese provides long-term healthcare through Wynhoven Healthcare in Marrero and Chateau de Notre Dame in New Orleans. These two properties incurred $4 million in damages. Both locations received FEMA funds for cleanup, repair work, and evacuation costs. Each facility has undergone extensive renovations. The two facilities served a combined population of 344.

• Notre Dame Seminary experienced significant damage to its two major buildings – Shaw Hall (administration offices, chapel, classrooms, resident facilities, and the lower level, which contained the Pastoral Center and a recreational area for seminarians and priests) and St. Joseph Hall (faculty and administrative offices, classrooms, resident facilities, and the seminary library). The damage from wind and water amounted to nearly $6 million. The seminary was able to reopen in January 2006. Cleanup and repairs continued for well over a year. Notre Dame remains in need of funds for capital improvements.

• Community centers, as well as the administration building (Chancery) suffered severe wind and flood damage. The damage inflicted by Katrina to these facilities amounted to $10.5 million. Community centers were restored quickly so they could resume providing emergency aid to those returning after the storm. The archdiocese, through Catholic Charities, was able to re-establish 12 community centers to meet the ongoing needs of the various communities in which they are located.

Seeing Is Still NOT Believing

Time after time, those who viewed the devastation wrought by Katrina usually offered one of two responses. One reaction was the sheer silence of disbelief. Visitors as well as residents just looked and shook their heads. Tears replaced words. As to the second way of reacting, people were often heard to say, "I can't believe it. I drove through some neighborhoods and I can't believe what I saw. It was as if a bomb exploded."

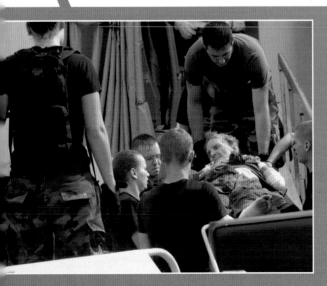

Chateau de Notre Dame offers a wide range of nursing care, from assisted living to skilled nursing care. Katrina made it necessary to evacuate 130 elderly residents, and after the storm passed, residents were placed in various nursing homes and assisted living facilities across central Louisiana. Chateau administrators placed a great value on the role of the employees' Christian faith. In the words of one administrator, "Our employees did not have to help us evacuate the elderly residents; they volunteered to come and help. Those who chose to evacuate with us chose to do so out of a deep caring for the residents and a feeling of family." In October 2007, final approval was given to reopen from the U.S. Department of Health and Human Services. John Tieperman, executive director of Chateau de Notre Dame, credited the Presbyterian Home Corporation (PHC) with a successful reopening. The PHC sent down key administrative staff who provided invaluable assistance. The assistance from the Mennonite community from Oregon proved valuable as well. The Mennonite members were willing to do the most basic tasks, from cleaning to moving beds. Yet these tasks, were essential for reopening.

Among the corporal works of mercy is burying the dead. Right after Katrina, this work was as necessary as it was difficult to achieve. The massive flooding, combined with the low sea level of the region, caused many caskets to emerge from their graves. Churches were closed and could not conduct funerals. The transportation of the dead to other parts of the state and outside Louisiana posed its own challenges. One of the churches to reopen early on was St. Louis Cathedral. Numerous funerals were conducted by Cathedral rector Monsignor Crosby Kern and a dedicated group of permanent deacons. Requests came from throughout the region. Not only did cathedral clergy and staff conduct religious services, but they also were heavily involved in the essential administrative details associated with funerals.

• Hurricane waters forced the walls of crypts to open at cemeteries throughout the region

For each person who lived through the hurricane, there is a blending of feelings, images, and words that will forever be a part of one's life story. Even those who were not personally touched by Katrina but were exposed through media reports were deeply moved. Many who came to volunteer with cleanup and recovery, as well as those who made other expressions of assistance, were profoundly moved by what they saw and read.

As the saying goes, a picture is worth a thousand words. The next two sections of this chapter are devoted to the images and signs of Katrina, free of commentary. There is a kind of tyranny exercised by the printed word. That is, one can be left with the impression that there is only one orthodox way of understanding an idea, event, or image. This is neither true nor respectful of the reader or, in this case, the viewer. One should experience these pictures without an imposed interpretation. The individual ought to be alone with the uniqueness of his or her own emotions and reflections.

The first part of what follows contains images of destruction. The word "image" is chosen with purpose. An image provides an immediacy of emotional impact that takes time to process. However, these images and the emotional response they evoke are just one side of the Katrina coin.

Part two presents signs of clean-ups, rebuilding, and recovery. As with the word "image," so the word "sign" is chosen with care. The term "sign" points beyond itself to something else. Signs provide information and lead one to a deeper reality than merely surface or sensory experience. In this case of Katrina, these photographs of recovery are signs of hope! The pictures of people cleaning up and reparing their homes, churches and schools tell a story far beyond the fixing of buildings. These pictures point to an unwillingness to be conquered. They point to a spirit of determination that seeks to triumph in the face of great odds favoring defeat. It is to images of destruction and the signs of hope that we now turn.

1 – 9th Ward view

2 – Circle Food Store at St. Bernard and Claiborne avenues

3 – The levee break at the 17th Street Canal led to the flooding of 80 percent of homes in Greater New Orleans

4 – Storm surge moved homes off foundations

5 – Sign indicates loss of life in home

1 - Louisiana Superdome and
   the New Orleans Arena under water

2 - Rescue teams search for survivors in flooded city

3 - Storm destruction

4 - Close to the London Avenue Canal

5 - St. Mark rectory in Chalmette

6 - St. Ann, Empire, after the storm

7 - High winds uproot massive oak tree

1 - Bishop Roger Morin's
residence fire

2 - 9th Ward destruction

3 - Katrina debris pile on Pontchartrain Boulevard

4 - West End Boulevard under water

5 - St. Ann Church in Empire was saved from further damage by impaling
on a tree

6 - Katrina debris piled on sidewalk

7 - Rubble at 17th Street Canal

8 - Archbishop Hughes thanks
Army soldier for rescue and
clean up work

1 - Flooded New Orleans cemeteries

2 - Buras

3 - Damaged home

4 - Chalmette oil spill

5 - Breach waters reach rooftops of homes

6 - FEMA Search and Rescue Team members
    search homes

1 - 9th Ward debris removal

2 - Youth and Young Adult Revival 2009

3 - Youngstown Bishop George Murry blesses a rebuilt home
   in Arabi

4 - Image of the Sacred Heart statue behind St. Louis
   Cathedral, missing several fingers due to falling branches,
   expressed powerfully the Lord's faithful love for us

1 -

2 -

3 -   4 -

1 – Good Shepherd Parish celebrates a eucharistic procession

2 – Catholic Leadership Institute, June 2009

3 – Contractors in hazard suits clean chemical-laden debris

4 – 17th Street Canal repair

1 - Lakeview debris removal

2 - Plaquemines recovery

3 - Archdiocese of New Orleans delegation at the National Catholic Youth Conference in October 2005 in Atlanta

4 - Heavy equipment moves in to help with recovery

1 - 2005 Katrina refrigerator is decorated with
   New Orleans recovery humor

2 - Borrow pit preparation to strengthen and repair levees

3 - Children at Cathedral Academy prepare for first Communion

4 - Archdiocese of New Orleans youth delegation at the March
   for Life in Washington, D.C., January 2009

Blackhawk
prepares to
evacuate refugees

Mississippi Gulf
Coast damage

Behind and Beyond
the Numbers

The world of finance within and outside the church and otherwise is highly fluid. Capital is created, distributed, lost, and remade every second of every day. The financial condition of the archdiocese presented in this chapter is a snapshot, a moment within an ever-evolving reality. The moment captured herein is a record of the effects of Katrina on archdiocesan economic resources. It is also, more precisely, an acknowledgment of the enormous generosity and goodwill of institutions and individuals who reached out to help a church whose mission is to help others. It is

a record of the recognition by the archdiocese that it could not meet every need, nor could it continue operating as it had before the storm.

The acceptance of post-Katrina realities necessitated the need for prudent stewardship. Those entrusted with making decisions about resource allocation, the continuation, suspension, or closing of ministry or facility always kept in mind Archbishop Hughes' first principle enunciated from the beginning: in every decision made, concern for people must be uppermost in all deliberations. Special care needs to be shown to those who are hurting and angry when their place of worship or schooling is no longer able to continue. When a particular ministry ceased to be offered, other ministries were called upon to provide creative, compassionate care. Out of a shared loss and caring a deeper sense of solidarity could emerge.

The archdiocesan commitment to prudent stewardship was not based on a simple cost/benefit calculation. Behind the numbers and charts are real people who had walked through the dark valley of Katrina. They desired to be uplifted once more, to remember home, to dream of a way of life that once was and could be again. They looked to their church for that light and life that beckons from beyond the present. They look to their church for the One who is Light and Life. May it be said in spirit and truth that they looked not in vain.

• First responders hunkered down at Our Lady of Holy Cross College.

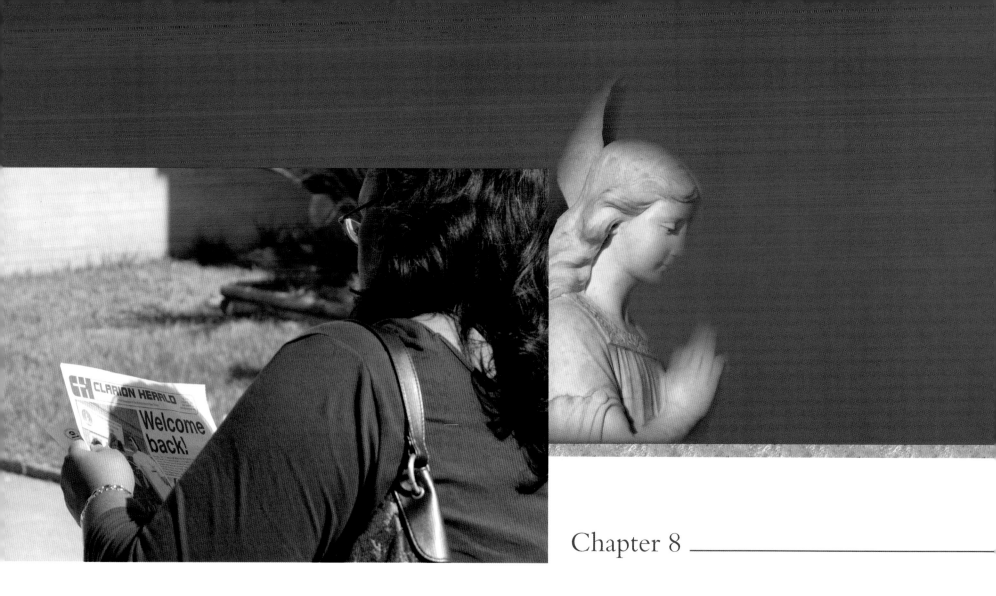

Chapter 8

LAITY: STORIES OF FAITH

The very title of this chapter raises a number of questions (if not objections) of which three will occupy our attention as prelude to the stories offered.

Why dedicate a whole chapter to the laity, especially one in which lay people are linked to stories of faith? Second, why employ story or narrative as the literary form in which to discuss faith as it relates to Katrina? Finally, if the foundational theme of this book is hope, why chronicle stories of faith rather than hope? All of these are important questions, and must be given a careful response if we are to honor those who open themselves to public viewing, and if we are to learn that their stories help us to better tell our own.

The Lay Vocation

To our first question – why stories of faith from lay people? The short answer is simple – why not? What is it about the lay faithful that excludes them, or at least gives pause, when it comes to appreciating lay witness on behalf of faith? This is a complex question that does not lend itself to a simple answer. Among the many factors in play, certainly a chief cause is the lingering belief that only the ordained and religious are gifted with a vocation. The lay state is still viewed, in some quarters, as a lesser state in the Church. Clearly such an ecclesiology was rejected by the Second Vatican Council. In the document *Lumen gentium* we read: "…the faithful, who by Baptism are incorporated into Christ and integrated into the people of God, are made sharers in their particular way in the priestly, prophetic, and kingly office of Christ, and have their part to play in the mission of the whole Christian people in the Church and in the World" *(LG31)*.

The document (LG) goes on to specify the "special vocation" which belongs to the laity. Lay Christians are called to holiness through their work in temporal affairs. Lay people are to be salt and light to those areas of social life they inhabit. It is through their personal and collective witness that God's kingdom is proclaimed. Not only are lay Christians called to bring the Gospel to that part of the world they influence, but they are to use their talents and skills to advance the living conditions of the general order. In effect, the faithful are called, through baptism and confirmation, to participate in the apostolate of the Church, that is, "individually or grouped in associations, (the faithful are) to work so that the divine message of salvation may be known and accepted by all men throughout the earth." This active role in the apostolic work of the Church becomes more pressing in those situations in which only lay people are in a position to make Christ known. *(Catechism of the Catholic Church, No.900)*

Rededication Mass at St. David Church
in the Lower Ninth Ward

"Faith is a personal act – the free response of the human person to the initiative of God who reveals himself. But faith is not an isolated act. No one can believe alone, just as no one can live alone…Each believer is thus a link in the great chain of believers." *(Catechism of the Catholic Church No.166)*

Before, and even more so after Katrina, the contributions of the laity to the mission and ministry of the archdiocese cannot be over-estimated. From finances to communications, from the vast network of social services to religious education, the professional expertise, dedication, and generosity of lay people were extraordinary. In addition to directing and working in various archdiocesan departments, the laity provides a powerful witness throughout the Catholic school system, as well as various parochial ministries in which they serve.

The degree of recovery within the archdiocese after Katrina, along with the numerous services provided by the Church, would not have been possible without significant lay involvement and leadership. Within a week after Katrina, lay department and office directors, along with staff members, assembled in Baton Rouge with Archbishop Hughes and appropriate clergy. The willingness to gather so quickly allowed the archdiocese to provide a rapid, well-organized response to those in need. This lay presence, so soon after Katrina, was a testimony to their depth of commitment to the mission of the Church. Furthermore, the faithful resumed their work, often at the point of great sacrifice to themselves and their families.

The stories of faith by the laity offered in this chapter do not come from the nuclear archdiocesan family (department and office directors and various administration officials). Rather, the stories that will unfold are from the Church's extended family that forms a vital part of the one community of faith of the archdiocese. These stories come from a cross-section of the faithful – people of different ages, races, life experiences, and socio-economic backgrounds. However, there is a common thread, beyond Katrina itself, which binds: an unshakable faith in the God who does not abandon his people in a time of testing. We will get to these powerful stories of faith and trust, but first we must address our two remaining questions.

The Power of Stories

Why stories? Why turn to narrative as a way into faith? Especially, why such stories of faith when it comes to Katrina? All are important questions that deserve a response.

The case could be made that to be human is to tell stories. The better we tell stories, the more we develop our humanity. From the first flicker of human consciousness there were stories. The earliest humans told stories, usually about hunting, gathering, and fighting against other groups, through etchings on cave walls. Stories are a uniquely human way of making sense of existence and dealing with contingencies of survival. We have the need to organize daily experiences, from the most mundane to the momentous. We crave coherence, an order that can provide us with meaning and truth. Stories confront one of the deepest of human fears – chaos. Stories provide us with a way to gain some control over the uncertainties of daily life. This need to feel secure,

St. Ann Mission Church in Empire was lifted from its cinderblock moorings by the rising water

to know that there is a power ordering events to a good end, is evidenced by the child who requests of a parent, "Tell me a story." The one who tells the story, usually at night before the child falls to sleep, has the power to confront the darkness and the unknown. The child can pass into slumber knowing there is someone who will protect. Stories assure us that we can pass into the darkness of unconsciousness, confident that the light will return.

The power of stories to provide order, security, meaning, and the confidence to face everyday life is clearly present in the Bible, the Book of Stories. It is not by accident that Holy Scripture opens with the stories of creation. Out of the primal chaos, God establishes order and sets boundaries. Into the original darkness God speaks light, the first gift of creation. The Bible proceeds to stories of humankind's fall and subsequent banishment from Eden, followed by stories of promise, liberation, forgiveness and redemption. The ultimate story, which gathers all others into a unified whole, is the story of God's self-disclosure, and humankind's response of faith or infidelity to the person of Jesus Christ.

Jesus is the ultimate story teller. Jesus came to proclaim the Kingdom of God, and he used parables to confound the learned and self-righteous, while teaching the humble and outcasts about the Father's love. The parables are told with a deceptive simplicity, drawing on everyday experience. Through Jesus' telling of stories, the ordinary reveals the oft-hidden presence of grace. Parables are dangerous because they challenge conventional ways of living and the proper ways of "being religious." If parables are upsetting, so is the teller of parables, hence, the establishment's hostility and

ultimate decision to kill Jesus and end the story. The Father of Jesus had a different plan.

• Our Lady Star of the Sea in New Orleans, now reopened, was dealt a heavy blow by Katrina

With the stories of Jesus, we are invited into the multiple layers of truth about God, ourselves, and others. One didn't need a formal education to understand what Jesus was revealing. As we know, the scribes and Pharisees often remained in the darkness of their refusal to accept the One who is Light and Truth. Theirs was not a failure of the intellect; rather it was a hardness of the will. They did not *want* to walk in the light of truth, of the One who is Truth. By contrast, those who followed Jesus, often the marginalized of the day, hungered and thirsted for the words of Jesus, for the very person of Jesus. Their hearts were eager to be satisfied in the mysteries of the kingdom of heaven.

"Where two or three are gathered in my name, there I am also"

It is not just the Judeo-Christian tradition that sets a special place at the table for stories. World religions, from the most primitive to the highly complex, preserve a collection of stories which are told and retold through the generations. Often the most revered members of the community are those who know and share the collective memory of the group contained in stories. Great care is taken to transmit the sacred stories of origin, life and death, rebirth and afterlife. Stories honor the past, inform the present, and guide the future.

Stories are not necessarily, or explicitly, religious in nature. All societies have stories, myths, legends, fables, and the like around which individuals become a people. The most obvious example is the founding of the American republic. History and legend often blend to shape a nation's narrative. America is formed around a set of ideas, events, people and texts (the Declaration of Independence, the Constitution, the Bill of Rights, and so on) in which succeeding generations are schooled. America would not be America without her stories.

At this point we must ask: why are stories so powerful? Why do they endure and move us so? The response offered at the beginning of this section is still operative – the telling of and listening to stories is an essential part of being human. We *have* to tell and listen to stories. After Katrina one of the most important things we did, just as important as cleanup and repair, was to share our "Katrina stories." When children returned to school, one of the first things to take place was the sharing of stories. Students needed to reconnect, to know they were not alone, and that life was continuing forward. Stories shared and listened to proved to be a crucial element of recovery.

Faith in the face of destruction puts trust to the test, and trust is real trust when all else counsels a different path. We cannot help others, and God cannot help us, if doubt prevents action. C.S. Lewis writes, "In getting a dog out of a trap, in teaching a boy to swim or rescuing one who can't, in getting a frightened beginner over a nasty place on a mountain, the one fatal obstacle may be their distrust." *(On Obstinacy in Belief, 23)*

Adults would stop their washing, sawing and hammering to greet returning neighbors not seen since the storm and share their stories. When so much was disrupted and lost, we looked for anything that endured, some common star that allowed lives to reconnect. When the waters of chaos, like those in the days of Noah, washed away so much, we desperately needed to make sense of the nonsense. We needed to listen to the stories of others so we might place ours in a larger context. The listening to others' experiences gave ours a depth it lacked if it remained a stand-alone narrative. Bonds of compassion and courage were established so that we could continue the work at hand.

This section began with a simple question – why stories? Hopefully, it is now clear that in the face of such massive destruction, when chaos and not order ruled the day, there was a profound need to find meaning and direction. Lives and communities were put back together one story at a time. No discussion about the archdiocese and Katrina would be satisfactory without appreciating the role of stories for recovery (in the next section more will be said about the *type* of story offered for reflection).

Again, why stories? The answer comes in the form of a question – how could one reflect about Katrina *without* stories? How indeed.

Faith: Radar That Sees Through the Fog

The final question to be answered before we turn to the stories themselves concerns the type of story offered. For a book in which hope is a major theme, wouldn't it be more appropriate to present stories of hope? At first blush the answer seems obvious – of course, the stories should focus on hope. The very title of the book leads one to champion hope, not faith. On closer inspection of what seems to be so obvious a choice, we may notice the favoring of hope over faith contains the fallacy of mutually excluding alternatives. This fallacy rests on a premise that must be exposed and rejected; the faulty assumption holds there is no essential relationship between the two theological virtues. If one favors faith, then hope is discarded. Likewise, if one opts for hope, there is no need to involve faith.

In this section, we will seek to answer two inter-related questions as a way of responding to our major inquiry – why stories of faith? The two sub-textual questions are:

How is the term "faith" understood? And secondly, what is the relationship, if any, between faith and hope?

From Fog to Sight to Insight

The theological virtue of faith plays a front and center role in holy Scripture. In the Old Testament, Abraham is held up as the Father of Faith. It is through his belief and trust in God's promise that the Messiah will enter human history. In the fullness of time, God, who is faithful and trustworthy sends his Son into the world. The *Logos*, who is the Word through whom all things come into being, is given a human face through Mary's *fiat*, her "yes" to the angel's announcement that she would bear a son and name him Jesus.

Throughout the healing ministry of Jesus – and healing is a primary sign of God's kingdom as present and active in the person of Jesus – faith plays a crucial role. For our understanding of faith, especially as it relates to our experience of Katrina, we turn our focus to a familiar story of faith and healing drawn from the Gospel.

The Gospel of Mark records the story of Jesus healing the blind man, Bartimaeus *(Mk 10:46-52)*. As Jesus is leaving Jericho with a large crowd following after him, Bartimaeus cries out to Jesus, "Master, have pity on me." The persistence of the blind man causes Jesus to stop and ask, "What do you want me to do for you?" The answer would appear to be obvious, "Master, I want to see." Yet, Jesus doesn't make assumptions, and requires the man to state clearly his need Maybe the blind man was just asking for alms. This was a common occurrence. Also, to be restored to sight radically changes the man's situation. He will no longer be the object

"Jesus falls the second time"... St. Patrick Church in Port Sulphur

of others' charity. Bartimaeus will be expected to assume more personal responsibility.

Jesus grants his petition, "Go your way; your faith has saved you." St. Mark goes on to tell us that "immediately he received his sight and followed him on the way." Notice that Jesus connects faith with healing. The power of faith has effected not just the regaining of his physical sight; the healing is also spiritual. Bartimaeus' faith starts out with his being able to see, but he progresses from sight to insight. He sees in a way he never imagined. Jesus is no longer a master who grants a favor. He is now seen as "the Master" who is worthy of being followed.

Faith involves a total trust of God in every situation. St. Teresa of Jesus captures this connection: "Let nothing trouble you Let nothing frighten you Everything passes God never changes Patience Obtains all Whoever has God Wants for nothing God alone is enough." (Poesias 30)

The faith-healing of Bartimaeus reveals an important dimension of belief, especially as it applies to life after Katrina. Faith is the process of an encounter with Jesus by which one moves from fog, to sight, and finally to insight. Faith is the process of having our vision informed by grace. Into the blindness, the fog caused by our need, comes the One who is Light and Life. New possibilities, creative ways of living, a new set of values and priorities take hold. A surprising source of strength comes upon us from a power beyond ourselves. Regardless of what others say or do, we persist in prayer, work, and a determination to meet the challenges at hand. It is often said, "seeing is believing," but when it comes to faith the reverse is the case: "Believing is seeing." With faith, we do not see in order to believe; rather, we believe in order to see, to see the God who is ever near.

When soldiers hit the beach in World War II, there was chaos as bullets flew and bodies fell. The eerie silence of pre-landing gave way to the sounds of guns, bombs, planes, and the anguished cries of men injured and dying. This experience is referred to as "the fog of war." No matter how well-prepared soldiers are for going ashore, the gun smoke blinds the eyes and fills the lungs. What was once so clear in the briefing room is now a blur in the reality of combat. Survival depends to a large extent on one's ability to break through the fog. Staying alive requires the ability to keep moving.

The spiritual writer, Corrie ten Boom, understands faith in the following way: "Faith is like radar that sees through the fog – the reality of things at a distance that the human eye cannot see." As with the fog of war, there was "the fog of Katrina." Upon returning home, people were met with

Even though San Pedro Pescador Church was designed as "hurricane-proof" and had its worship space on the second floor, Katrina's waters left their mark

massive destruction and numerous deaths. The mind swirled. Words could not be found. The body froze in disbelief. The human eye, often tear-filled, could not see past the present.

• The annual Boat Blessing in Yscloskey was an important event for the community

Out of the fog of Katrina came a voice asking, "What do you want me to do for you?" Countless returnees responded, "To see through the fog and be restored. We desire that grace of insight which allows us to be grasped by a vision of what can be." This petition for believing in order to see things that are as yet at a distance was not a desperate plea for some kind of

grand, divine intervention. It was a desire for the type of faith that looks reality squarely in the face, with all its ugliness, and can still say yes to life, can still experience love amid the ruins. Faith is not blindly grasping at straws or an irrational wishing that somehow all of this would just go away. Faith is an act whereby one surrenders in trust to the God who led his people out of Egypt into the Promised Land, to the God who returned and restored his people after exile in Babylon, to the God who sent his Son to be the Savior of all people, and to the God who abides through the Church until he comes and draws all things unto himself. In the midst of the fog of Katrina, faith could see that God was still present. And not only present, but God was doing what God has always been doing through the ages – creating, recreating, liberating, restoring, redeeming, and providing the courage to live in and through the challenges of the hour. As with our ancestors in faith, that great "cloud of witnesses," so it is with us now. God does not abandon his people. The stories in this chapter give powerful testimony to the God who calls us from the fog into his own wonderful light and life.

Faith Forward

The second issue that requires comment is the relationship between faith and hope. If faith is understood as passing from fog to insight, that is, seeing things as they are, and the reality of things on the horizon, then faith leads to hope. For faith is not static, but is a dynamic moving forward under the guidance of the Holy Spirit.

Faith is grounded in the truth of the past and an honest assessment of the present. The "pastness" of faith is the grateful acknowledgment of God's fidelity, revealed in

Faith is difficult in the face of evil. It is that very faith, however, which serves as the answer to this enduring challenge. The Catechism of the Catholic Church offers the following: "In time we can discover that God in His almighty providence can bring a good from the consequences of an evil, even a moral evil, caused by his creatures…From the greatest moral evil ever committed – the rejection and murder of God's only Son, caused by the sins of all men – God, by his grace … the greatest of goods: the glorification of Christ and our redemption. But for all that, evil never becomes a good." *(No. 312)*

his mighty works. Regardless of Israel's infidelity, God was steadfast to his covenant promises. Time and again, especially through his great prophets, God called his people back to their identity and strength, namely, the covenant. The everlasting fact that can never be revoked is this – they are his people, and he is their God. In famine and prosperity, exile and restoration, being conquered and conquering, the hand of the Lord is always upon them. Even in times of disaster, the Lord is near to his broken-hearted people.

In light of God's past fidelity, there is a confident trust that he will act in the present. The "presentness" of faith that

God is acting *now*, on behalf of his people, comes from knowing *and* believing what God has done before, he will do now. No matter the situation, God is reigning and his sovereignty is eternal. The forces of nature and the might of nations are subject to the will of the Supreme Creator and King of Kings. Faith clears away the fog of fear, uncertainty and timidity. The eyes of faith are able to see the reality of God. As in former times, so now God is ordering all things to his eternal plan in the here and now.

Faith does not stop at the water's edge of past and present. God lures his people forward. God is not only behind and alongside, he is before them with rod and staff. The "pastness and presentness" of faith is completed in its "futureness." And if faith thrusts us forward, then faith must be related to hope. In fact, we could say that the future face of faith is hope. If faith does not include hope, then a central tenant of biblical faith would be denied, namely, that God is the Lord of all history, and all of time is in his hands. The layers of time unfold according to his holy will and the wisdom of his providential care. To halt the dynamic of faith, either by freezing it in some golden past, or by seeing no further than a comfortable present, or even worse, by surrendering to a current injustice, in the name of peace and order, is to lock and limit God. To confine the dynamic of faith to past and present is an attempt to control God. It is an attempt to create God according to our specifications. The Bible calls this idolatry.

The desire to limit the dynamic of faith, and by extension God, is as old as Adam and Eve. The original disobedience of our first parents is often understood as being motivated by pride and the desire to be equal to God. That was certainly a factor, but not to be overlooked is the need for security

and absolute certainty. However, the God of Abraham and the Father of Jesus involves us in the dynamic of faith. The forward thrust of faith is always unsettling and filled with the unknown. We are challenged to live securely with insecurity. We can give ourselves to the adventure of faith only when we surrender in trust to the One who has been faithful, is faithful now, and will keep His promises into tomorrow. In the face of the daily contingencies of life, we must open ourselves to the rush of the Holy Spirit. Retreat and stagnation need to be rejected, for they lead to death. The God we profess as Father and Son is also the Holy Spirit, "the Lord and giver of life."

Katrina tested, in varying degrees, our willingness to be grasped by the dynamic of faith. The fog of Katrina understandably bubbled up serious questions that will be addressed in chapter 10. Isn't all this talk about the mighty deeds of God nothing more than myths, fables, and evidence

Welcome back Mass at Mary, Queen of Vietnam Church

Faith is not only a noun, a set of propositions that the mind understands and the will affirms. Faith is also a verb. Faith calls for action, a way of daily living. Philosopher and spiritual writer Gerard Reed highlights the active dimension of faith: "We Christians admire the great men and women of our faith, the heroes of our tradition, who lived bravely and well. They acted out their faith. Faith, not feeling, enables us to persevere. Faith, not feeling, glistens like a diamond, marking the last commitment that typifies authentic discipleship." (C.S. Lewis Explores Vice and Virtue, p. 133)

of the staying power of superstition? Where was God, as the winds blew and the water rose? Don't the enormous destruction and tragic loss of life prove that God is either indifferent to our plight or impotent to act in the face of this physical evil? Isn't all the talk about faith, hope, and the future nothing more than a defense mechanism, a psychological buffer of our own creation to help us get through the tough times? If we are honest with ourselves, don't we have to admit there is no wizard behind the curtain? Isn't it true that we are alone in facing the uncertainties of an unresponsive universe?

Doubts and questions after a great disaster are not unexpected. Yet doubts are not necessarily an indication of disbelief. The Pharisees had little doubt because they possessed little faith. Questions are not, of themselves, signs of a weak faith. Questions can often be a faith at prayer. To be spiritually troubled can be the quest for a peace that strengthens one's faith. The search for truth often requires a pilgrimage through the dark valley of doubt. No matter. The psalmist assures us that the Lord's rod and staff will lead to refreshing waters. To journey through the twin peaks of questioning and doubt is a personal odyssey each one must make in search of personal answers. However, while the answers are for each individual, we need not make our way alone. We need companions who share our burdens, know our struggles, and help us pass from fog into the light of his truth.

It is to a group of fellow travelers with their stories of faith that we now turn. The sharing of their journeys during and after Katrina will help us to better understand and tell ours. For it is in the telling of stories that the dynamic of faith moves us forward in hope.

New tabernacle at Our Lady
of Lourdes Church, Violet

Marc Soileau... *"Things will never be the same as before, but because of what we experienced, we can now be stronger and closer to God."*

Throughout my experiences from Hurricane Katrina and its aftermath, I have experienced struggles in faith. While working in the New Orleans 9th Ward and in the Superdome as a first responder, I did not have time to completely absorb what was happening around me. I had a numbing sensation throughout my experiences. Struggles that followed for the next couple of years would challenge my faith. This life-changing event has given me a new outlook on my faith, but only after forcing me to go through many struggles. Ultimately, my faith has become stronger, but there are still ongoing challenges that indirectly have come about because of these disasters. These struggles are my cross. When I fall, I must pick up my cross again and drive on to achieve God's will.

Before hurricanes Katrina and Rita, I had never had a true understanding of our vulnerabilities. My sense of security was strongly rooted in American hubris. We were the greatest nation on Earth. Things that happened to people in Third World countries did not, and could not, happen to us. I had faith in God and believed in his church. We were the smartest, most powerful and most resourceful people in history. Things that happened to others in the past or happened in Third World countries were not things that I truly understood. It was almost like watching a television show. I understood natural disasters happened but could not grasp the true vulnerabilities of the human experience.

As the storm approached, I was working in the Lower 9th Ward in a first-responder operations center. Because of our efforts, we had little time to reflect on what was personally about to happen to us. Because of my position, I was always up to date on the latest storm data. I remember calling my mother in the middle of the night before the storm because we had family in New Orleans and Slidell that did not plan to evacuate. Most of my family finally evacuated from the threatened areas, but I still did not grasp how our lives would soon change.

The morning of the hurricane at about 10 a.m. as waters were beginning to rise in the 9th Ward, I was speaking on my cell phone with my wife, who had evacuated to Baton Rouge. I was telling her that the water was rising and that we may get water in our Ford Explorer parked in front of my building. Soon after, my cell phone signal went out. I would not have communication with my family again until almost a week later. This loss of communication with my family and their knowledge of what was happening in the 9th Ward would bring great fear to my family. This fear led to many challenges that would affect my faith and family years after. When I turned around to return to my work station,

I noticed a wave coming down the hallway. I knew my office, just a few buildings away, was lost. Before I reached the stairwell 10 feet away, the water was already over my boots. Before the storm passed through, the first floor of our raised building had about five feet of water. All communications with our other elements had been lost. We had lost any sort of communications with our families that had evacuated, and we had no clue what was going on around us. We were completely isolated and helpless.

The evening after Hurricane Katrina passed, we were rescued by a combination of boat crews consisting of locals from St. Bernard Parish and soldiers from the 769th Engineers from the Louisiana National Guard. These boats drove into the stairwells of our building to the Mississippi River levee where flight crews from the 244th Aviation landed and flew us to the Superdome. At the Superdome, we would re-establish our operations center and also link up with our medical personnel who had been established before the hurricane to care for special-needs patients. As we flew through the darkness, we had no clue the amount of destruction that was underneath us. Electricity was out everywhere, and the only thing we could see was an occasional light from a police car and an occasional glimmer from reflections – like a faint light reflecting off water.

Upon our arrival at the Superdome, we had learned that the medical personnel in the Superdome had fared just as poorly. A makeshift aid station had been set up on the floor of the Dome where doctors, nurses and medics were to treat patients until the storm had passed and medical facilities and nursing homes reopened. The head nurse met me and explained the whole station had been moved because during the storm, large portions of the roof of the Superdome had been ripped off by winds exposing all the patients to the rains of the hurricane. The patients were moved into two banquet areas bereft of any light. One would serve for non-critical patients; the other area was for those who were expected to die. As the head nurse showed me where these facilities were located, I noticed the pitch-black rooms were filled beyond capacity. The medical personnel were frantically working to do whatever they could for their patients. I was brought into an area in a hallway where local nursing home facilities just dropped off elderly patients. I was told they were brought to the Dome to die. The medical personnel did what they could to save any patients they could. One patient could not breathe on his own, and the medics pumped airbags for hours to give him air. Miraculously, this patient began breathing again.

Later that night I walked alone outside, around the Superdome, looking at giant dark shadows over the city. Through the darkness you could just make out these buildings looking like giant skeletons with broken windows. Reality had just settled in. I questioned why God would let this happen to me. I did not know how my family was doing. Was everyone OK? I could not let them know I was OK. They were still thinking I was in the 9th Ward (although I would not discover the full extent of the destruction of this neighborhood until weeks later). I knew my place of work was gone. How much of the city was destroyed? Did we still have a home? Days later, I would find out that many of my friends working with us lost everything they owned. I started to question why God would let this happen to my city.

These events led to much pain which many from the area had to endure as well. Many lost loved ones. Many lost everything they owned. Countless jobs were eliminated. The archbishop closed what seemed to be viable church parishes that were deeply rooted in our city's history. There was much emotional pain and strain among those who had worked for many years to keep the parishes open. To this day, I am still commuting to a job that is located in another region of the state. These traumatic experiences led to years of not only emotional numbness but a slippage in my faith. Why would God allow this loss? Although I questioned, I knew I still had my faith. My faith would waver, but I would never stop believing in God.

In time, we would all begin to re-emerge from this emptiness. I saw people's struggles, but ultimately I saw that despite the losses, we would again be able to go forward. I do feel that my faith now is more personal than before. My relationship with God is reminiscent of that night I walked alone outside the Superdome. I still question, but the question has become more what than why. What route pleases God? What route does he want me to take? What is God's greater plan for me? The questions have changed because of the healing that has taken place by seeing the faith of my family and friends. But most of the re-emergence took place because I need God. I understand our weakness as humans. I understand the hubris of Americans. We are all God's children, and we are subject to the same trials as all his people.

Things will never be the same as before, but because of what we experienced, we can now be stronger and closer to God. We will struggle with the cross that God gives us, but when we fall, we will be stronger when we pick it up again.

Peter Le... *"I wanted to help those people but I couldn't."*

When my mom and dad were watching TV, my dad changed the channel to The Weather Channel for any hurricane information in the Gulf of Mexico. My mom and dad and I heard that it was a hurricane named Katrina and that it was getting larger and larger every day. When I heard this, I told my mom and dad. They said that we needed to pack up in case the hurricane hit New Orleans. So we started packing up slowly and watching the news at the same time in case Katrina curved to the east and hit Mississippi. It was several days until Katrina hit the Louisiana and Mississippi coasts.

I was very scared and so were my mom and dad. We packed the things that were most important to me and my family. We didn't know where to evacuate as we left. So my dad called his best friends in Dallas. He said we could evacuate to his house for several weeks until the hurricane passed. It was so tough to leave the house for so long. We started to pack the things that we really needed in the car. We have two cars, so we had to leave the little car behind. My parents said we would take the big van. After we finished packing, we started leaving the city of New Orleans.

It took at least 15 hours to get from New Orleans to Dallas because of really heavy traffic. My sister and I had to sleep in the van. It took a long time to get there. We got there sleepy, exhausted, and sick, too.

When Katrina passed through New Orleans, we were watching the news in Dallas. The scene was devastating with massive destruction to New Orleans and the Mississippi Gulf Coast, too. Everything was gone in hours. The wind destroyed everything in its path. Hundreds of people died because of Katrina. Many people had no water, food, shelter, rescue or anything. The levees broke and the waters flooded just about everything when Hurricane Katrina hit. Nothing survived in the storm's path. There was so much damage.

My family and I were heartbroken when we saw the destruction caused by the hurricane. We just wanted to cry, we were so sad. We saw our priest get rescued from the church roof and a couple of my dad's friends too. It was so shocking when I saw people waiting for help on the roofs of houses that got destroyed by Katrina. I didn't believe what I saw on TV. I never saw anything like that before. It made me sad and feel homesick. I wanted to help those people but I couldn't. Then I got really, really sick in Dallas because I was not used to living in a different state for so long. We lived in Dallas for one year after Katrina, and then moved back to New Orleans again.

My mom and a couple of her friends went back to New Orleans to see how our house and the house of her friend were after the storm. My mom told me our house was destroyed by 20 feet of water. Then when my mom went to throw all the flooded things out of the house, my dad, my sister, and I stayed back at my dad's friend's house until my uncle could come home from Dallas. My uncle didn't have any bad damage because he lived on the West Bank. It was good that my uncle's house didn't get flooded.

It was only the second week of school at St. Stephen Central School when Katrina hit. I was in the fifth grade at that time. I am glad to be back home. I never stopped praying. I still do.

Jeanne Pfefferle...
"Love for each other, our love for God and the belief that God was with us took over."

"Everyone who listens to these words of mine and acts on them will be like a wise man who built his house on rock. The rain fell and buffeted the house but it did not collapse; it had been set solidly on rock" (Matthew 7:24-27).

With a hasty evacuation to Baton Rouge, our feeling of security quickly ended with the news of the levee break. In a matter of a short time we became a family of need. Homeless, jobless, and exiled, we had no control over our lives, our future, our finances – or did we? Things were dire, but we needed to think clearly. We did have control over ourselves and our emotions, over our relationships with others, and over our love for each other. How we used our strength, our creativity, and our perseverance were all acts we could control. Our love for each other, our love for God and the belief that God was with us took over. My family was suffering greatly, but God had prepared us for this moment and he would guide us through. The bond between us and God remained strong.

Karl, our oldest son (26 years old), had started a new job after having taught economics at De La Salle High School. Three days prior he had knee surgery for a torn ACL. His job was now lost and he was in need of medical attention. Our two middle sons, Erik and Keith (23 and 25 years old) lost all they had worked for. They were young entrepreneurs building a real estate portfolio, and each owned his own grass-cutting business. Both were graduates of Our Lady of Holy Cross College with a bright head start on their future. Suzanne, our only daughter, was 20 years old attending OLHCC and transferring to LSU.

Karl Sr. lived in fear of having lost all his accounts. Karl is in paper sales with accounts in St. Bernard, New Orleans and Jefferson parishes and works for a local paper distributer in Destrehan.

We had very little cash; it was only supposed to be a three-day evacuation. Our bank froze all accounts. Thank God for credit cards. Diamond Paper Company sustained no physical damage and began resuming with five employees. Having lost our truck in the flood and with our Explorer having mechanical problems, Karl would leave Baton Rouge at 5:30 every morning with his boss and head to Destrehan. It had been only four to five days after the storm, so travel was difficult, involving snaking, back roads and going through road blocks.

Karl Jr. was pretty much laid up, but he needed to find an orthopedist to remove his stitches and evaluate the next step for recovery. Fortunately, my sister-in-law was able to help out in this situation. Erik and Keith, feeling that all was sinking, immediately started cutting grass in Baton Rouge for a landscaping firm, leaving at 6 a.m. It was a very different experience working for someone. The owner wanted to keep them as crew supervisors; instead they bought chain saws with the cash they made and would go back to Metairie to cut trees and look for any available work. Suzanne would be left in Baton Rouge while the rest of us moved to a trailer in Hammond. We were very thankful to be on our own again (10 days after), but the separation was very hard. Through a friend, a small isolated apartment was found for Suzanne and she began classes at LSU.

Life was tough, work was hard, but God continued to provide. Now I have a better understanding of the communion of saints. We, as a family, had tried to build relationships with the saints; now I see communion isn't just among those in heaven, but that we on earth are part of that communion. They were going to show us constantly that we are not alone. From the constant flow of living angels showing up with kind words, supplies, food, money, gift cards, love and support to the constant reminder of St. Joseph (our special family saint), to the intercession of aunts and grandmothers in heaven, we knew we were not alone. They were all there to help us to keep strong and uplifted.

We knew we would be OK. We were reminded of this daily by a sign placed up in front of a Lutheran church close by: "And all shall be made new again."

By now we had finished gutting and had begun rewiring and rebuilding. Our focus was on keeping our family intact and showing others they could, too. We cleaned the yard with the help of friends and started planting for spring - out of nowhere, stood this beautiful oasis, offering hope.

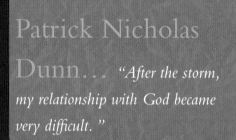

Patrick Nicholas Dunn... *"After the storm, my relationship with God became very difficult."*

August 27, 2005, I began packing for an event that would change my life forever. "Pack enough clothes for two days, three at most," my mother said. Thinking I would be returning Monday evening, I followed my mother's instructions without hesitation.

August 27, 2005 at noon, my mother, two brothers and I finished packing the car. Leaving Slidell at about 12:10 p.m., we were expecting an 8 to 10 hour drive to Houston. Arriving in Houston at about 2:30 a.m., I went directly to sleep. I awoke early to find a house filled with family watching CNN. I began to realize the seriousness of the threat approaching the Gulf Coast region. All Sunday, I sat around watching the news with my family in fear of returning to nothing. As the day went on, I began communicating with the rest of my family to make sure they were in a safe place.

Knowing my family was safe brought me a little happiness during a tough time. Before I knew it, Sunday was over and the big day had arrived. Monday morning, Hurricane Katrina made landfall, bringing extreme winds and rain into the Gulf Coast region. Flooded streets and severe damage to my city would be keeping me in Houston a few more days.

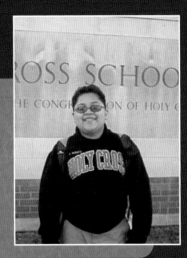

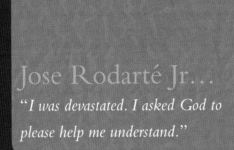

Jose Rodarté Jr...

"I was devastated. I asked God to please help me understand."

As Tuesday came, I sat around watching the news looking for any signal to be able to return home. But there wasn't any sign that I would be returning anytime soon. As Wednesday morning came, I found out horrible news; I would not be returning for the next few months. The levees had broken.

For the next few months, I would be residing in Houston. While living in Houston, I attended my first public school in my life, Labay Middle School. Leaving a Catholic school for the first time was a terrible experience.

After the storm, my relationship with God became very difficult. I experienced a car accident that almost took the life of my mother. I experienced the death of my grandmother, and my church life came to a halting stop. I was no where close to allowing God in my life.

I am Patrick Nicholas Dunn, I am 16 years old, and I am trying to let God back in my life.

I woke up on Sunday and heard noises. Mom and Dad said I should pack my things because the hurricane was coming. I didn't believe them until I heard the weatherman and saw a huge cloud coming toward New Orleans. I packed as soon as possible.

We jumped in the van and made it to the Interstate. Traffic was horrible. It took 14 hours to get to Shreveport, Louisiana. When we stopped at the gas station, we didn't know where to go. A young woman gave us the directions to LSU's shelter. There were at least 150 people there. My family was thankful for the shelter, but we all missed home.

My brother and I slept on the floor of the gym. I asked God to take care of us and our house in New Orleans. People were very nice at the shelter. The students at the college played games with us and brought us candy. Every day I was there, I only thought of home. We left the shelter and dad got an apartment. I prayed every night to go home, but I saw on television that the levee breached and my school and church, St. Frances Cabrini, were gone.

Mom registered me at St. Joseph Catholic School in Shreveport. The people were very nice, but it was not home. We stayed in Shreveport for one month and Dad found a way to get us back to New Orleans. I cried when I saw the neighborhood. It was as if someone had sucked the life out of it.

I started school at Cathedral Academy and finished third grade. I moved to St. Stephen Catholic School. We were still in an apartment, and every day Dad and Mom took us to see our house as it was being fixed. In the process of the house being fixed, they sold the land that the church and the school of St. Frances Cabrini sat on. I was devastated. I asked God to please help me understand.

Holy Cross School bought the land and promised to rebuild its school. Well, God helped me understand. You see, I may have lost a school and a church that I loved, but I've gained a school with honor, spirit, and virtue. On the St. Frances Cabrini land, Holy Cross School was built. I was blessed to be accepted to Holy Cross School where St. Frances Cabrini once stood. To me, God always has a plan. He knows just how to work things out. I put my faith and trust in God.

Andréa Nichelle Gros... *"So all I could do is pray and ask God to bless and keep my mom, my grandmother, and us safe."*

In 2005, as we know, the terrible hurricane of Katrina came through and destroyed New Orleans physically, mentally, and emotionally. The Friday before Hurricane Katrina was only my seventh day of the new school year as a fourth-grader. And by Saturday, all I knew was that I had to pack what I could and go. There was a problem. Sadly, my parents are divorced and it was my father's weekend, which means I had very few things. So, all I could do was pray and ask God to bless and keep my mom, my grandmother, and all of us safe. So by early Sunday morning, I was on my way to Lafayette with my dad and my sister. At first, I had no idea where we were going; all I knew was I wasn't going to see my mom and grandmother on Monday like I normally would.

We had a hotel room for a couple of days, then finally I found out my mom and grandmother were at the home of one of my mom's friends. I thanked God that they were safe and prayed to see them soon. Katrina was a destroyer. My mom's house, which was located in Gentilly, was destroyed, along with everything in it.

"I may have lost possessions, but what I found during those trying time was that my faith in God was so strong and that he was there for me even when I was questioning him."

I finally met my mom and grandmother in Baton Rouge at her friend's home. We stayed there for 11 weeks because everything in my house was ruined or gone. This broke my heart. So I said another prayer, which was to one day leave Baton Rouge and go back to New Orleans. My mom enrolled me and my sister in school, but the first school was not a good school for me and many people teased me about being from New Orleans and the hurricane. But I would pray and tell my mom and grandmother how I wished they would stop because it was not a laughing matter.

Around early November, my mom found us a beautiful townhouse and my prayers were answered again. I finally was taken out of the school and attended a different school which was nice. In July 2006, my mom received a job in New Orleans and my prayer to return to New Orleans was answered, although at the beginning, we had to live in the back of my grandma's house. She took her time and money to fix it for us. We had only one room, but I loved it because we were close to each other.

I thank God that he kept my family safe and continues to keep us safe. Yes, sometimes I was in doubt when things did not work out, but in the end, it all worked out.

Sunday, August 21, 2005 I took my husband to the airport. He was flying to Miami for business, the same day our daughter went back to LSU and our son to Denver. The weekend had been a wonderful, filled with happy moments, and our life was finally getting on track.

My husband was in Miami for Hurricane Katrina, and I was afraid that he would not be able to come home. I was mad at him because he was there. My husband made it back to New Orleans on Friday, August 26, late at night.

Saturday, we took my mother to the eye doctor and later to breakfast. During breakfast I received a phone call from my principal that we needed to secure the school because Hurricane Katrina was expected to come our way. After helping secure the school, my husband and I made the decision to stay at home. Sunday morning we received several phone calls from family and friends telling us that they were evacuating the city. Joe and I made the decision to evacuate mostly because of my 79-year-old mother and my sister-in-law, who was seven months pregnant.

All seven adults and three dogs took refuge in our daughter's one-bedroom apartment in Baton Rouge, expecting to be back the next day. But God had other plans for all of us. I remember praying and asking God why? What have I done wrong? Why was he punishing me? I was not able to see his answers, but they were coming. Our son drove all the way from Denver; he came to help us, and in the process of helping us he was able to work with his employer, setting up command centers in Baton Rouge, New Orleans, and Mississippi.

The next month was very difficult for all of us; the apartment building gave the residents a note, stating, "If you are housing Katrina evacuees, they must move out or you will be breaking your contract." What were we to do? God answered my prayer and we were able to secure our own apartment.

During September and October, I found myself very mad at God. I was not open to his presence; I was so mad at the world that it was destroying me. A lot happened to our family during that time. For the first time in my adult life, my mother and I had a fight that drove my husband and me to move in with a friend. That day God answered another prayer, but I was not open to see it. Moving back to the New Orleans area helped me some, but I was still looking for God and it did not matter where I was going; it did not feel the same. I continued praying and asking our Father for forgiveness and for guidance.

Two weeks before Palm Sunday, we attended Mass at a little chapel near UNO; it was a small chapel that parishioners from St. Raphael and St. Frances Cabrini were able to use. That day sitting in that small chapel, I felt a peace and love that was unexplainable. The following week we attended Mass again, and from that day forward that chapel became my new home.

From the little chapel we moved to our present location and the new parish was created – we are called Transfiguration of the Lord. Today I am a eucharistic minister for our parish; for a year that was my dream. My husband is an usher, and our daughter who God so gratiously brought back home is a lector and eucharistic minister.

Today I know that God never left my side, that he was there next to me holding my hand every single step, that he answers all my prayers and has given me more than I could ever imagine. Yes, he also has given me sorrows. I lost my mother in October 2006, but before her death she was able to see how we were rebuilding our home, how our family had become stronger and close to each other, how with God's mercy and help we all learned to love each other more and to forgive each other.

My faith is stronger than ever. When I look into my new grandson's eyes I see the pure love of God, and I thank him every moment for all he has done. I could write forever –

Sheila Chatelain…

"At this time I am not sure if I am mad, sad, happy or even OK."

how we rebuilt, what we lost – but those are stories that most of us have. I was not the only person who lost her home, furniture, etc.; no, I may have lost possessions, but what I found during those trying times was that my faith in God was so strong and that he was there for me, even when I was questioning him. I am a better person today, and I only have God to thank for that.

Things were going pretty well in my life. On Friday, August 26, 2005, after I finished thanking God for my wonderful day and everything that had happened that day, I turned the television on, just to relax. The next thing I knew, we were told to keep a close watch on the weather. There was a major hurricane in the Gulf of Mexico named Katrina, and she was headed for New Orleans. Next, we were under a mandatory evacuation. I started asking God to spare us. But I think he had another plan for us.

On Monday, August 29, 2005, Hurricane Katrina hit the New Orleans area. Hoping to find minimal damage and getting back to our lifestyle were not going to happen. Two days after Katrina hit, things started to change. It seemed like no one's life was going to be the same. Asking for God's help and direction on what to do, I knew he would answer me. But it would take awhile. Some of my prayers were answered, others were not. I did not know whether to keep praying or stop. Confused and knowing that I lost everything in my life but I still had my children, I decided to keep asking God what was next. I knew in time that my prayers would be answered. Slowly things were starting to happen again in my life. Progressing slowly, my life and the lives of my children were starting to get back to normal.

I prayed to God every day, asking for guidance and thanking him for what we have. At this time I am not sure if I am mad, sad, happy or even OK. There have been many other events that have happened in my life since Katrina. But I still thank God every night for letting me wake up, for the wonderful day I had, for my four special children, my grandson, my family and friends, my job, my co-workers, people who have helped us, touched our lives, or shared something with us. I also thank him for the things that I have to share with others, or help others with, or how to touch someone's life.

I also ask him to help me understand why this happened. And I know that one day my prayers will be answered.

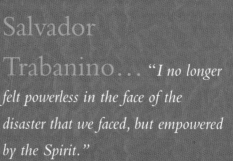

Salvador Trabanino... *"I no longer felt powerless in the face of the disaster that we faced, but empowered by the Spirit."*

Hurricane Katrina came roaring into my rather placid life on Friday, August 26, late in the afternoon when the weatherman on one of the local television stations said that "everything has changed" and Katrina was heading toward New Orleans with the potential to develop into a very destructive hurricane. I lived and still reside in the French Quarter, having moved to New Orleans in 1980 from the Central American country of El Salvador at the beginning of what was to be a long, bloody 12-year civil war.

By 1985 I had moved to the Quarter and started attending Mass at St. Louis Cathedral. By 1986 I owned a house in the French Quarter, a neighborhood that I had loved since I first visited it when I was about 12 years of age. It was an ideal place for me and my many quirks, including the fact that I don't drive, and most everything one may need could be found in the Quarter. This eccentricity of not being able to drive a car is a symptom of something I battle with to this day: a high degree of anxiety when placed in new situations.

Hurricane Katrina did just that: it was a totally new and terrifying situation. As I frantically consulted with my close friend Mark about what to do on that Friday before the storm, we made the decision that we would prepare the house for the coming hurricane early on Saturday, and then make the final decision to stay or leave. By the end of our preparations, it was obvious that the wisest thing would be to leave.

Thankfully, Mark does drive and had a jeep that could accommodate not only our luggage, but also two inside cats, an outside cat, and a noisy cockatoo named Joey that I was caring for while a friend was away. I didn't want to go because of my reluctance to face change, but I knew that I had to. We left New Orleans convinced that we would be back in a few days. We left on Saturday afternoon, heading toward Florida where Mark had a mobile home that was sitting empty, but completely furnished. We made it as far as Fort Walton Beach that evening and settled in a room with the confused mix of pets. It was when I woke up on Sunday and turned the TV set on that I saw a monster heading toward New Orleans and felt for the first time the almost complete certainty that I would soon be homeless.

On Monday morning as we watched the hurricane approach the city and veer a bit toward the right, we were thankful that the city had been spared, but decided to go on to Florida – following the advice from Louisiana officials – to the town of Eustis, the location of Mark's mobile home. When we arrived in Eustis, we found that the levees had failed and the city was flooding. The images I saw on TV reminded

me of some lawless Third World country as people could be seen looting stores while splashing in the rising water. Pick-up trucks driven by armed men controlled the streets. It became evident then that we would not be going home anytime soon.

Considering the choices that many evacuees had, I was living in the lap of luxury with my own bedroom and kitchen and laundry facilities, while my cats roamed freely through the house as if they were on some kind of holiday. But I faced the question of what to do.

What to do? I had approached this question not only from the practical point of view, but firmly anchored in my Catholic faith. I had been a Communion minister at St. Louis Cathedral since 1998, and consulting over the phone with my mother who still lived in El Salvador, I decided that I would go to the only Catholic Church in the little town of Eustis, St. Mary of the Lakes, and see if the priest could use me as a Communion minister. And so I went to church on the Sunday after the storm, after a surreal week of seeing the desperation of those in New Orleans caught on film trapped in flooded attics, and the plight of those stranded at the Convention Center and the Superdome.

During Sunday Mass, I found out that the priest in charge was Pastor Manuel Fernandez. He said after a long list of announcements that the following weekend there would be a special second collection for the victims of Hurricane Katrina. It was then that I turned to Mark and told him that I wanted to talk to the priest after Mass, and so I did. We met at Father Fernandez's office and he asked in Spanish some pertinent questions about who I was. Then I told him I wanted to speak at each of the Masses where there would be a collection for the victims of Katrina. He asked me, "Who gave you the idea to speak at the Masses?" And without hesitation, I answered, "The Holy Spirit." He seemed to ponder my answer with skepticism; after all, I was a stranger who had arrived without credentials and was claiming to be moved by the Spirit to address his congregation. After a few uncomfortable seconds, he agreed to give me the chance to speak at five Masses the following weekend: a vigil Mass, three Masses for the English-speaking congregation, and one Mass for Hispanics that same Sunday.

As I revealed to you in the beginning, I have this secret anxiety that could be disastrous in facing a large group of unknown people and trying to deliver a message that would open their hearts to give to those in need in New Orleans and the Gulf Coast battered by the same monster. But the Spirit came to my aid.

While in constant contact with my mother — a pillar of strength and faith in my life — I decided to make an outline of touch points in my speech and leave the rest to the Holy Spirit. I simply knew that I wanted to use some quotes from the Bible, particularly from the Book of Jeremiah, the Gospels, and the Psalms.

The day of the vigil, the priest invited me to the microphone and I simply became a vehicle for the Spirit to touch the hearts of those who filled the church. I could see that there were people crying and that the collection baskets were full. As I told the congregation, I embraced the non-politically correct term of "refugee." I had found refuge among them, and then I noticed the stained-glass window behind me showing the flight of the Holy Family into Egypt, and pointing to it, I said that I was in good company. I also talked about the yearning of people of New Orleans to go back home so that God could again be praised and worshiped in the city. I quoted Psalm 137, which says, "By the rivers of Babylon we sat down and cried as we remembered Zion" and "How can we sing songs to the Lord in a strange land?" No offense meant to the good people of Eustis, but we were in a strange land, and we yearned to go back to New Orleans, as the Jews yearned to go back and rebuild Jerusalem and its temple. I told the congregation that God challenges us to go out of our comfort zone, and if they had come ready to give five dollars, then to give 10; if one dollar, then give two. And people responded and gave and gave.

After one of the Masses celebrated by Father Fernandez, he walked over to me and said, "I can see now that the Holy Spirit is indeed speaking through you." It was all very touching for me, and very humbling. The Hispanic congregation – on average, of less financial means – who heard my message in their native language, responded even more effusively, and at the end of the Mass I was surrounded by well-wishers pushing money into my pockets while I was trying to tell them that I was OK, that I didn't lack anything, and to please give money to the priest.

Once I was done with the five Masses, I went back to the mobile home and collapsed. I slept for several hours thankful for the experience of seeing the Holy Spirit in action, not only through me, but also through the faithful in Eustis. I was later told that the amount of money raised for the victims of Katrina exceeded every other collection for charities outside the parish in the remembered history of St. Mary of the Lakes.

I no longer felt powerless in the face of the disaster that we faced, but empowered by the Spirit. There was only one thing I had to do: in spite of my fears and anxiety, my inadequacies and my sins, I had to surrender to the Holy Spirit, and let him stir me and stir those who heard his voice.

Bettina Buval...

"I felt branded as a victim of the storm: an evacuee, a survivor, a dislocated person, and abandoned"

It seemed appropriate and ironic that I moved back into my home during the fourth anniversary weekend of Katrina. I would never have believed that it would have taken me four years to end the Katrina-enforced exile from my Broadmoor home of 15 years. As anyone who has lived the post-Katrina life knows, my world has revolved around higher prices at the stores, higher taxes, sky-high insurance rates, crazy utility bills, bad contractor stories, Road Home program horror stories, and the stressful interaction with the bureaucratic quagmire associated with rebuilding agencies. I can just imagine that Jesus' ears must have been red from all the times I had to invoke his name, and called on him to keep from losing my temper, my mind, and my "religion."

Before Katrina hit my life and tore it apart, I had an unshakeable faith and love of God. My mother brought me up in the church from an early age and gave me the foundation of a Catholic education: St. Matthias School, Xavier University Preparatory High School, and Loyola University. She always made sure my brother and sisters were also active in our Catholic faith. From early childhood, I was involved in the music ministry of St. Matthias Church. I was a lector, a member in the Ladies Auxiliary of the Knights of Peter Claver, active in parish council, and other church ministries. I also participated as a delegate for the Black Catholic Congress and several archdiocesan committees. My church family was as much a part of my life as my treasury of close friends and family.

My Katrina survivor story is like those of thousands of others who witnessed the insanity and moral breakdown of a city. Within an hour of the waters flooding into streets and homes, the criminal element of the city threw a party. In almost a Mardi Gras atmosphere, people began looting businesses and homes. It soon became clear that with streets flooded, the police couldn't stop criminals from helping themselves to whatever they wanted. They broke into shops and stores for cigarettes, alcohol, drugs and anything else of value. They even desecrated the Rhodes Funeral Home, stealing from the dead. From my home you could hear gunshots, but who was shooting the guns? Some guys hot-wired a forklift to pry open the Universal Furniture Store's metal shutters. I watched in amazement as thieves used mattresses to float living room and dining room sets, flat-screen televisions, and electronics down flooded streets. It was a "flood sale"; everything was for the taking. It was a free for all, a scene from the Wild West, and utter madness.

By dusk it wasn't safe to stay in my home with waters still rising. My sister Nicole and I helped a neighbor from across the street get to higher ground. His wife and two daughters could not swim. With difficulty, we made it to the Broad Street overpass. National Guard members were also on the bridge and I had a brief feeling of rescue. However, I was told that their priority was to get the Orleans Parish prisoners to safety. It was more important to move prisoners than the elderly, young, and pregnant women who had also sought refuge on the bridge. The guardsmen told us that they would try to come back for us, but even the young man who said this didn't sound convincing. Night fell, and it was pitch black. The prisoners in Central Lockup had set fire to mattresses in their cells and you could see the flames. I was very afraid sitting on that bridge with nowhere to go. As I prayed to God to keep us safe, he answered my prayers with a "get out of town card."

My neighbor's relative was with the RTA, and the company was evacuating their employees and families using high-water trucks to transport them to safety. With my neighbor's help, we became "cousins" and could ride with them to a Baton Rouge shelter. If not for this divine intervention, we would have been in the hell that was the Louisiana Superdome and the Ernest N. Morial Convention Center.

They dropped all of us at the River City Arena which was next to a riverboat casino and hotel. My first night at the shelter was spent shivering in my wet clothes on a bed of paper boxes and a garbage bag for warmth. I prayed a lot that night. Not for me, but for the people we were hearing stories about on the radio and television. (The broadcast 911 call from the woman who drowned, trapped in her home, still haunts me to this day.) The shelter quickly swelled from about 500 people to almost 3,000. We were issued wristbands; National Guardsmen carried AK-47s; and we despaired when we heard the horrible news coming out of New Orleans. No one was going home anytime soon. I remember at one point, shelter volunteers began putting an "X" on our hands to designate who had received a meal. I had never felt so low or so alone. I felt branded as a victim of the storm: an evacuee, a survivor, a dislocated person, and abandoned. I wanted to wake up from this bad dream.

Workers were overwhelmed with the sheer volume of people in the shelter. Rumors ran rampant about what was going to happen to people in the shelter. Were they going to put us on planes and buses and ship us out of state? Were families going to be split up? Even with the chaos of the shelter, there were compassionate and kind people trying to lessen our grief. Volunteers from all over the state and the southern region came in spite of and despite the stories about lawlessness in the shelters. They amused the children and brought toys. People came with blankets, clothes, and money. Area churches made hot meals and tried to feed as many people as they could.

I met a woman named Julie who used all of her company vacation time to fly down to Baton Rouge because she could not stand watching what she saw on television and not act. Her kindness and encouragement were a balm to my spirit. I never saw her again, but I believe God puts people in your path, and we have to be open to receive their message. I also remember Archbishop Hughes and some other New Orleans priests came to visit the shelter one day. While I could not get close enough to talk to him because so many people clamored to just touch him, it was comforting to see a familiar face from home and know that the church community was not lost in the flooded city.

After the initial shock wore off, it finally dawned on me that I had my cell phone with me. I tried to call my family, but all the towers were down in the 504 area code. I worried about them and my friends constantly. A 12-year-old taught me how to text and I was able to make contact with friends. A family friend sent a plane ticket to bring my sister to New York to be with her while I figured out my next step.

My job required that I stay near New Orleans and get a major part of the state's infrastructure back up and running. As a sub-district manager of a workforce office, I was responsible for getting as many offices in the New Orleans region staffed and reopened in order to allow people who had lost their jobs and livelihoods due to Katrina to get unemployment compensation. The only offices in Greater New Orleans not severely damaged were in Metairie, Slidell, and Gonzales. I felt compelled to put my personal situation aside and help the Katrina survivors who were in worse shape than I was. So five days after Katrina hit, I was waking up at 5:30 a.m. and traveling the Interstate in a state car along with construction crews, supply trucks, National Guard units, insurance agents, disaster teams, FEMA trailers, and every other vehicle known to man. What was once a 45-minute to an hour drive became two or more hours due to congested roadways and military checkpoints. On the first day I was able to locate enough staff to open our Metairie office. More than 1,000 desperate people showed up trying to file unemployment claims. They wrapped around the parking lot and building and stood in the hot sun for hours. Our staff skipped breaks and meals because we recognized how much people were hurting. We didn't have our homes either, but at least we had jobs and could expect a paycheck. I wouldn't get back to Baton Rouge until about 7:30 p.m., exhausted but knowing this would be the cross I needed to carry for those suffering great loss. I bounced between three co-workers' homes in Baton Rouge until I could reach my insurance agents and find housing close to New Orleans. I was able to locate an apartment in Metairie with the help of friends, Lauren and Donna, in October 2005 and was a step closer to getting home.

From 2005 until 2007, everything was a blur of activity: filing applications for disaster assistance, fighting with Road Home, working six-day workweeks as the city moved from recovery to rebuilding mode, and trying to get my life back to "normal." Until 2007, I had focused on caring for others and ignored my own needs. One day I collapsed from exhaustion and couldn't get out of bed. It was my wake-up call in a number of ways.

Katrina's effect on first responders and "essential" workers after the storm has never been fully addressed. However, hundreds of people have lived with the aftermath just like me. I had been so busy trying to do my job, deal with Road Home, FEMA and SBA, and rebuild my church family that I had not dealt with Katrina on a personal level. When I would get discouraged or exhausted, I would just tell myself all the platitudes we are so fond of saying in a crisis. "God doesn't give you more than you can bear"; "Be strong taking heart – all you who hope in the Lord"; "The Lord is my strength and my salvation"; "What doesn't kill you only makes you stronger"; "I am too blessed to be stressed." I just felt empty. When St. Jude's choir director asked if I could help bolster the numbers in their choir (which I had done in the past), I'm sure I completely surprised her when I responded that I was "too sad to sing anymore." Singing, which had once been a great joy to me, had become painful. I visited my doctor trying to find answers. He bandied around words like "Katrina burnout," "stress" and "rest" during my visit with him. While the doctor helped me to heal my body, where was God to heal my soul?

I was finally dealing with the new post-Katrina reality of living in New Orleans. While in Baton Rouge, I had made a mental deal with myself that once I got back to St. Matthias I would be happy. But my church family where I had celebrated my first Communion, confirmation, and other milestone sacraments, no longer existed as I had known it. St. Matthias is now Blessed Trinity – a merger of Our Lady of Lourdes, St. Monica, and St. Matthias parishes. It is almost too much to know I will never be married in "St. Matthias Church," and it hurts my heart. While I love my church, it was just another blow to my spirit. Right now I am a church nomad, not really calling any particular church my home. For that, I feel guilty. I ask myself if what I believed to be a strong faith in God before Katrina was really an untested faith. Am I a "doubting Thomas"? Will I ever feel that spiritual strength and faith again? I have never felt that I have left God, but I do feel that I have not truly let go and let God work his will with me.

There were 20 college students who gave up their school break to assist in gutting my home. They packed themselves into a van, drove for several days to get to New Orleans, and lived in a hostel in order to do backbreaking physical labor for strangers. I thanked them for giving up their time and resources. They commended me for my determination and courage in returning home after a disaster which in all probability could happen again. But I called it my "pit bull" attitude that I was not going to let a girl named Katrina

take away everything that I had loved my entire life - my family, my friends, my city, and my faith. My faith that things happen for a reason kept me going. While I had not figured out the "why" of Katrina, I was too busy with more important things to spend much time on the question.

I am starting over in my life. Only my sister and I have decided to stay in New Orleans. My brother calls from Texas to constantly remind me that there are houses and jobs there. He wants me to leave New Orleans. My closest friends have been scattered to the winds. While we try to stay in touch over the phone or e-mail, it is only a matter of time before that, too, fades and contact is lost as life moves in other directions and new friends are made. I've retired after 23 years of public service. People thought I was crazy for not staying until I got my 30-year pension. However, post-Katrina, I have new priorities in my life and am searching for what that new purpose might be. I'm trusting in the Lord to show me the way. I am stepping out on faith to become renewed by the Holy Spirit.

Now that I am home, I sleep better in my own bed. I have even begun singing in the house again, which I have not done for quite awhile. I opened my Bible the other night, and my eyes lighted on this passage from Matthew 6:34 in the New Standard Bible: "…So do not worry about tomorrow for tomorrow will care for itself. Each day has enough trouble of its own." This passage brought a verse from Jeremiah 29:11 to mind: "For I know the plans I have for you, declares the Lord, plans to prosper and not harm you, plans to give you hope and a future."

So Lord, I am letting go. I will pray to the Holy Spirit for discernment in following your plans, for you are the light in my darkness. You strengthen me, help me and uphold me in my trials.

Harry Jumonville Jr. . . . *"The city has changed, people are different, most now realize what is most important in life. It's not stuff."*

After my wife and I evacuated to Mobile, Alabama, for a week, my friend drove down from South Carolina and met us there. He brought chainsaws, generators, plywood, gas and water (a truckload of supplies he thought we might need). We couldn't get any information on road closures from either Mississippi's or Louisiana's state police or department of transportation. We decided to drive until we were down to half a tank of gas and then re-evaluate our plan. My wife Shirley and I took my truck, and my friend went in his truck. We left Mobile and drove all the way to Pearl River, Louisiana, north of I-10 where my home is, with no problem at all. The roads had been cleared of all debris.

There didn't seem to be much debris on the highways, but when we turned into my neighborhood there were trees everywhere. The streets had been cleared by neighbors who had stayed and who had cleared them to be able to get out. Most of the damage was from fallen trees. I lost about 40 trees; a few fell on the house and two fell on cars we had left behind. The three of us spent the next week clearing yards and boarding up holes, and Shirley cleaned the refrigerators of family and friends – a nasty job after over a week with no power.

We had no electricity, running water, or communications. Gas was hard to find, and the line for getting gas could take as long as two hours. The National Guard would pass by and offer ice and water, and a location in town was set up to pick up ice, water and MREs (meals ready to eat). You would drive up in line and the Guard would put what you needed in your vehicle. You didn't even need to get out. The spirit of help was great.

I worked for a utility company in New Orleans and knew that I couldn't get there, so I reported (after two weeks away) to the office in Slidell. After a few days there, all the displaced workers were told to report to Kenner – no easy feat because I-10 and Highway 11 and Highway 90 were all closed. In fact, the city of New Orleans was closed off by the military. No one was allowed in. After a few days in Kenner, we were moved to Metairie, where we surveyed the plant for a few more days. We were finally allowed back in New Orleans to survey damage during daylight hours only. We rode two to a truck. There was only one way in or out. Military check points determined who could go in and who would be kept out.

The city was unreal. Debris was pushed to the side of major streets so vehicles could pass. Tree branches and utility wires were down, but the scariest thing was the water lines on buildings marking where the water levels had stayed for awhile. Everything below that line was either gray or dead.

Parts of the city looked like a black-and-white photo: no color, no signs of life, no movement, not even noise. It was dead still. Over the next few weeks we went in different parts of the city. The destruction varied from flood water damage to total destruction. Lakeview, Chalmette, the Lower 9th Ward and parts of New Orleans East were devastated. Lake Catherine was virtually wiped out. My understanding is that there were more than 400 structures before the storm; after Katrina there were 30 left and most of those were damaged beyond repair. This is the area in which Father Red Ginart resided; his home was washed away, and he was never found. I met many people who knew him and were very upset that he was missing. The church was still standing, but all the walls and contents were gone.

Help poured into the city almost immediately. Some said it wasn't enough, but there was so much that needed to be done, it was hard to know where to start. Help came from all over the country. I even met people from Canada. Many were here because it was their job, but unknown numbers were volunteers from church groups along with elderly people helping any way they could. Some people walked the city, feeding pets that were starving and couldn't be rescued. To this day (more than five years later), it's still heart-warming to see people give up their free time to help.

The city has changed, people are different, and most now realize what is most important in life. It's not stuff.

Ellan F. Vavrick...

"Always our faith in God kept us going. Believing that what nature had destroyed, God would help us rebuild. His providence was daily evidenced in our lives."

The horror, destruction and painful sadness of a major city devoured by wind, rain and flood struck us in one moment of television reporting: a rescue boat cruising down our Mid-City street rescuing neighbors! The boat's wake sent lapping waves across the front porch of our raised camel-back home. We watched in silence from our exile in Jackson, Mississippi, surrounded by the comparative comfort of my mother's home. Not just our home or our area of the city. No, it was the realization and heartache of our beloved New Orleans, its culture, and rich traditions ripped apart and strewn across the nation. New Orleans was like pieces of a giant jigsaw puzzle waiting to be put back in place. A seemingly impossible task loomed before us. "Oh, my God!" was the only uttered prayer in that moment of silence.

The question was how many hands, how many years would it take to make us whole again? Would we have enough time to see it done?

My husband, Richard Vavrick, had been in failing health for several years. Moving from Chicago as a young man to attend Loyola University, he fell in love with the city and found his faith in Christ here as well. He had devoted more than 55 years to New Orleans. He worked tirelessly to support church, charity and community. The tears in his eyes were a reflection of those in his heart. For a moment, only a moment, he wondered if he could return and bear witness to what had become of his beloved city. A moment followed by firm resolve and utter faith. We would go home. We would renovate, rebuild, and restore what was now lost.

Friends and family provided our first line of support. The Internet became our communication link with the world, allowing us to locate friends, contact family, notify insurance companies, and maintain financial data. Mississippi became Chicago, Chicago became LaPlace, our center for rebuilding activity. The generosity of fellow exiles, the extended hands and hearts of our neighbor churches, and the care given by dear friends gave us the strength of purpose to continue the cleaning and rebuilding process.

Always our faith in God kept us going, believing that what nature had destroyed, God would help us rebuild. His providence was daily evidenced in our lives. The Roesers, who were on an extended tour of America at the time of the storm, drove cross country to LaPlace to share their home and hospitality with us for the six months of our rebuild.

Construction professionals, who appeared out of nowhere, put us first on their list. Electricians, plumbers and air conditioning professionals seemingly appeared as needed.

Most especially, insurance adjusters who met us less than 60 days after the flood and only days later, hand-delivered checks that maxed out our insurance policies, giving us the financial resources to rebuild immediately.

Delays, trials and trauma merged with sweat, prayers and fortitude until in May 2006, Dick and I stood once again in our living room, looking around at fresh paint, clean floors, and new furniture. Turning to me, Dick said, "We're home."

Less than two months later, Dick's heart would finally give out. He had somehow held on to see me safe again at home in New Orleans,

Dark clouds do indeed have a silver lining. That silver lining proved to be faith, family and friends, which combined through the worst of times to bring us once again into the light of a bright new day.

St. Joseph Abbey provided a temporary home for Notre Dame Seminary and Archbishop Hannan High

The Rest of the Story

For many years Paul Harvey was a fixture on American radio. His signature closing of each broadcast – "Paul Harvey… Good Day!" – was as familiar as Walter Cronkite's "and that's the way it is" and Ed McMahon's "Here's Johnny." Harvey, in addition to his regular program, developed a spin-off segment entitled, "The Rest of the Story." The format was simple, yet fascinating. He would recount a little-known incident that left listeners to wonder why he would spend airtime with the telling of the story. After the commercial break, Harvey would let his audience in on the surprise twist which made this seemingly unimportant story anything but. Listeners couldn't wait to find out "the rest of the story."

The Gospels are filled with stories about Jesus that would fit perfectly in a "rest of the story" format. For example, whatever became of the woman caught in adultery in John's Gospel *(Jn 8:1-11)*? She was about to be stoned in accordance with the Mosaic Law. Jesus intervened and she was spared. At the end of the story of this unnamed woman, Jesus tells her, "Go your way, and sin no more." Rest-of-the-story addicts can't help but wonder whatever became of this woman. Did she return to her sinful ways? Did she follow Jesus' instruction and remain pure the rest of her life? Did she and her husband reconcile? Whatever became of the man with whom she had the affair? Who knows? We are left to wonder. And maybe that's how it should be. When God deals with us, there is always a rest of the story. To be touched by grace is not to be extracted from life with

all its temptations, trials, joys, and gifts. Jesus does not tell the woman to hide, or even follow him. Rather, Jesus tells her to "go your way," but where is she to go? Back home, to her village, or to her parents? All of these choices are dangerous and embarrassing. Jesus challenges her to re-enter life in whatever shape it takes, not as the woman caught in adultery, but as the woman who encountered him and was given back her life, physically and spiritually. While there may be no second acts in America, as the saying goes, such is not the case with God. The curtain is always rising, falling, and rising again.

Katrina is one of those generational stories that profoundly alters a person's perspective on the whole of life. As the actual event recedes deeper in memory with the passage of time,

it is easy to overlook the rest of the story. The people who have just shared their stories serve as a powerful reminder that each of us who lived through Katrina has a story. More accurately, each of us is a story, a living narrative of ordinary people confronting extraordinary circumstances.

The stories of faith in this chapter are more powerful than the fury of Katrina. The force of these stories is not of nature, but grace; what is stirred is not water, but the Spirit; and what abides is not destruction, but the dynamic of faith, guided through the fog by the beacon of hope. And it is that faith, thrust forward by hope, which shapes the rest of the story.

• A sculpture of Jesus with the woman at the well outside Notre Dame Seminary

Immaculate Conception Church, Marrero

Chapter 9

CHURCH AND STATE:
HEALING THE WALL OF SEPARATION

Hurricane Katrina provided us with a teachable moment in the complex and unfortunately contentious area of church-state relations. Specifically, what emerged was a hopeful sign of church-state cooperation between the archdiocese and FEMA (the Federal Emergency Management Agency) for the common good.

What became clear was the vital role faith communities could play in recovery, and at the same time, not run the risk of establishing a particular religion. Church and state, it was shown, could work together with each sphere preserving its proper integrity and freedom within the social order. It is to that story that we now turn.

Embedded within Hurricane Katrina were numerous tornadoes, hidden, but just as powerful. Likewise, contained within the story of Katrina are a number of sub-plots often lost or veiled, but no less important than the main storyline. One such sub-plot is the relationship between church and state, religion and politics. To be sure, this issue is not new. From the earliest colonial times, throne and altar have played a prominent role in shaping this *"Novus ordo seclorum."* American history reveals a marriage of religion and politics with varying degrees of closeness and separation. In the aftermath of Katrina, we witnessed a new phase in the fascinating story that is religion's place in the American public square. For in order to respond effectively to the challenges of a post-Katrina world, there needed to be a working relationship, and at times even an intimate one, between civil and church authorities. It is this complex dance of sacred and secular that will occupy our attention.

Before diving into the story at hand, honesty requires that the reader be alerted to the following: this chapter will be presented with a different emphasis and manner than you have come to expect. Previous chapters were attempts to lay out in a straight-forward way the response of various archdiocesan agencies to Katrina. The record of the archdiocesan response was presented in a more descriptive, rather than an evaluative or normative manner. The approach that will now be employed is one that calls for a greater reliance on political philosophy, history, theology, sociological and normative analysis. Such a shift ought not to surprise the reader, since the nature of the issue – church and state relations – requires such an alteration. Furthermore, the reader should be informed that what follows makes no pretension of being neutral when it comes to a set of religiously grounded social teachings. To be specific, the author will advance those parts of the Catholic Social Teaching that are relevant to our topic, specifically, the role of the state, religious liberty, and the principles of subsidiarity, solidarity and the common good.

• In God We Trust

The sub-plot of our focus – the relationship between church and state – did not arrive with Katrina. There is a long narrative that precedes ours and of which we are of a part. If we are to gain some understanding of the Katrina story and the role played by the Church (in this case the archdiocese), a brief excursion into our past is required.

The Colonial Face of Religion

There are two colonial Americas, one steeped in myth and one in fact. The image of colonial America etched in the popular mind goes something like this: those first arrivals were deeply motivated by the desire for religious liberty. They understood themselves through the Old Testament stories of bondage, exodus, and being led by God to a new land. The Puritans expedition into the wilderness was guided by the hand of Divine Providence. Early colonial life was characterized by a high degree of uniformity and conformity concerning religious beliefs and practices. Religion permeated every aspect of the public and private dimensions of life. Orthodoxy, not dissent, was honored.

As with all myths that are effective and enduring, there is enough truth to mask the inaccuracies; hence, the simplistic distortions stick. There is little doubt that those who left England were motivated by the desire for religious freedom. However, the quest was for religious freedom of a specific kind; namely, the Puritans who came sought the freedom to practice their own brand of Anglicanism. The idea of universal religious freedom was not part of the cargo deposited on these shores. If a group wished to enjoy a free exercise of their faith, there was a freedom – the freedom to move to another part of the new world. This geographical freedom in pursuit of religious liberty is precisely what occurred. Colonists from New England began to migrate and establish new settlements with a variety of religious expressions. Other nations as well began to colonize, which added to the diversity of nationalities and denominations. In time, two of the original 13 colonies, Rhode Island and Maryland, actually passed laws in favor of religious toleration. It was in these two states where Catholics were concentrated.

In colonial times, the churches and meeting places served as locations for religious services, as well as for conducting the secular affairs of the settlement. Not surprisingly, there was a comingling of the things of God and the business of Caesar. It was not uncommon for public monies and resources to be used to fund the religious activities (and the salary of clergy) of a community. Clergy exercised great influence in the day-to-day life of people, and this influence was not confined to things sacred. Public life in early colonial times was deeply intertwined with all manner of things religious.

As the early colonial generations passed further into the rearview mirror of history, subsequent generations would assume the reins of culture and the business of daily life. These succeeding generations would be more concerned about the things below (survival, security and assorted commercial enterprises) than the things above. Compounding the declining influence of religion in public life was an intellectual and cultural revolution sweeping continental Europe, Britain and the British Isles: the Enlightenment. While there were various national manifestations

• The dome of St. Augustine Church in Tremé felt Katrina's wrath

Flooded hymnal
at St. David
Church

(the Scottish and French varieties for example), there were a number of common themes.

The three core ideas of the Enlightenment are reason guided by the method of experimental science, freedom as the ability to determine one's future without external influence or coercion, and the recognition of natural rights that limit the power of the state. These core ideas found a receptive audience in the generation that would embark on the path of revolution from the mother country. The influential French novelist Victor Hugo once remarked that there are few things as powerful as an idea whose time has come. This cluster of Enlightenment ideas – reason, freedom, and natural rights – exploded in the minds and hearts of 18th Century colonists. Even before the first shot was fired at Concord, the fires of liberty were ablaze, and they would not be extinguished until this new nation was born.

The first fundamental idea of the Enlightenment focused on the nature of reason. The human person endowed with reason could arrive at truth without the aid of revelation, religion or tradition. In fact, if reason was to mature, the individual must be liberated from the shackles of religion and any inherited beliefs from the past. The human mind, guided by the method of experimental science, could explore, understand, and *change* the world. Human dignity required each individual to think for himself or herself.

Closely related to the Enlightenment's view of reason is the demand for freedom. Enlightenment thinkers held a negative view of freedom; that is, the dignity of the human person requires a liberty from, if not against, tradition and authority. The past must be rejected and overcome in the name of scientific progress. Knowledge is not a fixed set of truths or beliefs received from past luminaries, or from on high through the pronouncements of some divine; rather, knowledge is ever evolving and always open to the new. For the Enlightenment, tradition enslaves while science liberates. Reason, unchained from the dead faith and learning of past generations, is able to explore what was once treated as mysteries but now can be explained through natural or physical causes.

The cross and the flag came together after Katrina

• The south Louisiana Pieta reminds us that love involves suffering

The human person does not exist as an instrument of the state. Being made in the image and likeness of God, each person enjoys a transcendent dignity, which government does not grant and cannot remove. In the words of Pope John Paul II:

"What is at stake is the dignity of the human person,
Whose defense and promotion have been
entrusted to us by the Creator,
And to whom the men and women
at every moment of history
are strictly and responsibly in debt."
(Sollicitudo rei socialis, No. 47)

The Enlightenment's scorn for tradition extends to its treatment of authority. Those who exercise authority, usually the clergy and those under their control, continue to hold onto the past in order to protect their positions of privilege and power. The Enlightenment mindset views authority as authoritarian in all its traditional forms. Appeals to a past wisdom are automatically viewed with suspicion precisely because it is from the past. Only through the use of experimental science can the corrupting grip of authority be broken. Courage will be needed to walk into the light of this new day.

The third core Enlightenment idea is the belief that the individual is endowed with natural rights. These rights (life, liberty, property, etc.) are not granted, nor can they be taken away, by the state. These natural rights are essential to what it means to be a human being. The role of the state in terms of natural or human rights is to safeguard and honor these rights, and they can only be suspended by substantive due process (a trial in a court of law). There was an acknowledgment that these natural rights had their origin in the creator or nature, but belief in a supreme being was not required for their recognition.

The Founders and Religion

While it is clear how Enlightenment ideas influenced the Founders' thinking, there is a crucial modification that must be kept in mind. The Founders, however uncommitted to the creed of a specific denomination, were explicit in their support for the public expression of religion. If this experiment in republican democracy (a unique attempt at self-government in the history of political experience) was to endure, religion would play a vital role. Consider the words of George Washington and James Madison, the so-called "Father of the U.S. Constitution":

Of all the dispositions and habits
which lead to political prosperity,
Religion and Morality are indispensable supports.
In vain would that
man claim the tribute of Patriotism,
who should labor to subvert
these great pillars of human happiness,
these firmest props of the
duties of Men and Citizens. The mere politician,
equally with the
pious man, ought to respect and cherish them.

(President George Washington –
Farewell Address to the Nation, 1796)

We the People of the United States, in Order to form a more perfect Union, establish Justice, insure domestic Tranquility, provide for the common defence, promote the general Welfare, and secure the Blessings of Liberty to ourselves and our Posterity, do ordain and establish this Constitution for the United States of America.

Article. I.

Section. 1. All legislative Powers herein granted shall be vested in a Congress of the United States, which shall consist of a Senate and House of Representatives.

Section. 2. The House of Representatives shall be composed of Members chosen every second Year by the People of the several States, and the Electors in each State shall have the Qualifications requisite for Electors of the most numerous Branch of the State Legislature.

No Person shall be a Representative who shall not have attained to the Age of twenty five Years, and been seven Years a Citizen of the United States, and who shall not, when elected, be an Inhabitant of that State in which he shall be chosen.

Representatives and direct Taxes shall be apportioned among the several States which may be included within this Union, according to their respective Numbers, which shall be determined by adding to the whole Number of free Persons, including those bound to Service for a Term of Years, and excluding Indians not taxed, three fifths of all other Persons. The actual Enumeration shall be made within three Years after the first Meeting of the Congress of the United States, and within every subsequent Term of ten Years, in such Manner as they shall by Law direct. The Number of Representatives shall not exceed one for every thirty Thousand, but each State shall have at Least one Representative; and until such enumeration shall be made, the State of New Hampshire shall be entitled to chuse three, Massachusetts eight, Rhode Island and Providence Plantations one, Connecticut five, New York six, New Jersey four, Pennsylvania eight, Delaware one, Maryland six, Virginia ten, North Carolina five, South Carolina five, and Georgia three.

When vacancies happen in the Representation from any State, the Executive Authority thereof shall issue Writs of Election to fill such Vacancies.

The House of Representatives shall chuse their Speaker and other Officers; and shall have the sole Power of Impeachment.

Section. 3. The Senate of the United States shall be composed of two Senators from each State, chosen by the Legislature thereof, for six Years; and each Senator shall have one Vote.

Immediately after they shall be assembled in Consequence of the first Election, they shall be divided as equally as may be into three Classes. The Seats of the Senators of the first Class shall be vacated at the Expiration of the second Year, of the second Class at the Expiration of the fourth Year, and of the third Class at the Expiration of the sixth Year, so that one third may be chosen every second Year; and if Vacancies happen by Resignation, or otherwise, during the Recess of the Legislature of any State, the Executive thereof may make temporary Appointments until the next Meeting of the Legislature, which shall then fill such Vacancies.

No Person shall be a Senator who shall not have attained to the Age of thirty Years, and been nine Years a Citizen of the United States, and who shall not, when elected, be an Inhabitant of that State for which he shall be chosen.

The Vice President of the United States shall be President of the Senate, but shall have no Vote, unless they be equally divided.

The Senate shall chuse their other Officers, and also a President pro tempore, in the Absence of the Vice President, or when he shall exercise the Office of President of the United States.

The Senate shall have the sole Power to try all Impeachments. When sitting for that Purpose, they shall be on Oath or Affirmation. When the President of the United States is tried, the Chief Justice shall preside: And no Person shall be convicted without the Concurrence of two thirds of the Members present.

Judgment in Cases of Impeachment shall not extend further than to removal from Office, and disqualification to hold and enjoy any Office of honor, Trust or Profit under the United States: but the Party convicted shall nevertheless be liable and subject to Indictment, Trial, Judgment and Punishment, according to Law.

Section. 4. The Times, Places and Manner of holding Elections for Senators and Representatives, shall be prescribed in each State by the Legislature thereof; but the Congress may at any time by Law make or alter such Regulations, except as to the Places of chusing Senators.

The Congress shall assemble at least once in every Year, and such Meeting shall be on the first Monday in December, unless they shall by Law appoint a different Day.

Section. 5. Each House shall be the Judge of the Elections, Returns and Qualifications of its own Members, and a Majority of each shall constitute a Quorum to do Business; but a smaller Number may adjourn from day to day, and may be authorized to compel the Attendance of absent Members, in such Manner, and under such Penalties as each House may provide.

Each House may determine the Rules of its Proceedings, punish its Members for disorderly Behaviour, and, with the Concurrence of two thirds, expel a Member.

Each House shall keep a Journal of its Proceedings, and from time to time publish the same, excepting such Parts as may in their Judgment require Secrecy; and the Yeas and Nays of the Members of either House on any question shall, at the Desire of one fifth of those Present, be entered on the Journal.

Neither House, during the Session of Congress, shall, without the Consent of the other, adjourn for more than three days, nor to any other Place than that in which the two Houses shall be sitting.

Section. 6. The Senators and Representatives shall receive a Compensation for their Services, to be ascertained by Law, and paid out of the Treasury of the United States. They shall in all Cases, except Treason, Felony and Breach of the Peace, be privileged from Arrest during their Attendance at the Session of their respective Houses, and in going to and returning from the same; and for any Speech or Debate in either House, they shall not be questioned in any other Place.

No Senator or Representative shall, during the Time for which he was elected, be appointed to any civil Office under the Authority of the United States, which shall have been created, or the Emoluments whereof shall have been encreased during such time; and no Person holding any Office under the United States, shall be a Member of either House during his Continuance in Office.

Section. 7. All Bills for raising Revenue shall originate in the House of Representatives; but the Senate may propose or concur with Amendments as on other Bills.

Every Bill which shall have passed the House of Representatives and the Senate, shall, before it become a Law, be presented to the President of the

The Constitution of the United States

Madison is no less supportive of the need for religion, especially by those who exercise public authority or influence in the community:

> I have sometimes thought
>
> that there could not be a stronger
>
> testimony in favor of Religion
>
> or against Temporal enjoyments,
>
> even the most rational and manly,
>
> than for men who occupy
>
> the most honorable and gainful
>
> departments and (who) are rising in
>
> reputation and wealth, publicly
>
> to declare their unsatisfactoriness
>
> by becoming fervent Advocates in the cause
>
> of Christ, and I wish
>
> you may give in your evidence in this way.
>
> *(James Madison – Personal Letter to William Bradford, 1772)*

The above-quoted words of Washington and Madison, along with the other Founders (even the more skeptical such as Jefferson and Franklin), reflect the belief that religion would play a vital role in the stability and longevity of the new republic. The desire for religion to play a vital role in public life ought not to be unexpected. The very nature of a republican form of government requires a virtuous people – citizens and officials. The Founders looked to religion to provide those moral resources if "the miracle at Philadelphia" was to endure. The hope for religion to supply the necessary moral foundation for the republic was powerfully stated by Charles Carroll of Maryland (the only Catholic to sign the Declaration of Independence):

> Without morals a republic cannot
>
> subsist any length of time;
>
> they therefore who are decrying
>
> the Christian religion, whose
>
> morality is so sublime and pure,
>
> and which insures to the good
>
> eternal happiness, are undermining
>
> the solid foundation of morals,
>
> the best security for the duration of free governments.
>
> *(Personal Letter to his son, November 4, 1800)*

"One of the most religious of America's Founding Fathers was the son of an intensely religious man… When the son became one of the richest men in colonial Maryland, and one of the most powerful, he was still denied the right to hold office or even to vote. This man was Charles Carroll of Carrollton, the last living signer of the Declaration of Independence and the only Catholic among the fifty-eight signers." (*The Faiths of Our Fathers*, p. 124)

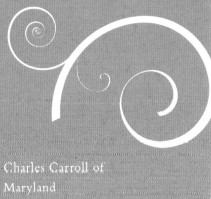

Charles Carroll of Maryland

The importance of religious freedom is captured in the Bill of Rights, the first 10 amendments to the Constitution. The need to protect religious liberty was demanded by newly formed American citizens who remembered with bitterness the European practice by those on the throne of appointing religious leaders and enforcing the crown's view

The Bill of Rights

the attempt than those who covered their ambitious designs under the garb of a fiery zeal for religious orthodoxy." The Gazetteer went on to support the Bill of Rights as necessary in order to protect religious freedom: "…to secure…by the most express stipulations, the sacred rights of conscience." All natural rights and civil liberties are in danger if the first liberty – the right to follow one's conscience – is not fully protected.

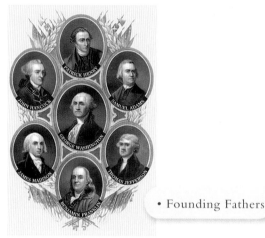

• Founding Fathers

The Founders were not blind to the threat to freedom that an official, state-sponsored religion poses. Once again their experience in Europe was instructive. The wedding of cross and crown served poorly the interest of liberty. When one denomination ascended to the pinnacle of power, a persecution and suppression of other faiths was not long in coming. The Framers and the vast majority of citizens wanted to avoid the tragic mistakes of the Old Country. The Fathers of the Constitution believed the way to achieve their goal was by means of a two-part, interrelated amendment: the first clause would prohibit Congress from establishing an official state religion, and the second part would prohibit Congress from inhibiting the free exercise of religion. By prohibiting the federal government from establishing its own church, and by encouraging the widest

of orthodox belief. This was not to happen here. While there was no royalty in America, it was not unexpected for politicians to try to wrap their ambitions in the robe of religion. The danger of religion being co-opted by a particular political faction, and the need to protect against this, was captured in a 1787 editorial in the *Philadelphia Independent Gazetteer*. The newspaper noted that the devious use religion to advance their own power, while disturbing the peace and liberty of the community. The editorial went on to opine, "…none has been more frequently successful in

possible expression of faiths, liberty would flower for both church and state. There was to be no theocracy or divinely anointed monarchy; rather, each citizen was to be free to follow the dictates of conscience, and one was at liberty to worship as one pleased. Equally important, one was free to not worship at all.

This constitutional safeguard for both religious and political liberty was understood by the courts to mean that support for religion did not, on its face, mean the establishment of a church by the state. At times, the wall of separation was breached; some states continued to favor a particular religion to the exclusion of others. The wall of separation was more like a line that displayed a great deal of mobility and accommodation for religious expression. No one seriously suggested that the establishment of an official state religion was underway. Likewise, when there was a co-mingling of church and state, no one was prevented from exercising their religious faith. Even when an occasional complaint reached the courts, it was dismissed. The two elements of this first freedom – non-establishment and the free exercise – were understood as supporting each other, and they were not viewed as being mutually exclusive or antagonistic.

• Unfortunately, FEMA funds could not be used for church repair. The inside of St. David Church was turned upside down.

U.S. Supreme Court
Justice Hugo Black

A profound, though very subtle, change took place in 1947, with the case, *Everson v. Board of Education*, argued before the United States Supreme Court. The Everson case was direct: Could taxpayers' money be used to provide services, in this case, the transporting of parochial students to school? The High Court ruled that this practice was constitutional and did not rise to the level of establishing a state religion. So far, so good. However, the court opinion written by Justice Hugo Black went on to indicate that while this arrangement was acceptable, every precaution must be taken to preserve the constitutional principle of the separation of church and state. Justice Black, several times, used the Jeffersonian metaphor "wall of separation," except that now, this image was raised to constitutional status. What had been used by Jefferson in a letter to Danbury Baptists was now anointed by Justice Black with the sacred oil of the Constitution and would be used numerous times by radical separationists in subsequent years. The seeds of the "Naked Public Square" – a place devoid of any religious influence or comment – had been planted.

The seeds of total separation would begin to sprout in the 1960s (the school prayer case being the most profound) and flower into full bloom in subsequent decades. Over time, what would have been unthinkable to the Framers became constitutional orthodoxy. Namely, Supreme Court jurisprudence after Everson evolved in such a way that the two clauses – non-establishment and free exercise – were now understood in such a way that any state accommodation of religion was declared to be an unconstitutional establishment by the government! In a complete ignoring of original intent, any public expression of faith, however marginally it was associated with the state, was ruled unconstitutional. Such a reading of the Constitution, along with rulings by federal courts, gave rise to an America the Founders would neither recognize nor intend. The late Chief Justice of the Supreme Court, William Rehnquist, after a school prayer case, was moved to write that the court now interprets the Constitution in such a way that the Constitution itself is hostile to public expressions of religion.

The above brief history is essential if we are to understand what occurred after Katrina in terms of church-state relations. The aftermath of the storm necessitated a cooperative spirit, one akin to the kind the Founders' would have approved, between the church and various levels of government. From a lowering of the wall of separation, might we not learn, or better relearn, the ways in which church and state can work together for the common good? Might we now, several years removed from Katrina, find creative ways of addressing enduring problems without establishing a national religion, or inhibiting the free exercise of religion? Is this not what the "generation of genius," which produced the Philadelphia miracle, had envisioned?

• St. Bernard Cemetery across from St. Bernard Church

The Persistence of Populism

Dark humor for a dark time was much in evidence after Katrina. Just a sample of such dark humor will reveal the mood of many in the days and months after the storm: What were the three destructive forces brought by Katrina? Answer: wind, water, and FEMA. And the worst was FEMA, since the headaches associated with FEMA lasted longer. Perhaps this is the chuckle needed to stave off the crying. However, one can discern a deeper force at play: a suspicion of and hostility toward government. This anti-government sentiment has been an enduring part of the American DNA. The flames of revolution were ignited and fueled by the passion for freedom from an oppressive government (the crown).

• TEA (Taxed Enough Already) Party bumper sticker

The American political landscape is dotted with eruptions of populism (the Tea Party Movement is just the most recent example); that is, a deep feeling of resentment, frustration and alienation by certain segments of society that feel left out of the decision-making process. Populists believe that those in power are indifferent or even hostile to their concerns. Whether the protest is over a perceived economic or social injustice, the common thread that connects assorted movements is a strong dislike for government. The battle cry of the Populist is

"Thoreau-esque" – the government that rules best is the one that rules least, or better yet, not at all.

The Achilles heel of all populist movements is the lack of an institutional foundation, an organizational structure which allows the protest to endure beyond the moment. No doubt Populists would not accept this observation as valid. After all, the ire of the protestors usually is aimed at big government or big business. Organizational structure is at the core of the problem and must be dismantled. Yet history teaches that without an institutional structure, an organizational chart, and a set of rules for leaders, Populist movements splinter and easily fall into fanaticism, lose their focus, and lack the discipline necessary to unite members for the realization of the desired outcome.

TEA Party. Picture by Herb Galloway

Espccially in a time of crisis, Populism has little to offer. In order to respond effectively to a national or regional catastrophe, society needs more than voices of angry protest, no matter how loud. In a time of testing, a nation must employ the power of manifold institutions and organizations. Citizens look to and have a right to expect their government leaders to meet the emergency at hand. Different governmental institutions are also expected to put communities and individual lives back on the road to recovery. Even the most cursory review of historical experience teaches us to be wary of the simplistic "either-or" approach to the question of government. Either one favors the establishment of an all-powerful central government which enters every aspect of public and private life, or one supports the elimination of government *in toto*. There is a better path than totalitarianism or anarchy. Catholic Social Teaching offers an instructive perspective on the role of the state. It is to this teaching we now turn.

The Enduring Need for Government

Catholic Social Teaching regarding society and state must begin with the human person. Catholic Social Teaching, following the witness of Scripture and the dictates of reason, holds that the human person is by nature a social being. That is, an essential dimension of human nature is matured by being in relationship *with* and *for* others. From the social nature of the human person, people come together to pursue those social goods, one of which is government, that enhance the quality of life in light of the common good (more will be said about the common good). It is crucial to keep in mind that society is an outgrowth of the social nature of the human person, and the state proceeds from a particular society in accord with its needs, values, and aspirations. Because society is prior to the state, the state must be limited in its scope and reach if liberty and human dignity are to be protected. Totalitarianism results when the state and society become one; hence government is not walled off from any area of life. The mediating structures of family, school, church, clubs, and numerous volunteer organizations are swallowed up in the omnipotent and omniscient state. All of life is reduced to the political, and the human person is treated as a mere instrument of government.

> "Certain societies, such as the family and the state, correspond more directly to the nature of man; they are necessary to him. To promote the participation of the greatest number in the life of a society, the creation of voluntary associations and institutions must be encouraged 'on both national and international levels, which relate to economic and social goals…(voluntary associations) express the natural tendency for human beings to associate with one another for the sake of attaining objectives that exceed individual capacities.'"
>
> *(Catechism of the Catholic Church, No. 1882, Mater et magistra, 60)*

The evils of totalitarianism were clearly present during the last century (communism, fascism and National Socialism) and remain into the present day (North Korea, Iran, and Cuba, to name the most obvious). However, the slide of a regime into totalitarianism is not a valid argument in favor of anarchy. The absence of government and civil society poses its own dangers to freedom and human dignity. Anarchy yields the Hobbesian condition of "all against all." The strong will exploit the weak. Various factions will be in a condition of constant conflict in which the notion of domestic tranquility is an elusive good. History reveals that over time, anarchy gives way to totalitarianism because, at some point, people will trade any natural right for security. The irony is inescapable – the condition of anarchy brings about the very political reality anarchists detest.

Because Catholic Social Teaching begins with the dignity of the human person, the evils of totalitarianism and anarchy are avoided. Catholic Social Teaching is grounded on the following principles:

1. The human person, made in the divine image, is deserving of respect by the sheer fact of one's humanity.

2. The dignity of the human person is derived from God, and not something bestowed by the state. God endows each person with intellect and will, the human faculties for truth and freedom.

3. Each human person is the recipient of certain natural or inalienable rights, among which the right to life is primary. All other rights, natural and civil, are secure to the extent that the right to life is protected.

4. The social nature of the human person gives rise to society as a natural condition, and not the result solely of a social contract or general will.

5. Human society, if it is to be well-ordered and serve the needs of its members, invests some people with the legitimate authority to guide its institutions, promote justice, and advance the general welfare.

6. At its core, political authority is the moral permission, granted by the citizens of a state, to conduct the people's business under the rule of law. Those in positions of political authority are themselves under the same laws which obligate the body politic. No one is above the law, and no one should fall below the law's power to protect and grant justice.

7. Citizens have the right, privilege and responsibility to participate in the sundry aspects of personal and public life. Each person must take charge of those areas which come under one's immediate control – the well-being of the family and engaging in just labor for the good of society. Citizens have a responsibility to grow in civic virtue, which uplifts the moral quality of public life. The right to participate at every level of public service is essential to the moral well-being of a society. Unjust exclusion must be eliminated, and laws enacted which promote the widest range of involvement by all citizens.

8. The life of the individual, the well-being of society, and the moral quality of the state require the promotion of the common good. Beginning with the individual citizen, and extending throughout the many levels of our complex social order, there is a fundamental duty to promote respect for human life.

In reviewing the above principles, and stated clearly in the last one, we learn that the pursuit of the common good is essential to human respect and the moral health of the commonwealth. The promotion of the common good is reflective of the social nature of the human person. If a society and its institutions are to respect the human person, the general good must be advanced, and not the privileged interests of the few. It is to this fundamental requirement for a just society, the common good, that we now turn.

• Local police and firemen provided much assistance to churches and schools

Rebuilding the
floodwall at the
17th Street Canal

The Common Good and Solidarity: To Bear Another's Burden

A number of influential modern political and economic philosophies view the human person as an essentially isolated individual, motivated by self-interest, who enters into temporary arrangements with other isolated individuals in order to obtain one's desires. As soon as the goal is realized or other desires arise calculated to be more advantageous, the bond is broken in order to satisfy the new objectives. There is no thought of lasting, faithful relationships which often require sacrifice, self-denial, the willingness to relinquish a right in order to do the right thing, and the ability to commit to a work in service of the common good. Society, from the perspective of liberal political and economic thought, is nothing more than a collection of isolated individuals who come together and form a contract in order to realize a desired end. Such a society highly values what is novel and disdains tradition. It is assumed that what is new is better than what has gone before. Too often, it is a society without a memory.

The above articulated view of the human person, relationships, and society as nothing more than an aggregate of self-interested individuals or atoms is contrary to Catholic Social Teaching. As we have seen, rather than begin with atomistic individuals, Catholic Social Teaching's stepping-off point is the human person positioned within a set of natural relationships, beginning within the family and extending outward to the larger society of one's fellow citizens. The human person requires this social networking in order to realize his or her potential as a human being. To grow in one's humanity, one must be in and for community. Solitary confinement is one of the severest punishments a prison uses to control inmates. Why? To be only with oneself, and only for oneself, is hellish because it is truly inhuman, that is, contrary to our social human nature. Jean Paul Sartre is wrong: hell is not other people; hell is being without others.

There is, to be sure, within human nature the capacity for inordinate self-love, indifference to the plight of others, and conducting our daily affairs according to the "ethic of the sharper elbows." Such is the reality of Original Sin. The recognition of this capacity, too often actualized, has guided political philosophers from Aristotle to James Madison. Much of Western political thought, influenced by St. Augustine, viewed the state as the Great Restrainer on the prideful and destructive passions within human nature. At the same time, that state itself was in need of restraint. Those who are given political power must be placed under the rule of law, made accountable to the electorate, and subjected to a system of checks and balances as a safeguard against the abuse of power.

This Augustinian realism should not blind us to what Lincoln called "our finer angels." There is the capacity, both

• Churches in New Orleans East suffered much but continue to serve

ST MARIA GORETTI CHURCH

Abraham Lincoln

terms of Catholic Social Teaching. Our definition guide will be the Catechism of the Catholic Church (see sections 1905 and 1939).

A helpful way to begin our discussion of the common good is to recall the familiar parable of Jesus entitled, "The Good Samaritan"(Lk 10:30-37). The core issue raised by the lawyer to Jesus is direct: "Who is my neighbor?" There was an accepted and well-known response: The neighbor is the one who is part of one's group, race, gender, creed, and so on. The neighbor is the one with whom one has much in common. That concept of neighbor is highly restrictive. Likewise, that restrictive meaning limits one's duty to show compassion. One is required only to extend help to one's

individually and by the state, to promote justice, seek peace, and extend freedom. Through personal witness, the laws, and the institutional makeup of society, it is possible to labor for the common good and enter into solidarity with the weak, vulnerable, and powerless. The responsibility for advancing the common good and being in solidarity with and for others proceeds from the social nature of the human person. In terms of the state, it proceeds from the requirements of justice that government is not for the elite few, but for the overall well-being of society as a whole. Government is also required by justice, not charity, to protect and provide for those basic human goods which promote respect for human life.

As we shall see in this chapter, the ideas of the common good and solidarity are crucial if we are to understand two key elements guiding the archdiocese's response to the devastation caused by Hurricane Katrina. Hence, it is necessary to be clear on the meaning of these important

· Katrina victims disembark an Army Chinook helicopter

God's people), Jesus is expanding the notion of who is to be seen as neighbor (remember those who passed by the stricken man did not stop because they did not see him as a neighbor, as one deserving "pity"). The meaning of neighbor is now expanded to include anyone who is in need. The old restrictions no longer apply.

Jesus is also offering an expanded meaning of exactly who is part of God's people. As with the concept of neighbor, God's people include anyone who shows pity, compassion, mercy, and care to another in need. The former qualifications of race, nationality, and a specific form of religious practice must give way to a new covenant of love written on the heart. It is no longer enough to define neighbor as one with whom one has things in common. Jesus' parable troubles the comfortable with the face of violence that must be seen, with the reality of an unexpected loss of resources that challenges one to share, and with the wounded who end up in a ditch that requires one to make provision for their recovery. There is more than having things in common if one is to be part of God's people; one must be moved to pity and work for the common good. The person in need, whom one can help, is no longer invisible. Human need, addressed by the ability to show compassion, now predominates.

Within the parable of the Good Samaritan there are a number of underlying principles that have been formulated into a unified concept, which Catholic Social Teaching terms the "common good." It is to this key component of the teaching that we now turn.

The Catechism of the Catholic Church's (CCC) presentation of the common good begins with what is primary:

A post-Katrina cross at St. Thomas Church in Pointe a la Hache serves as a symbol of God's faithful love

neighbor, and the understanding of neighbor is narrow in scope. One can remain indifferent to the plight of those in need by taking refuge in an anemic conception of neighbor.

Jesus' parable challenges the conventional wisdom on who is one's neighbor, and in so doing, pulls the comfortable rug of moral apathy from underfoot. By holding up a most unlikely candidate for showing "pity" (in the Hebrew Scripture, the showing of pity is one of the main actions of Yahweh, and one of the fundamental requirements for the social nature of the human person. No one in isolation can achieve, much less enjoy, those genuine human goods (for example, friendship), which promote personal flourishing. The very nature of the human being calls for inclusive participation in public life if the truly good life is to be realized. The banding together of individuals for some purpose and good, beyond individual self-interest, is the work of the common good. Advancing the common good is the concern of all, guided by prudence, but a special responsibility falls to those who are entrusted with offices of authority. The CCC, drawing on the Second Vatican Council's document, *Gaudium et spes*, defines the common good as "the sum total of social conditions which allow people, either as groups or as individuals, to reach their fulfillment more fully and more easily."

Contained in this rather direct, if not abstract, definition of the common good are three essential elements.

First, the common good requires respect for the human person. Those who hold the different offices associated with civil authority must promote respect for the basic and inalienable rights of the human person. Of great importance is the need to protect and promote the exercise of the natural freedoms associated with one's human vocation. Among those natural rights or freedoms, great care must be taken to protect freedom of conscience, the right to privacy and to be secure in one's person and home, and the rightful freedom in the exercise of religion.

Second, following upon the duty to respect the human person, is the need to promote the social well-being and development of the group. The CCC goes so far as to teach,

"Development is the epitome of all social duties" *(Section 1908)*. Those in authority are called upon to see that no one special interest, or segment of a group, advances at the expense of others' right to participate and obtain those goods necessary for a truly human life. Among these essential goods associated with well-being are the following: food, clothing, health, work, education and culture, suitable information, and the right to establish a family.

Finally, the common good requires peace. Several key aspects need to be kept in mind. The peace to be sought should not be confused with quietism or moral apathy. For a genuine peace to be experienced there must be a just social order. The absence of justice, or a workable means of correcting grievances, is the absence of the social good of peace. Jesus blesses the *peacemaker*, not necessarily the peacekeeper. There are times when the call for peace comes at the expense of human dignity and various rights. In such instances, protest and civil disobedience are legitimate means to right the wrong. Furthermore, peace is not an absolute moral value but must be balanced by other, prudently considered values. A nation, unjustly attacked, has the right, if not the duty, to provide for the common defense as part of the common good. Individuals and certain groups, often religious in nature, have the right in conscience to advocate and practice pacifism. However, public officials have a fundamental obligation to provide security for the citizenry and protect the right of a nation to achieve legitimate ends.

The concept of the common good and its three major elements are grounded in the social nature of the human person and the need to honor human dignity. In the stunning words of the CCC: "The common good is always oriented towards the progress of persons… (A just social order) is founded on truth, built up in justice, and animated by love" *(Section 1912)*. This is an easy wisdom to forget, especially in modern times, but one we fail to remember at the loss of liberty and the denial of human dignity. The human person must always be an end and never merely a means to some social or political goal. The social order is structured to develop the potential of each person. The human being is not created to be an object of the state. The dignity of the human person requires the individual to be treated as a subject, a thou and never an *it. (M. Bubur)*

The notion of the common good can easily come to be understood exclusively in terms of material well-being and the proper structure of society in order to secure a fair distribution of goods and services. The spiritual dimension of the person can be overlooked. The person becomes reduced to a mere list of physical goods and services that society distributes. Lost in the essential unity of the human person, the material and spiritual needs must be fulfilled. The principle of solidarity, so key to the social thought of Pope John Paul II, provides the necessary component for any discussion of the common good.

As far back as 1938, during the pontificate of Pius XII, the call to solidarity was voiced. The Holy Father spoke of the error.

"…today abundantly widespread, is disregard for the law of human solidarity and charity, dedicated and imposed both by our common origin and by the equality in rational nature of all men, whatever nation they belong to. This law is sealed by the sacrifice of redemption offered by Jesus Christ on the altar of the Cross to his heavenly Father, on behalf of sinful humanity."

(Summi pontificatus)

• Pope Pius XII

While not ignoring the requirements of a just social order, "the virtue of solidarity goes beyond material goods" *(CCC, Section 1942)*. The spiritual goods of faith, ministered through the church, are not in opposition to providing material goods; in fact, the spiritual can open new ways to use and distribute the goods of this world. Attention to the material and spiritual needs of the person is necessary if the human person, as a unitary being, is to be properly respected. To focus solely on the physical goods of life overlooks the transcendent origin and destiny of every person. A spirituality that is exclusively directed toward heaven can too easily become indifferent to injustices within the social order. The Church throughout its history has sought to seek first the Kingdom of God, while addressing the material needs of people here below. Again the words of Pius XII are to the point:

> For two thousand years this sentiment has lived
> and endured in the soul of the
> Church, impelling souls then and now
> to the heroic charity of monastic farmers,
> liberators of slaves, healers of the sick, and messengers
> of faith, civilization, and science
> to tell all generations and all peoples
> for the sake of creating the social
> conditions capable of offering to everyone possible
> a life worthy of man and of a Christian.
>
> *(Pius XII, Discourse, June 1, 1941)*

The archdiocese's response to Katrina, as hopefully this book shows, continues the long story of ministering to the physical and spiritual needs of person and society.

For every instance of providing food, water, clothing, shelter and financial support, there were countless instances of prayer, pastoral counseling, sacramental ministry, and the offering of the Eucharist. The needs after Katrina were obviously, but not exclusively, material. It should not be lost, however, that there was a deep desire for the gifts of the Holy Spirit, the word of the Lord through Scripture, and a deep hunger and thirst for the Body and Blood of Christ.

After Katrina, the Sacred Heart provided comfort at St. David Church

In addition to meeting the physical and spiritual needs of individuals, the archdiocese raised a prophetic voice on behalf of social justice. After Katrina, the archdiocese took great care in crafting a message of "welcome home" to those who had been displaced. Times of crisis, especially on the scale of Katrina, understandably cause nerves to be on edge, vision to narrow to the needs of self and family, and a resentment that saps good will toward others. The archdiocese through its multiple ministries – from education to social services to medical care and job training – sought to make all welcome regardless of the recipient's religion. The archdiocese knew that more than tone and pious words would be needed if people were to return. While a returning population was indispensable for recovery, still more was required. With people coming back, the need for adequate housing would be a significant challenge. In addition to providing financial resources for rental payments, the archdiocese, through a variety of partnerships between Catholic Charities Archdiocese of New Orleans and other entities (public and private), began a number of creative housing programs to meet this crucial need. Finally, the archdiocese, again through Catholic Charities Archdiocese of New Orleans and other partners began operating a number of job-training programs. The labor market post-Katrina has greatly changed in terms of skills required for employment, as well as those sectors experiencing a high level of need for trained workers. The ability to work – the finding of employment – enhances a person's self-respect. Work allows a person to contribute to the common good and feel a sense of accomplishment. By empowering people to take hold of their lives and participate and contribute to society, the archdiocese is being faithful to the Gospel, offering hope and working for the common good.

Mediating Structures and Subsidiarity: Little Platoons of Hope

Thus far, two concepts of Catholic social teaching have been discussed in this section: the common good and solidarity. These principles were clearly in play as the archdiocese responded to individual and regional needs. There is one remaining principle, subsidiarity, and its close relative, mediating structure, which is germane to our discussion.

• The Great Depression: National Archives and Records Administration, Records of the Office of the Secretary of Agriculture

In the face of crises and disasters, such as Katrina, it has come to be that we look to government at every level for assistance. For example, in the last century our nation faced a Great Depression. It was beyond the ability of any one state or region to solve problems. The national government needed to act. Most recently, the nation, along with a vast majority of the world, faced a serious recession. The federal government responded with various stimulus packages in order to prevent a financial collapse (the wisdom of such a response is not the issue). The same federal response is expected during times

Debris removal, October 2005

of natural disasters. The scope of devastation and the depth of need are simply of a magnitude that no one community, state or region can adequately respond. The intervention and resources of Washington are needed.

Yet, we have learned from experience an important lesson: government, no matter how powerful or extensive the resources, cannot do everything. Nor should we expect government to solve every problem. Often our level of frustration is proportional to the degree of our expectations. There are limits to the reach of the political arm. A second hard lesson we had to re-learn was the importance of what sociologists call "mediating structure," that is, those levels of organization which buffer the individual from a total management by the state. Mediating structure includes the family, school, club, volunteer and civic organizations. Among the most important are churches and synagogues. These important levels of social life are more intimate and less intrusive than the larger, more complex social arrangements that form much of modern life. Mediating structures are closer to the needs, goals, and resources of a local community or region. These lower levels of social complexity put a "human face" on local needs which are more likely to be responded to in an impersonal and bureaucratic way by highly complex and far-removed social structures.

Commanding General Carl A. Strock, middle, and Brigadier General Robert Crear
of the U.S. Army Corps of Engineers at the 17th Street Canal

None of what has been said so far should be taken to mean that, for example, the federal government has nothing to offer to a local community in need, or that a central school office has no place in the educational practices of a particular school. We have also learned from experience that what passes for "local wisdom" can disguise a bigotry and provincialism that excludes a just participation by certain groups in public life. One need only think of the struggle for civil rights and equality in the last century (which continues into our time). Under the banner of "state's rights" and local autonomy, elected officials supported racial discrimination. It was necessary for the federal government to establish laws against the order, for the social structures in place violated the requirements of justice and respect for human dignity. This federal intervention by means of law and troops, along with the moral witness of so many – Dr. Martin Luther King Jr., the most notable – stirred the conscience of a nation and effected a profound social change.

The good society – one in which human dignity is honored, equality of opportunity is operative, liberty is cherished, natural rights are protected, and goods and services are justly available to all – fosters mediating structures. Edmund Burke, the 18th century British political philosopher, termed these structures "little platoons of virtue." For our purpose, a specific theological virtue can be added – hope (more will be said about hope in Chapter Ten). The family, school, places of worship, and the numerous associations to which we belong exert enormous influence in shaping character. The virtues of justice, equality, freedom, compassion, civic involvement, and prayer are indispensable resources for a society. It is within the home, school, church and club that each generation learns and practices how to show respect for others, advance the common good, and promote the value of being concerned beyond the "puny self." (de Tocqueville). The good society activates those habits of the heart (again de Tocqueville) that move us to be brother and sister to one another.

When faced with a crisis, personal or collective, the lesson learned from these mediating structures is crucial for recovery and the building of something better. Mediating structures are platoons of hope, for out of these webs of relationships we learn the *skills* of hope. That is, we learn through observation and practice how to face challenges, setbacks, disappointments, and failures without easily surrendering to circumstances. Through various platoons of hope, we are schooled in how to look beyond the immediate and problematic and put forward creative, imaginative approaches. By grace and temper of character we grow strong at the broken places.

The mediating structures of a society provide empirical evidence for the Catholic social teaching's principle of subsidiarity. The articulation of this principle was provided by Pope Pius XII: "… a community of a higher order should not interfere in the external life of a community of a lower order, depriving the latter of its functions, but rather should support it in case of need and help to coordinate its activity with the activities of the rest of society, always with a view to the common good" *(Quadragesimo anno)*. Subsidiarity highlights a number of important themes presented throughout our discussion. All authority is derived from God who rules with perfect justice. This holy, just will of God should be done on earth as it is in heaven. Hence, those who are entrusted with authority exercise it

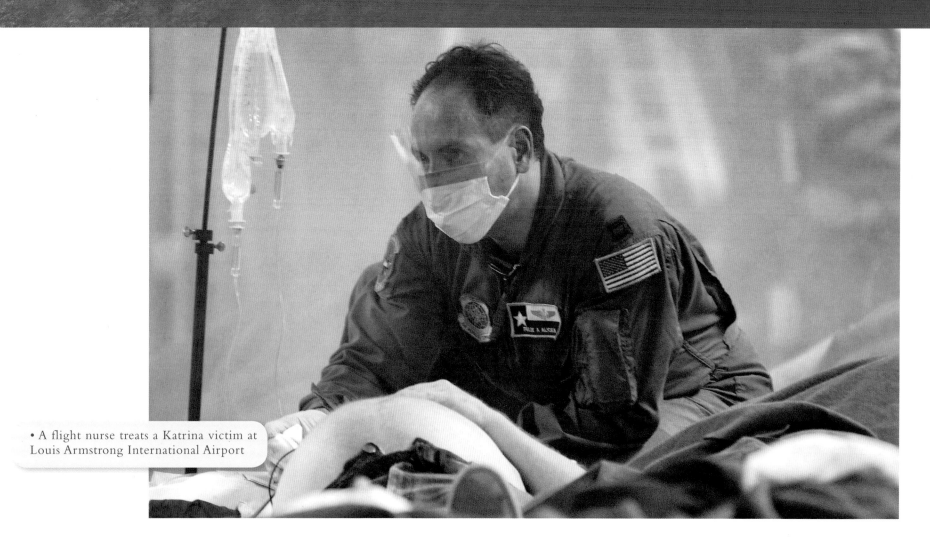

• A flight nurse treats a Katrina victim at Louis Armstrong International Airport

as ministers of God's providential care. This means, among other things, respect for and enhancement of responsible human freedom. The protection and promotion of liberty is in accord with human nature, the dignity of the person, and the advancement of the common good.

Secondly, the principle of subsidiarity advocates limited government, and the extent to which the state should involve itself in lower levels of organization. Subsidiarity stands in opposition to the various forms of collectivism which diminish overall liberty, creativity, innovation, and personal responsibility. The more levels of society the state reaches into and controls, the more dependent on the state citizens and communities become. Over time the state, walking on cat paws, becomes all encompassing. The oxygen

of a democracy – liberty – becomes polluted with the smog of impersonal bureaucracy and endless regulations.

Finally, the promotion of limited government does not mean the elimination of government. Subsidiarity is a prudential teaching as to the scope and reach of the state. There must be a harmonious balancing between the individual and society. Such a balance is an ongoing task of every properly ordered society. Individual citizens and groups can disagree as to the point of proper balance. In a free society these arguments are necessary and a sign of political well-being. Not all civic tension is unhealthy; in fact, the debates within a society, when done with civility and mutual respect, often serve as the spark for needed change.

This chapter has been concerned with church-state relations against the backdrop of Katrina. The discussion has proceeded through the lens of Catholic social teaching, to be specific, the principles of the common good, solidarity, and subsidiarity (with a view to the importance of mediating structures). Before concluding, it would be helpful to offer a case study as to how these principles were in play in the aftermath of Katrina. The thesis advanced is simple: the response to Katrina by the archdiocese and the federal government were different due to the core operational principles that guided each entity. Without an understanding of these fundamental elements, resentment, suspicion, and ineffectiveness will hinder any cooperative efforts in the ongoing process of recovery. Dialogue and collaboration are not luxuries but fundamental requirements if we are to move forward with recovery and rebirth.

Responding to Katrina: FEMA and the Archdiocese – A First Step Together

In the weeks and months after Katrina, a frequently heard question went something like this: Why were private organizations, especially faith-based ones, seemingly more effective in meeting individual and regional needs than government agencies? (The scope of this important question will be limited to the archdiocese and FEMA.) If one is to give serious thought to the above question, one must not indulge in a knee-jerk anti-government sentiment that poisons civic life with a deadly cynicism. The urge to romanticize the response of the private sector to the storm also must be resisted. Good will and mission-vision are necessary, but not sufficient, in responding to great disasters. Without adequate resources, the urge to help gives way to frustration, soon replaced by feelings of impotence. Finally, the things that government did well – and there were things done well – should be acknowledged, and where possible improved. To simply "go negative" when it comes to evaluating the various levels of governmental response is counter-productive. If we are to address the many challenges which lie ahead, solutions will come from those who are able to build bridges (and not just levees) between the government and the private sector. Faith-based communities and religious institutions can be given a greater role in public affairs without endangering our non-establishment provision. We need those with the vision and courage to heal the breach that for too long has festered division that denies us, and succeeding generations, a future to hope in.

For those who lived through Katrina, FEMA is a symbol of all that is wrong with government: big, out of touch, ineffective, bureaucratic red tape, impersonal, and overwhelmingly incompetent. No doubt the examples are legion which give credence to those who believe that FEMA is a house divided, that is, the Federal Emergency part is accurate; the Management Agency is not. Unfortunately, many went on to say, "Yes, FEMA is the federal emergency agency which managed to make things worse and provided little assistance." Ouch! Such a view, dripping with bitterness and frustration, often came from those who were overwhelmed by the storm and who felt just as overwhelmed when turning to those who were supposed to help. Also, the depth of dissatisfaction is proportional to the level of expectation. The level of expectation was raised to a high pitch when President George W. Bush congratulated FEMA director Michael Brown "for a job well-done." These premature kudos offered at Jackson Square were interpreted as nothing more than the exploiting of a terrible disaster for the sake of a "photo-op."

If we are to avoid the corrosive acids of cynicism or apathy, if we are not to let the ideal become the enemy of what can reasonably be achieved, then a fundamental distinction must be made between the work of government (in this case FEMA) and that of the mediating structure (for our purposes, the archdiocese). Broadly speaking, government is an *institution of supply,* while a mediating structure is one that is best understood in terms of *distribution* or *dissemination.* The failure to appreciate this distinction is one of the key driving forces in producing anger, distrust, and a general disdain for government and the relevant public officials. A brief word about an institution of supply and a structure of distribution would be helpful.

Hurricane Katrina provided a prime example of understanding the distinction between institution and structure, supply and distribution. To begin with, an institution of supply, in this case FEMA, is entrusted with responding to various emergencies and disasters that affect an individual state or an entire region. The obvious strength of FEMA is its access to resources – materials, professional and administrative personnel, and money. In the case of Katrina, FEMA was that extension of the national government responsible for providing the necessary resources for cleanup, recovery, and rebuilding. However, while obtaining materials is necessary, it is not sufficient. Too often missing was FEMA's inability or unwillingness to connect with local and regional mediating structures for distribution, for making resources available where they can

do the most good for those in need. Without this network of distribution, vital materials do not effectively reach the local communities. In disaster situations timely delivery to those who are hurting is of the essence. The sheer complexity of FEMA, along with the severity of Katrina's after-effects, made it imperative that FEMA, an institution of supply, develop a good working relationship with numerous structures of delivery. The failure to make this connection only increased anger, frustration, and deep resentment toward a government that seemed to be incompetent, powerless, and even worse, indifferent.

Archbishop Alfred C. Hughes provided consolation to Susie Morris, wife of former Slidell Mayor Ben Morris, outside the collapsed Our Lady of Lourdes Church in Slidell.

Archbishop Hughes converses with military personnel at Louis Armstrong International Airport

If the strength of FEMA was its access to resources and its weakness was on the delivery side, the opposite was the case with the archdiocese. The archdiocese, having experienced a significant blow to its own resources, was unable, on its own, to meet the overwhelming volume of need. The archdiocese, even though having suffered extensive damage, was able to maintain the delivery part of its organizational structures (this was clearly evident through the work of Catholic Charities Archdiocese of New Orleans; see Chapter Three). In addition to the operational status of various archdiocesan distribution structures, the principle of subsidiarity played a key role. Unlike FEMA, which is centered in Washington, D.C., and far removed from local and regional needs, mores,

values, and centers for decision-making, the archdiocese is a major presence in the region. There is a wisdom to be honored that comes from those who are most intimately involved in the everyday life of a community. Particularly in southeast Louisiana, the Catholic Church, with its parishes, schools, and numerous social service ministries, is ideally positioned to deliver goods and services. Among the major lessons taught in the aftermath of Katrina, few were as important as this: in responding to a disaster or emergency, especially one with the magnitude of a Katrina, the common good requires a prudent partnership between the public (government/FEMA) and private (mediating structure/archdiocese) sectors according to their spheres of competence. The supply strength of government and the distribution ability of mediating structures (such as the archdiocese) must be joined for an effective, compassionate response in helping to rebuild lives and communities.

FEMA and the Archdiocese – Part II

In the years after Katrina, there has been an important sea-change in the relationship between FEMA and the archdiocese - and for the better. Both sides have made significant strides in mutual understanding and respect. The experience of entering a new culture is unsettling at first. The unfamiliar easily evokes feelings of fear, alienation, and the urge to defend one's own ways of living, all the while discrediting and rejecting other ways. Getting past these initial feelings usually comes with the passage of time and a genuine openness to learn from those who operate differently.

Hurricane damage at Christopher Inn

National Guard tag at Villa St. Maurice

• Damage and mold at St. Bernard Manor

The archdiocese and FEMA, while having some degree of organizational similarity, are vastly different cultures. These two institutions operate from a set of particular first principles, assumptions, values, beliefs, missions, and operational norms that can easily give rise to misjudgment and conflict. For example, the numerous requirements imposed by FEMA for obtaining reimbursements can be interpreted as an unnecessary delay in the face of pressing human needs. Likewise, pressure from the archdiocese to streamline the process for funds can be viewed as a lack of respect for governmental regulations and accountability. Without dialogue and the willingness to forge shared goals and procedures, too much time can be wasted on the battleground and too little on the common ground, which is the place where solutions are reached and people helped.

Great credit should be given to both FEMA and the archdiocese for moving to end the dialogue of the deaf – parties speaking at and about each other, but not *to* or *with* one another. This developing collaborative spirit has borne fruit for both entities.

Through a long process, one covering four years and still ongoing, the archdiocese has received $61,980,774 from FEMA for numerous construction projects and reimbursements for cleanup, evacuation, demolition, repairs and a series of new construction. In addition, the archdiocese is anticipating a further reimbursement totaling $108,157,322, which is to be used for schools, community centers, and assorted archdiocesan projects. The total reimbursement received and anticipated from FEMA totals $170,138,096. This total figure does not include future applications by the archdiocese as they relate to Christopher Homes and Catholic Charities Archdiocese of New Orleans.

The four-year process (and the one that is continuing) was achieved through a highly fruitful collaborative process involving representatives from the archdiocese (the Office of Catholic Schools, Finance Council, Building Office, Property Management Office, and numerous

• Storm damage at St. Bernard Manor

• Villa St. Maurice

church parishes), FEMA and the state of Louisiana. While acknowledging the process was a challenge, Jeff Entwisle, chief operating officer of the archdiocese, expressed deep respect for the government officials involved, noting how indispensable their guidance was in completing this first phase of the process. These officials also provided valuable assistance for further FEMA reimbursements. "We have a very cooperative working relationship with FEMA and the state," Entwisle said. He went on to add, "Through our collaboration, we've been able to maximize our available funding for projects that will allow us to do what the archbishop thinks is important for education and for the

Debris from Katrina at Metairie Manor

community. The FEMA and state representatives have been incredibly helpful."

While a sizeable reimbursement has been received and put to use, there is much left to do in the ongoing process of recovery. The timetable for starting and completing various building projects remains uncertain because the FEMA review and reimbursement process is ongoing. Entwisle believes it is reasonable to expect construction to be completed over the next several years.

• Blue tarp covers the roof of St. Martin Manor in New Orleans

• St. Bernard Manor after Katrina

Just as important as the FEMA funds is the improvement in the working relationship between officials representing an assortment of government agencies and the archdiocese. This collaborative spirit has not only been valuable for past accomplishments, but also can be the foundation

the challenges and responsibilities each faces in the highly complex process of recovery. Nonetheless, like the mustard seed spoken of in the parable by Jesus, this small beginning may mature into new ways of cooperating for the good of many. If such be the case, another most welcomed sign of hope has emerged out of a time of destruction.

A number of archdiocesan offices were able to productively collaborate with appropriate government agencies. Such cooperative relationships proved extremely helpful in the areas of education, building repairs, food and nutrition, and social services, all of which significantly advanced recovery efforts for the archdiocese and the wider community.

Wind damage to Wynhoven Apartments on the West Bank

Wind damage to the Nazareth Inn building in New Orleans East

for future partnerships in service to the common good. The fostering of professional and, perhaps over time, even friendly relationships can serve as a model for what can be achieved with mutual goodwill, respect and appreciation for what each side has to offer, as well as an understanding of

The Enduring Challenge

Hurricane Katrina brought into sharp focus a challenge and an opportunity that are as old as the founding of this Republic and as current as the latest Supreme Court ruling on the proper exercise of religion in public life. Katrina afforded us the opportunity to revisit the foundations of Catholic social teaching and the American constitutional order. Too often in the contemporary context, a discussion about church-state relations has taken on a harsh tone. If we are to move beyond a barbed-wire wall of separation mentality to one more akin to the accommodationist approach of the Founders, then we must appreciate how congenial, in significant ways, are Catholic Social Teaching and the truths we hold to be self-evident. A most appropriate guide for this valuable undertaking is the late Jesuit theologian, Father John Courtney Murray.

The relationship between throne and altar, crown and cross, extends deep into Western history. Since Constantine brought Christians out of the catacombs and established Christianity as the religion of the Empire, the proper role of religion and politics in the social order has been debated. Sometimes the debate was rhetorical; too often it has been accompanied by the shedding of blood.

The Founders of the American Republic knew well the constructive and destructive effects of religion in the public square. The challenge they faced was to allow for the widest possible free exercise of religion, all the while keeping the state neutral as to favoring a particular denomination. This balanced constitutional order would protect the liberty of both church and state. By fostering both free exercise

and government neutrality, social unrest over religion and politics would hopefully be lessened, if not eliminated.

Father Murray thought deeply and wrote profoundly about church-state issues as they affected the American context. His book, *We Hold These Truths*, is a modern classic and must reading for anyone interested in this crucial area of public life. Father Murray's wisdom would serve us well today as we continue to work through the enduring challenges and opportunities posed by religion in a free society.

Father Murray held that the nature of a democratic republic, such as America, required discourse. The vital oxygen supply for the life of American society is conversation (democracy, Murray believed, is a conspiracy in the true sense of the term; that is, the "breathing of a common air"). The vibrancy of America was not only its economic and military might, but also in the willingness of citizens to engage in a free, public, and ongoing dialogue about who we are as a people, who we wish to become and what kind of future we want to bequeath to succeeding generations.

As Father Murray insisted throughout his writings, public discourse about the leading issues of the day is necessary but *not* sufficient. The conversation within a society must be characterized by *civility*. Tone is most important when the issues for debate are momentous and different points of view are deeply held. Without civility, there is too often more heat than light; unruly passions drive out reasoned analysis; and the common good is sacrificed for some special interest advanced by those who shout the loudest. A shrill discourse drowns out those thoughtful voices that endeavor to lift a society to new possibilities. Those who exercise

authority, whether in the public or private realm, bear a special responsibility to promote civil conversation. Leaders provide the example that others follow. Civility by those in leadership positions filters down and permeates the social order. The converse is also true. Incivility at the top signals to one's followers or associates that such a way of conversing is not only acceptable but encouraged and rewarded.

Father Murray's call for civil discourse is not just a plea for good manners. Civility is reflective of the nature and dignity of the human person. Speech in the service of truth is grounded in the social nature of the human being. By nature, each person is oriented to truth and away from falsehood. It is through ongoing civil conversation that a society progresses in truth and away from error. Truthful speech strengthens social bonds and furthers those virtues (justice, equality, freedom, domestic peace, and compassion) that enhance the common good. When the manner and substance of conversation in a society is civil and truth-seeking, the dignity of each person is honored.

• Churches in the Ninth Ward of Orleans Parish were badly damaged

An abandoned jet ski at
St. Bernard Manor

In the aftermath of Katrina, we have come to see how important truthfulness and civil discourse are in a time of crisis and recovery. When the initial shock of the storm began to wane, the hard physical and emotional work of cleanup, rebuilding, and recovery became paramount. Over time, frayed nerves and sheer exhaustion became a constant condition among those recovering and those responsible for helping with recovery. The need for civility and truth were powerfully revealed for the social, human goods they are. The advancement of the common good was greatly aided by those individuals and social agencies (public and private) that proved to be respectful of human dignity, compassionate to those in need, and trustworthy when it came to promise keeping. From the building contractor to the parish priest to the helpful government official, respect and reliability lightened many a burden.

The qualities of civility, truthfulness, compassion, reliability, and trustworthiness were much needed after Katrina by various social entities involved with recovery. Those entities that exhibited such virtues were most effective in meeting the needs of a recovering population. Those lacking in these qualities were viewed in a most negative light. It is not enough to provide materials for recovery; the manner in which resources are provided also matters. Governmental agencies that tend to be impersonal and removed from the communities they are called to aid need mediating structures such as churches and faith-based organizations to put a human, compassionate face on bricks, cement and wood.

The connection between government and a mediating structure is greatly facilitated when both sides engage in a civility of discourse, which conveys mutual respect. Civility, respect, and appreciation for the expertise each side brings do much to help build *structures of cooperation* in service of the common good. As was highlighted in the previous section of this chapter, FEMA and the archdiocese were able to establish such a civil dialogue. The result benefited both entities, and more importantly, those in need. The prospects for further collaboration are much more hopeful than if the barriers of old stereotypes and assumptions had remained in place. The example of FEMA and the archdiocese working together can serve as a model for future efforts and provide guidance to those who seek to build similar bridges.

• Those in need of Catholic Charities' services line up at St. John the Baptist Community Center

Finally, Father Murray went on to address the broader context of church-state relations by proposing the following bold thesis: Catholicism and the American constitutional order envisioned by the Framers have more in common than is often assumed. Among the points of connection, too often unappreciated, the following areas are relevant to our purposes:

1. Both the founding documents of the Republic (Declaration of Independence, Constitution and Bill of Rights) and Catholic teachings are one in their respect for the social nature of the human person and the need to honor human dignity.

2. Essential to human dignity is the need to respect natural rights. These rights are not bestowed by church or state, nor can they be taken away by popular will or religious edict. Natural rights are endowments from the Creator, which church and state are obliged to protect.

3. A fundamental dimension of human dignity is freedom. Both the Founders and Catholic teaching share a common understanding of liberty: freedom is the ability to do as one ought and not as one pleases. Liberty, if it is not to become license, must be guided by the truth of the natural moral law. For Catholicism, the natural law is written on the human heart and in conformity with the eternal and divine laws of God. The natural moral law, though given by God, can be known by reason without the aid of divine revelation. For Catholicism, and the Framers influenced by the Enlightenment, the human person is authentically free when he or she obeys a law not of one's making. By obeying the natural moral law, one properly guides one's personal conduct and directs the proper ordering of public life.

4. If a free society is to progress, it must be guided by the rule of law. The establishment of a just legal system is fundamental to domestic tranquility and the necessary social conditions that allow peaceful daily interaction among citizens. Furthermore, the weight of law applies to all and not just to regular citizens. A just social order is one in which the rule of law, and not the will of a privileged few, determines access to and opportunity for those goods that promote true human development.

5. Catholic social teaching speaks of promoting the common good. The American constitutional framework advocates the need to promote the general welfare. Both of these concepts obligate the individual to be involved with more than the self or one's parochial interests. To be Catholic and a citizen requires more than the claiming of rights; responsible living recognizes social obligation.

The intersection of Catholic teaching and the constitutional framework could develop in a most fruitful way. It will fall to those who are directly involved with various governmental and church agencies to develop creative ways of collaboration. An important role will be played by those responsible for formulating social and church policies. That is especially true in the area of federal regulations and guidelines for application and participation in various governmental programs. Individual dioceses and the United States Conference of Catholic Bishops have the vital duty of writing pastoral letters, statements concerning numerous moral issues, and establishing sound principles for guiding the level of cooperation by the church in order to safeguard its ultimate allegiance to the Gospel. Church leaders, clergy and lay persons can further advance a "Murray Project" by engaging in ongoing dialogue with government officials about areas of common concern and points of disagreement.

Church-state relations are an enduring challenge, regardless of whether one favors lowering the wall of separation or erecting it even higher. Daily experience, however, teaches that neatly drawn divisions and staked-out positions seldom remain unchanged in the face of everyday realities and great crises. In this post-Katrina world, as we have seen, new alliances are being formed and old divisions are crumbling. Creative ways of church-state cooperation are emerging on behalf of the common good. All of this is cause for hope. And hope, in any measure, is most welcomed.

It is to hope, the persistent theme running through this book, that we now give sustained attention. What has been left largely implicit will now be made explicit in the next and concluding chapter.

So, onward with hope in our hearts...

• Bell tower at St. David Church

St. Maurice Church, New Orleans

Chapter 10

HOPE IN A TIME OF DESTRUCTION: A THEOLOGICAL NOTE

In the beginning, the reader was informed the story to be told was not about Hurricane Katrina, at least not as the major theme. As is hopefully clear to the faithful who have persevered to this point, what has gone before has been the story of a people in a time of crisis.

Katrina served as a backdrop, for a witness to hope, when despair was so inviting. The preceding pages offered an account of a people, a church, who drew on a courage and generosity that point beyond any human power to a grace bestowed by the God who is Love. No one can have lived through Katrina, and have read these pages, without concluding that God does not abandon his people. As with our Jewish ancestors in faith – that "little flock" in Jerusalem formed by Jesus and that "great cloud of witnesses" through the centuries – the Lord is close to the broken-hearted. Throughout history God "looks with favor…and does great things" for all who look to his countenance in times of individual and community need. So in our own time of testing, the words of the Magnificat speak to our hearts: "… the Almighty has done great things for me, and holy is his name."

Shattered residence on the Mississippi Gulf Coast shows the effects of wind and water

How can a people who have lost so much and experienced such horrific destruction and death make these words their own? The short answer is simple: we are a peculiar people. From the first moment that one accepts Jesus' invitation to "follow me," one is viewed by the world as "strange," not quite like other folks. This distinctiveness is evident when one considers that in the face and fact of enormous destruction, the "reasonable" thing to do was move on. The road home should be "the road less traveled." Why start anew when

the same fate is possibly just a hurricane season away? Why rebuild lives, homes, and communities when "prudence" would seem to dictate putting down roots elsewhere? Those who advocated such "reasonableness" and "prudence" seem to be in agreement with Dante's inscription over the gateway to hell, "Abandon Hope, All Ye Who Enter Here."

At the same time, there were those who chose a different response, a response that is at once a "stumbling block," even a "scandal," to common sense and conventional wisdom. They chose to re-enter and not abandon hope. And not just any brand of hope, but a *spes contra spes*, a hope against hope. Hope is that toughest of virtues, for it lures us beyond the present into a future which can only be hinted at, a tomorrow not yet seen, a vision forward from a mirror that only now reflects darkly. The power of hope is the power to see light at the edges of darkness, to seek a love that drives out all fear, a resolve that overcomes despair and the rumor of angels beneath the rubble. Again, all this is possible, but by no means guaranteed, for those who dare risk to hope. The banner over Dante's gateway to hell is replaced by the words of the Apostle Paul to the Romans. "For we are saved by hope: but hope that is seen is not hope: for what a man sees, why does he yet hope for? But if we hope for that we see not, then we do with patience wait for it" *(Rom 8:24-25)*. The strength of that patient hope is anything but an invitation to passivity and quietism.

There is energy and expectant eagerness exhibited by those taken forward by the grip of hope. Hope does not plant us as much as it empowers us to bloom where we are planted.

Our story is not primarily about a destructive storm but rather about the *response* to that event by a people of faith. And hope is the tough side of faith. More powerful than the winds of Katrina, deeper than her waters, was the will to return, rebuild, and recover. At the deepest of levels, our story is one of longing for home and that hope which kept the longing alive. For many, the experience of home is similar to Mr. Mole in Kenneth Grahame's, *The Wind in the Willows*. Mr. Mole and Mr. Rat are fleeing danger when the thought of home grips Mr. Mole, "…when suddenly the summons reached him and took him like an electric shock."

• Salvaged family photos became precious after Katrina

"The Church must transmit hope, proclaiming that suffering is not absurd, that it is meaningful, because there will be a resurrection after death. She must give the reason for the hope that she has…it is only in the light of Christ's resurrection and in the hope of ours that we can understand the meaning of suffering and death. The cross is better understood by its effects than its causes, which often remain mysterious and inexplicable to us."

(*Mary, Mirror of the Church*, p. 111)

It was one of those mysterious fairy calls
from out of the void
that suddenly reached Mole in the darkness,
making him tingle
through and through with its familiar appeal,
even while as yet he
could not clearly remember what it was.
He stopped dead in his tracks,
his nose searching hither and thither
in its efforts to recapture the
fine filament, the telegraphic current
that had so strongly moved
him. A moment, and he had caught it again;
and with it this time
came recollection in fullest flood.
Home! That was what they meant,
those caressing appeals, those soft touches wafted through
the air, those invisible little hands pulling
and tugging, all one way!
The home had been happy with him,
too, evidently, and was missing him,
and wanted him back, and was telling him so,
through his nose, sorrowfully,
reproachfully, but with no bitterness or anger;
only with plaintive reminder
that it was there, and wanted him.

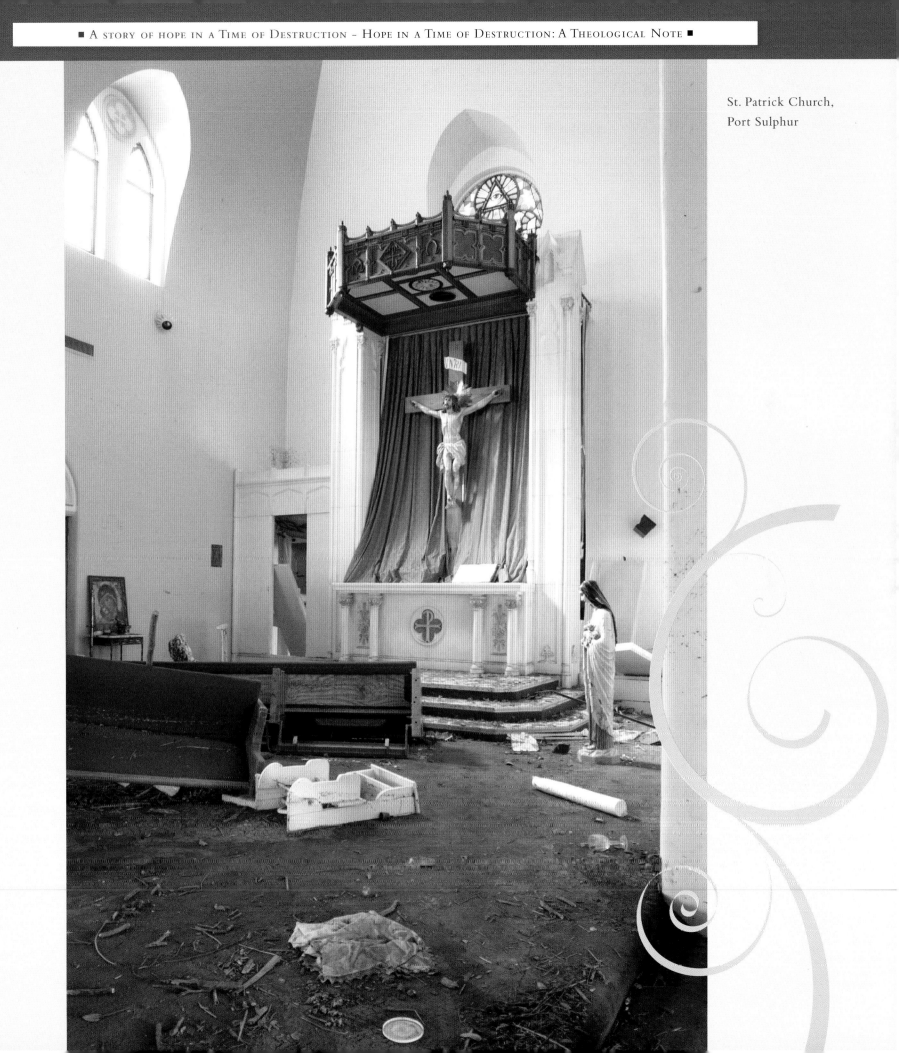

St. Patrick Church,
Port Sulphur

For many who had fled the dangers of Katrina and found themselves in exile like the children of Israel, the Psalmist's words are most poignant:

> By the waters of Babylon
> there we sat down and wept,
> when we remember Zion...
> If I forget you, O Jerusalem,
> let my right hand wither!
> Let my tongue cleave to the roof of my mouth
> if I do not remember you,
> if I do not set Jerusalem
> above my highest joy!

The archdiocese sought from the beginning to be a witness to hope. It is only fitting that we conclude our narrative with a reflection on hope, especially hope in a time of destruction. For it is by that theological virtue, infused in the human heart as gift, that we "live and move and have our being." Three questions, prompted by hope, lay claim to our attention: What is hope? Where was God to be found in this time of destruction? Is hope possible after Katrina?

What is Hope?

Within the pages of Scripture, most prominently in the Gospel of St. Luke, and Catholic theology, the virtue of hope is most often associated with the Holy Spirit. Yet, it must be acknowledged that the relationship is not easily comprehended. Of the Three Persons of the Blessed Trinity, surely the Holy Spirit is the most neglected (even considering the Charismatic Renewal movement in recent decades within the Catholic Church). The image of God as Father and Creator finds an analogy through the human experience of family life. Jesus clearly strikes the most intimate note since he is often described as friend and brother. The Gospel of John, in the Prologue *(1:1-19)*, proclaims the Logos, the Word, "became flesh and dwells among us." God, in the person of Jesus, takes on a human face *(1:14)*. When it comes to the Holy Spirit, things radically change. The image of the Holy Spirit is often that of a dove or a tongue of fire. The *work* and the functions of the Holy Spirit are featured prominently. The Holy Spirit is an advocate, defender, source of joy, the Father's power of creation, revealer of the Father's will, and so on. Clearly the relational aspect of the Holy

The purple cloth drapes the broken window at St. Thomas Church in Pointe a la Hache

Spirit is secondary to the performative dimensions of the Third Person of the Blessed Trinity. The very name, Spirit, conveys an abstractness, which easily turns the mind to the more personal Father and Son.

The virtue of hope often fares no better when it comes to being understood. In order to comprehend this virtue, so essential and evident after Katrina, we must first indicate what hope is *not*.

Although often used interchangeably, hope is not optimism. The optimist operates by a creed which holds that everything must turn out well ("well" understood as the way the optimist desires or demands). The creed of the optimist demands a short time horizon; that is, everything must turn out well, and it must do so *now*! If the demand for instant results is not met, the optimist can easily become disillusioned, if not despairing. Over time, absent instant gratification, the optimist becomes a cynic, a perpetual nay sayer who deconstructs rather than constructs something good or better than what is. Finally, the optimist wears a set of "rose-colored glasses." The vision of the optimist allows one to see only what is desired. Reality is selectively engaged; hence, real challenges can often go unattended, or if responded to, they will be done in a superficial, incomplete manner.

By contrast, hope is a virtue, a *theological* virtue, rather than a psychological disposition or a Pollyanna cheerfulness of temperament. Any fruitful discussion of hope must begin with an understanding of virtue. The word virtue is derived from the Latin *virtus*, meaning "strength." Hope is a virtue, a strength or excellence toward some true human good. The object or aim of hope is for human happiness. This desire

for happiness is placed within the human heart by God who is our ultimate, eternal happiness. Hence, hope is not an acquired virtue (the cardinal virtues – prudence, temperance, fortitude, and justice – are acquired through habit or practice as with any achieved human skill) but an infused virtue. That is, hope, by its nature, must be theological. Hope has as its goal the very attainment of God. Hope is that gift of grace which moves us to dare life with God!

> "The virtue of hope responds to the aspirations to happiness which God has placed in the heart of every man; it takes up the hopes that inspire men's activities and purifies them so as to order them to the Kingdom of heaven; it keeps man from discouragement; it sustains him during times of abandonment; it opens up his heart in expectation of eternal beatitude. Buoyed by hope, he is preserved from selfishness and led to the happiness that flows from charity."
>
> *(Catechism of the Catholic Church)*

Daily experience teaches that lasting happiness is not found in the world. To be human is to be in a constant state of *status viatoris;* that is, we are in a state of being on the way. We are in a state of pilgrimage until we arrive before the

One for whom we are made. What impels us to that final goal is the grace of hope. Hope teaches that this earthly sojourn is not futile or meaningless. The virtue of hope is not in agreement with King Lear: "Life is a tale, told by an idiot, filled with sound and fury, signifying nothing." Hope is more akin to C.S. Lewis' longings:

> At present we are on the outside of the world,
> the wrong side of the door. We discern the freshness
> and purity of morning, but they do not make
> us fresh and pure. We cannot mingle with the
> splendors we were. But all the leaves of the
> New Testament are rustling with the rumor that it
> will not always be so. Someday, God willing,
> we shall get in. When human souls have become
> as perfect in voluntary obedience, then they will
> put on its glory, or rather that greater glory of
> which Nature is only the first sketch.

Honesty requires that we stare into the reality of Katrina, with all its destruction, and acknowledge that despair is a real option. So much damage and death, broken homes and hearts, would seem to make a compelling case for hopelessness. All the evidence, clear to the naked, natural eye, leaves one with only one sensible response – move out and move on. There is a waste and futility in returning to the metro area. Yes, there is no real hope, if hope is reserved only for things seen. In Hebrews 11:1, it states, "Faith is the substance of things hoped for; the proof of things not seen." After Katrina what was seen were the effects of a great natural disaster. The brokenness was not in dispute. The grace that needed to be received was a faith, propelled by hope into what could be. Faith strengthened by hope sharpens the ear to the sound of the rustling leaves of the New Testament, "with the rumor that it will not always be so." Destruction, abandonment, and desolation need not pronounce the final verdict. A wise and not vicious circle is offered to us. Where there is life there is hope; and where there is hope there is life.

This talk of faith and hope in response to Katrina can easily seem beyond our poor powers. We can only believe and hope so much until the acid of doubt eats away at our resolve. To be sure, such can be the case. Left to our inner and outer resources, we are powerless to rebuild, to envision a future not of our making. It is in the honest recognition of our limitations that the Holy Spirit and hope unite to take up residence within the heart.

Long after the wind, water and debris departed, Katrina left a residue that was not easy to remove. The residue left behind by the storm was discouragement. And this was most understandable. The most ordinary day-to-day activities presented huge challenges. From finding an open grocery or service station, to a place to eat or bank, the long lines and delays were like salt on open wounds. Bigger frustrations and anxieties were experienced by those who were able to return and rebuild because of the numerous delays from contractors and insurance companies, not to mention the seemingly endless hours spent filling out a flood of government forms. All of these issues and countless other burdens left people with a deep weariness.

There was also a discouragement known to those who wanted to come home but couldn't for many reasons. This pain of being in exile was acute for the poor and elderly.

Holy Cross School
in the Lower
Ninth Ward

The poor often lacked the resources to return, much less rebuild. A good number of the elderly not only faced financial burdens but also had health issues that demanded medical attention. Compounding the plight of the poor and elderly was the shortage of adequate housing. The place they once called home was no more.

The challenge to hope and start anew amid the ruins, the challenge not to lose heart in a new place, can seem to be a mountain too high to climb, a cross too heavy to carry. Yet it is precisely at this point, in the shadow of the valley of darkness, destruction and death, that the Holy Spirit dwells in us most deeply and the grace of hope is most available. It is at the broken places that the God of the crucifixion is revealed. It is in our weakness that God's strength reaches perfection. It is in abandonment and the passing of all our securities that God can become our riches; God is our all in all.

The difficulty with the Holy Spirit is that the Third Person of the Trinity often falls victim to an abstraction that the mind finds hard to grasp. The Holy Spirit can seem far removed from the blessings and burdens of everyday life. This situation is more than a little troubling, since it is the Holy Spirit who is to be sent by the Father and the Son to indwell with the faith community until Jesus comes again. The abstractness of the Holy Spirit is overcome when we call to mind the Apostle's and Nicene Creeds. In both professions of faith, the Holy Spirit and the Church are intimately linked. The Holy Spirit, Jesus' gift to the Church, becomes visible, tangible, and historical through the sacramental and pastoral ministries of the Church. This incarnational reality was keenly felt by those touched through the various ministries of the archdiocese during and after Katrina. From meeting

• Christ still reigns despite damage to Immaculate Conception in Marrero

the most basic needs for food and water, to caring for those with medical issues, to providing sacramental and pastoral ministry for both evacuees and aid-workers, the Church was present not as an idea, but as a healing, comforting, hopeful presence in a time of loss, dislocation and destruction. The old theological debate over Church as institution or Church as Spirit-filled community dissolved into insolvency. The Church is *both* institution and community guided by the indwelling Paraclete. The structural and organizational make-up of the archdiocese was an essential component in

Hymnals and missalettes once used for worship at St. David Church carry the scars of Katrina

its ability to minister to so many who found themselves with varying needs and circumstances. The sheer magnitude of Katrina's destructive effects necessitated a complex multi-dimensional response – in other words, an institutional response. At the same time, the Church is entrusted with the Gospel, the Good News; hence, the Church cannot be reduced to a mere organizational or sociological entity. The Church carries on its work in and through the power of the Holy Spirit. And the Holy Spirit, in the words of the Nicene Creed, is "the Lord, the giver of life." As was said previously, where there is life, there is hope, and where there is hope, there is life. The archdiocese, in the power of the Holy Spirit, serves as witness to life and hope, especially in a time of destruction.

Is There Any Word from the Lord?

There is an issue that lingers, a kind of subliminal doubt that is not easily put to rest; namely, where was God? Where was God when the wind and water of Katrina brought destruction and death? Why was God seemingly so silent and absent? Even more troubling, was Katrina God's punishment for our alleged wickedness, the removal of his protective hand in order to bring about a change of heart, as some have suggested?

None of these questions, which at times can seem more like indictments against God's love and power and moral condemnation of an entire region, are easily answered.

(Is God cruel and vengeful? Is God powerless in the face of nature's wrath?) And when answers come, they often make things more confused and unclear.

Perhaps a way out of this thicket of inquiry is to employ the distinction proposed by the French existentialist philosopher, Gabriel Marcel. He holds that the situations of life can be categorized in two basic ways: situations which are *problems* that lend themselves to solutions, and situations which are *mysteries* that can only be pondered in the depth of one's being with the aid of grace. The Katrina event can make clear what Marcel is writing about. The waters of Katrina breached the levees and then finally burst through to flood large parts of the city. This is an example of a problem to be solved. We turn to engineering and construction experts for solutions. We look to them in order to begin repairs and ensure that such devastation will not happen again. By contrast, when we ask, "Why did the city flood? Was this God's punishment for sin?", we find ourselves moving from the realm of problem to the realm of mystery. Such events as Katrina give rise to religious and existential issues. We lay aside our charts and slide-rules in order to take up our Bible, enter our churches to pray, and seek enlightenment in order to understand the ways of the Almighty. Intellectual certainty eludes us in the presence of mystery. In place of talk and activity, we find ourselves in holy silence, listening for any word from the Lord.

When searching for meaning and truth in the presence of mystery, especially the mystery of evil, it is essential to ask the right question from the start. Too often the question of evil is posed this way: Why do bad things happen to good people? The answer is simple — we don't know, any more than we know why good things happen to bad people. To persist in the above question is to get lost in an endless game of theological and intellectual speculation. Even the Bible in its most sustained treatment of evil in the Old Testament, the Book of Job, leaves us less than satisfied. At the end of the Book of Job, we are left with this: God is not answerable to humans. The all-powerful God of creation does not need human approval to carry out his will.

The better question to ask goes like this: How do good people respond in the face of evil? This question invites us to be lured into the mystery of evil and the deeper mystery of God's faithful love. The New Testament does not provide a catechism answer to evil. Rather, we are called to ponder a life, the life of Jesus Christ. For Jesus, the Father's beloved Son, though innocent, suffers for the sins of many. In the crucifixion, suffering, death, and evil are not denied but transformed by love. In Jesus, we are given the grace of hope in the face of all suffering and evil. In the life of Jesus, we once again witness the coming together of life and hope. The Holy Spirit continues to bring order out of chaos, light to darkness, and the Divine Word into the void. All who wait in patient hope for God will never be disappointed. In the powerful words of Isaiah:

> ...those who wait for the Lord shall renew their strength,
> they shall mount up with wings like eagles,
> they shall run and not be weary,
> they shall walk and not faint (Isaiah 40:30-31)

In the face of evil, good people open themselves to the transforming power of the Holy Spirit, who offers the grace of hope. It is this grace of hope, through the Holy Spirit, which moves us beyond the present reality of destruction to a vision of what can be. We are liberated and empowered to start anew. The old order has passed away, and in the grasp of the Holy Spirit we are united in helping to build a new dwelling place. The past and present need not blind us to the possibilities of tomorrow. The words of the great French spiritual writer, Péguy, are germane:

> Faith sees only what is,
> and hope sees what is to be.
> love loves only what is,
> and hope loves what is to be.

The ultimate hope which lies deep in the human heart is to be in the presence of God for all eternity. We have hints and rumors of what awaits those who trust in the Lord. T.S. Eliot's *Murder in the Cathedral* has Thomas Becket saying, "I have had a tremor of bliss, a wink of heaven, a whisper, and I would no longer be denied; all things proceed to a joyful consummation."

St. Maria Goretti Church, New Orleans

In the midst of Katrina and its aftermath the question raised by many believers was direct: Where was God? The answer is equally pointed: He was in the very midst of the storm, saying to us, "Do not lose heart. Stand firm and know that I am God. I will not abandon you. My word is faithful and eternal. Look up in hope and dare to follow me. Behold, I make things new." Numerous people were grasped by hope and rebuilt their lives, homes, and communities. This openness to hope became contagious. One rebuilt house encouraged others to follow suit. The news of a reopened church or school moved other infrastructure components to return. Through the Holy Spirit, the archdiocese became a sower of the seeds of hope through its various ministries. The ongoing work of the archdiocese is fundamentally the work of hope – "be not afraid, you are not alone." Through the personal witness of countless, often-unknown individuals and the presence of the Church as Church, the weeds of destruction were replaced by the seeds of hope with their promise of the harvest of new life.

Before leaving this section, a word must be said in response to those, including a number of clergy from various denominations, who have linked God's anger over sin with the visitation of Katrina. The position that Katrina was God's wake-up call to sinners in the metro area and along the Gulf Coast runs into an empirical problem, as well as conceptual confusion. As to the empirical difficulty, the "Katrina as God's wrath" approach must be able to explain why a goodly part of the French Quarter (often considered the epicenter of moral depravity) experienced relatively minor damage from the storm. Further compounding this approach is the fact that the French Quarter was one of the first sections in the city to reopen! If this is viewed as God's wrath, one can only wonder what his blessings must be like! By contrast, some of the poorest areas, and those with highly vulnerable populations, experienced the worst effects of Katrina. This fact is hard to square with the idea that God extends a special caring for the widow, orphan, stranger, and poor. It has become part of the standard Christian theological furniture to propose that God exercises a "preferential option for the poor." On the basis of Katrina, the poor couldn't be faulted for thinking that God exercises a "preferential option against the poor!"

• Severe water damage rearranged even the most solid of fixtures at St. Mary of the Angels Church, New Orleans

Besides the above-mentioned empirical hurdle, the "Katrina as God's wrath" position suffers from a failure to distinguish between a physical and moral evil. A physical evil, such as Katrina, is the result of an imperfection or disorder in the natural forces of the world. No one is responsible for or the

cause of the destructive effects and death resulting from a natural disorder. With a physical evil, there is no moral actor present; no one planned or willed Katrina. To pronounce Katrina as retribution for sin would place God in a rather strange, to say the least, moral position. It would be hard to acquit God of mass murder and human suffering.

A moral evil, on the other hand, requires a moral actor, a being capable of knowingly and willingly bringing about the evil in question. If God be the moral actor, then it would be more than reasonable to conclude that God teaches with a punitive, even vengeful, hand. God's punishment, in this case, Katrina, was indiscriminate as to the innocent and the guilty. At best, God is unjust; at worst, God is an immoral monster! The "Katrina as wrath of God" perspective usually tries to escape by claiming that God's ways are unsearchable. We can't understand the actions of God through our poor human powers. While not denying the limitations of all our human faculties, it could be held that a God who would use Katrina to teach sinners a lesson is not a God whose ways are above us, but *beneath us,* and deserving of our contempt and rejection.

To be sure, the pages of Scripture attest to God's wrath and his ability to punish sinners. However, a significant new age enters human history with the sending of his Son, the Savior. The supreme self-disclosure of God takes place in the Incarnation. God's response to sin becomes visible in the ministry of Jesus, especially through his table fellowship with sinners and those who exist on the margins of society. Jesus continually seeks out the lost and rejected in order to express the Father's unbound love. At the same time, there are significant words and episodes in the New Testament which reveal Jesus' anger toward sin (Jesus' love for sinners never wavers) and a willingness to confront the religious establishment over their self-righteousness, their moralistic condemnation of those deemed unworthy, and their ritualistic formalism in which the externals of worship and dietary requirements trump the much-needed change of heart. The witness of Scripture, when taken as a whole, is clear: Jesus proclaimed the kingdom of God and commissioned his followers to preach and teach the Good News to the ends of the earth. Those who suffered from Katrina were not "sinners in the hands of an angry God" but brothers and sisters who have experienced a great suffering. The God who is "close to the broken-hearted" looks for all his people, – his Church – to be close as well … what does he see?

Is Hope Possible After Katrina?

The question which opened this final section must have been raised countless times in the minds and hearts of all who experienced Katrina. It is a natural question pondered by even the most determined. The mind swirls at the thought of rebuilding and starting over. The will to begin again grows weak in the face of so much destruction, not only of property, but of what it symbolized – houses that over time became homes; places of memory that connected generations; places of hope that welcomed new lives; businesses that were developed through hard work and sacrifice to service a community; churches where Word and sacrament nourished the faithful; and schools which shaped tomorrow by forming the young today. After Katrina, an entire way of life seemed in ruins. What was thought to be so solid was washed away in a brief period of time. Now, the talk of hope sounds like a break with, even a downright

refusal to acknowledge, the hard realities of a post-Katrina world. Few, if any, would deny that the needs were many, and the resources appeared so meager. What to do?

While Katrina was historic, the clash between many needs and meager resources is not new. Jesus and the disciples faced just such a dilemma. In the 14th chapter of the Gospel of Matthew *(Mt 14: 15-33)*, we read of Jesus feeding the multitudes. After a long day of Jesus healing the sick and teaching, night was fast approaching. The disciples were ready to send the crowd home, but Jesus had a different idea. Before sending them away, Jesus instructed the disciples to feed the people. Immediately the disciples thought this impossible, since there were at least 5,000, not counting women and children, and only five loaves and two fishes. The classic case of too many mouths to feed and not enough food was evident. The reaction of the disciples is as one might expect – resistance at being asked to do the impossible.

The disciples' resistance was met by Jesus' persistence. The disciples were fixated on a seemingly impossible problem. Being locked into the dilemma, the disciples became frozen in one-dimensional, horizontal thinking. The resources before them were static – five loaves of bread and two fishes cannot go into more than 5,000 people. End of story. However, for Jesus this was just the beginning. Jesus refuses to be paralyzed by the problem; hence, his thinking was vertical. After getting the crowd to recline, which no doubt heightened their expectations, Jesus receives what resources are available, lifts his eyes heavenward, and gives thanks. Jesus expresses gratitude for what is at hand rather than bemoaning what is lacking. The impossible not only

• Poydras Street in front of the Superdome

becomes possible, but the crowds are given all they want. Jesus' prayer of thanksgiving, in fact, yields abundance. It would seem that the refusal to hold fast to problems, to expand thinking beyond the merely horizontal, and to express prayerful gratitude for what one has, together yield an abundant harvest.

The story of Jesus feeding the crowds was played out many times after Katrina. The hurricane produced its own brand of many needs in the face of meager resources. It was understandable, maybe even prudent, to get locked into purely horizontal thinking. Lying before us were vast areas of destruction. Numbness, as a kind of anesthetic, rushed through mind and heart. For the longest time all we could do was stand frozen in disbelief. Thoughts of rebuilding only added to the disbelief, sorrow, and anger. Many couldn't rebuild if they wanted to. Any talk of a Road Home grant took on the tone of a cruel joke, producing no laughter, just tears.

Former Archbishop Philip Hannan was 92 when he flew over a city flooded by Katrina

Theologian Richard John Neuhaus writes lyrically about hope, "As Christians and as Americans, in this our awkward duality of citizenship, we seek to be faithful in a time not of our choosing but of our testing. We resist the hubris of presuming that it is the definitive time and place of historical or tragedy, but it is our time and place. It is a time of many times…a time for walking together, unintimidated when we seem to be a small and beleaguered band; a time for rejoicing in momentary triumphs, and for defiance in momentary defeats;…a time for generosity toward those who would make us their enemy…"

If there was to be a rebuilding and a willingness to follow the road home, the first stirrings of recovery would have to begin inside one's heart. This is precisely that holy place where our spirit is addressed by the Holy Spirit. For it is that renewal of the human spirit by the Holy Spirit which empowers one to hope; and where there is hope, there is life. The moving of the Holy Spirit, mightier than anything produced by Katrina, at first gently blows away the shock, sense of loss, and feelings of futility. Once we began to imagine a new beginning, once the seed of hope found fertile ground in the heart, the winds of the Holy Spirit picked up momentum and moved the mountain of despair. The human heart, once constricted and shriveled by despair, expanded as hope began to flower. This flowering of hope did not remain confined within the individual heart. Hope bloomed outward to yield a garden in which people came together, united in a common grief, now uplifted in a shared hope.

The Holy Spirit, as the Lord and Giver of Life, is, the One who bestows the gift of hope and abides not only in the human heart, but also in and through the Church. The Church is that tangible herald of a hope that will never ultimately disappoint us because the One Spirit remains until Jesus comes again. The Church, in the power of the Holy Spirit, is entrusted with the message of hope for those who feel themselves beyond hope, to those who are broken-hearted.

The Church, for what has been for our purpose the Archdiocese of New Orleans, had to be present during and after Katrina if the Church was to be true to her mission: proclaiming the Good News of Jesus Christ, the One who is Life and Hope itself. This proclamation is not just informative, but also must be performative. The Gospel is not exclusively a noun; the Church understands the Gospel as a verb, a perennial call to be the sacrament, the revelation, of God's boundless love. St. Francis of Assisi put it nicely: – Preach the Gospel always, and when necessary, use words. The various ministries offered to those in need after Katrina were a combination of word and deed. From the simplest act of offering consolation, to the celebration of the Eucharist; from handing out food and water, to feeding the faithful with the Word of God and the food of eternal life; from opening hearts locked by fear, to opening wide the doors of church and school; the archdiocese was administering the balm of consolation, a healing oil that would provide strength for the journey through the indwelling presence of the Holy Spirit.

The roof of Notre Dame Seminary shows the effects of Katrina

In the years after Katrina the scars are still evident, as are unclosed wounds. A large number of former residents have not or could not return. The damage from the storm is still evident, with houses remaining abandoned and streets badly damaged. Areas once busy with commercial establishments go unoccupied. There are churches and schools once alive with the joyful shouts of praise and children's laughter which now stand silent. Of course, all scars are not external. There is an ache that is still felt in many hearts, a tenderness that draws back from the slightest touch. There abides in memory images of destruction and death that powerfully rush to consciousness as if Katrina was only yesterday.

While the shadow side of Katrina abides, much has changed. As indicated above, scars remain, yet a scar is a sign of healing, a wound in the process of recovery. Scars can be more than signs of past injuries; they can become scars that indicate the promise of new growth. The buds are already emerging, if not yet flowering: a new set of leaders in civic and governmental spheres are emerging; the old barriers of race, ethnicity, gender, class and religion are being toppled; and those who are able to build upon the energy of a people determined to begin anew will be rewarded with the mantle of leadership.

The Church has experienced new ways of being Church. To many for whom the Church was something remote, a weekly visit to a building for a religious ritual, the Church has become much more. Church became their community of worship in which the Word was heard, the Eucharist received, and fellow believers shared stories and offered support to one another. New worshipers, often from parishes that were not or could not reopen, were made

Jesus on the
Via Dolorosa,
enroute to Calvary
but ultimately to
the empty tomb …
at St. Patrick
Church,
Port Sulphur

of each school, there was the expression of a deeply felt gratitude to God by all involved. School administrators and teachers employed creative ways to meet the educational needs of returning students, both former as well as new students. Schools engaged in an unprecedented degree of cooperation by sharing facilities and educational resources and even loaned faculty members to schools in need. The imaginative and cooperative experiments conducted by school leaders left a lasting impression. Students returning after Katrina had a number of emotional and psychological challenges. Throughout the archdiocese, Catholic schools

• St. Patrick Church, Port Sulphur

welcomed and consoled. Families and individual church members reflected in a deeper way on the things that really matter. In the midst of having lost so much, people began to give thanks for what remained – life, faith and loved ones. Clergy themselves found their priestly ministry expanded in ways unexpected. Along with the traditional expressions of ministry, priests and deacons found themselves increasingly called on to meet counseling and social service needs. The clergy's presence and prayer were more requested and valued than in so called "normal times."

Much the same was occurring with schools. Often with the threat of loss, or actual loss, there comes widespread appreciation of the item in jeopardy. With the reopening

as familiar, safe places allowed students, family members, and teachers to tell their Katrina stories, receive feedback, and when necessary, make arrangements for professional psychological counseling. Above all, Catholic schools provided the spiritual resources and support that proved to be indispensable as students and families made the transition from evacuee to returnee status.

We began this section with a question – Is hope possible after Katrina? From what has been presented above, and from this book as a whole, the answer is supplied by asking a different question: Is it possible not to hope after Katrina? If one believes that we live by hope, and life is stronger than death, then we cannot help but hope. This hope offered by the Holy Spirit is anything but escapist. Holy Spirit hope gives us the strength to start again. In our trials and sufferings God will not forsake his people. The words of the Apostle Paul fill us with confidence: "We also boast about our sufferings, knowing that suffering produces endurance, and endurance produces character, and character produces hope, and hope does not disappoint us because God's love has been poured into our hearts through the Holy Spirit that has been given to us" *(Rom 5:3-5)*.

Commencement Exercises

History teaches that to each generation there comes a time of testing, as gold is tested in the furnace. The founding generation of America pledged their all in order to bring forth a nation conceived in liberty, equality, and justice for all. This new nation of high ideals was more a hope than a realized achievement. Another generation engaged in a tragic Civil War as a sign of its commitment to a new birth

of freedom. Two world wars and numerous global conflicts would test succeeding generations' belief that life without liberty is not befitting the human person.

Not all testing comes by way of armed conflict. The Great Depression tested the resolve of a nation, which had known great prosperity, to remain true to itself in a time of deep want. Would America follow the example of many European nations that were experiencing similar economic hardships by trading democracy for bread and security? Would America be another instance of a nation, gathered on the ash heap of history, which blindly followed a "leader," a Führer into oblivion? Hardly. America would lead the forces of freedom against the ideologies of enslavement. In the years after World War II, America experienced a sustained period of economic prosperity while the seeds of profound social change were being planted.

The seeds of social change flowered in the decade of the '60s and presented that generation with its own time of trial. A new urgency and commitment to civil rights was sweeping the conscience of a nation. The prophetic voice of Dr. Martin Luther King Jr., along with many others, was troubling the waters of the comfortable. These voices were challenging America to be America. The result of this great moral awakening was a further movement toward realizing the founding vision and hope of a country pledged to liberty and justice for all.

The above examples share a common theme: the importance of hope in the face of great challenges and opportunities. The history of America would have been different without the courage to hope and the willingness to bear every cost in the cause of freedom and human dignity. Katrina has been, and will be for some time to come, our moment of testing. There are miles yet to run before we rest and pronounce "mission accomplished." The temptations to despair, grow weary, and forget our highest ideals and deepest spiritual truths must always be resisted. As the pages of this book reveal, our temperament runs in favor of courageous hope. The final chapter of our time of testing is not yet ready to be written. The words of the Psalmist can spur us onward together so that in a time of destruction, hope is our enduring decision. "All time, O Lord, is in Thy hands." *(Ps 31:15)* And so are we.

Spiritual writer Ignacio Larrañaga, O.F.M. Cap., in his book, *Sensing Your Hidden Presence, Toward Intimacy with God,* writes a dialogue between discouragement and hope.

Discouragement: I look back and everything is in ruins. I look at my feet and everything is a disaster…No one can go back. What I do know with certainty is one thing: there is no hope for me.

Hope speaks: If, up until now, there were ruins, from now on there will be castles of light pointing their towers to the heights. If, until now, you have harvested disasters, remember: Spring showers are coming.

Behind the silence breathes the Father. The solitude is inhabited by a presence, and above us waits rest and liberation. Walk. The Lord God will be light for your eyes, breath for your lungs, ointment for your wounds, goal for your path, and reward for your effort.

Come. Let us begin again. (pp.281-283)

• Rededication of Our Lady of Lourdes Church, Violet, in 2009

AFTER WORD:
THE BONDS THAT ENDURE

As this book nears completion on a particularly cold January 2010 morning, this last entry was not part of the original plan. Its origin lies elsewhere. Upon completion of the intended text, instead of a sense of relief that the heavy lifting was in the rearview mirror, present was the irritation of an incompleteness beyond the usual anxieties that fill every author. Something more needed to be said without which the work would be known more for what it did *not* contain. Beyond mere vanity, there was a sense of obligation to the reader, as well as to the project. After due prayer and reflection, it became clearer as to what was lacking, namely, a word to those who by choice or circumstances, have not returned to the New Orleans metropolitan area.

A book about the archdiocese and Katrina must also honor its debt to those who are not among us, yet are still *with* us; and the acknowledgment that we abide with them.

The continued displacement of those who were once near – family, friends, neighbors and associates – does not mean they are lost to memory or beyond our reach. The realities of those who are away provide us with the opportunity to be drawn into a deep mystery, specifically, the mystery of the church as the Mystical Body of Christ. To understand the Church as Mystical Body is not a model that comes easily to us. The vast majority of our relationships and associations involve a physical presence, rather than a mystical or spiritual one. We greet one another with gestures of love, affection, friendship, and welcome. We identify places such as home, church, school, office building, and other landmarks by their location and physical structure. The loss of someone dear or the destruction of a significant place in our lives fills us with sadness and a longing to reconnect or rebuild.

Those who after Katrina are no longer among us can leave us, and *themselves*, with a void. We feel that essential chapters in our life's story have been taken, and with them parts of our identity. Katrina not only washed away our possessions, but the waters also carried away significant parts of who we were. There is a longing for restoration. There is a deep desire to believe that while things have changed they are not ended.

It is into this feeling of separation, disconnection, and emptiness — a void once so wide and deep — that the reality of church as Mystical Body of Christ is so powerfully experienced.

The Church is at once historical and transcendent, in time and beyond. The visible manifestation of the Church takes the form in its various structures and hierarchical orders (parish to diocese, priest to bishop, and so on). This historical, earthly manifestation of the Church is not the whole of the Church. The Church enjoys a divine dimension, the spiritual reality of grace which she offers to all. The sacred reality of the Church, like its head, Jesus, seeks to draw all people into communion with God. This communion in grace, the mystical union and oneness in Christ of the many members, cannot be reduced to a purely human understanding. Another dimension must enter our thinking. Namely, there is a spiritual kinship between members of the One Body which the worldly forces of nature and history cannot break. These bonds in the living Church are gifts of God. They endure beyond the contingencies of the moment. The members of the Mystical Body of Christ endure into eternity.

With the "here and now" aspect of the Church, the bonds we form as a people of faith are present even when we are no longer physically with one another. The great prayer of the Church, which unites all members, regardless of distance, is the Eucharist. This is the great sacrament of our unity and encounter with Christ and one another. In our participation in the Eucharist, the earthly barriers that divide us and the miles that separate are overcome. Through our gathering to pray at the Lord's Table, we are sacramentally one with the universal Church. Through our membership in the Mystical Body of Christ we draw strength, courage, and the resolve in faith to go forward in hope. As when Jesus multiplied the loaves and fishes and gathered the fragments so nothing was lost, so now in the Eucharist all are gathered and made present. No one is to be lost.

The reality of the Mystical Body of Christ, which includes the historical, earthly Church, speaks a powerful word to all of us, especially after Katrina. We are drawn into the visible and invisible dimensions of the Church. We are reminded of those human and spiritual bonds which unite us in faith, made most visible at the Eucharist. On further reflection, we come to understand the Mystical Body of Christ holds out a special message of solidarity and hope to three particular segments of the community.

First, to those who have not returned by design, you are forever a part of New Orleans and Katrina. We have every right to view you as our gifts to the new communities of which you are now a part. The faith and talents with which you blessed us, you now bless others. No matter, the Body of Christ is enriched. You now flower on some different shore. We rejoice, however distant you are and unknown your future, in the knowledge that God is glorified.

Second, to those who have not returned because of life's circumstance, distance cannot diminish the affection with which you are held. We hope, not according to our schedule, but God's, you will be united with those who love and cherish your presence. Your gifts are lent to others with the hope that upon your return, we will be blessed the more. God's time always brings forth abundance beyond our expectation.

Finally, to those who have suffered the death of a loved one or a friend, with Jesus nothing is ever lost forever. The Mystical Body of Christ makes ample room for our dearly departed; in the Lord they are welcomed as the newly arrived. Through our prayers and memories, contact continues and grows deeper. For the ultimate sting of death has been removed with the Risen Lord. As we commend them to the Triune God, so our departed pray for us until we are all reunited at the Banquet which never ends.

The winged chariot of time indicates that we have just passed the fifth anniversary of Hurricane Katrina (August 29, 2005). Anniversaries invite a looking back and forward. It should be no different with Katrina. However, as a people of faith, we view events through a special pair of glasses. For us, we look back with sadness, tempered by a spirit of faith that moved us from then to now. We look forward with a hope that empowers us, in our time of destruction, to know that seeds of Resurrection abound.

St. Louis Cathedral,
spiritual icon of New
Orleans, 2008

Publisher:

Éditions du Signe

1, rue Alfred Kastler - Eckbolsheim

B.P. 94 – 67038 Strasbourg, Cedex 2, France

Tel: ++33 (0) 3 88 78 91 91

Fax: ++33 (0) 3 88 78 91 99

www.editionsdusigne.fr

email: info@editionsdusigne.fr

Publishing director: Christian Riehl
Director of publication: Joëlle Bernhard
Publishing assistant: Marc de Jong

Author: William F. Maestri
Layout: Anthony Kinné - Éditions du Signe
Copy editor/front cover design: Bettina Buval
Photoengraving : Éditions du Signe - 108397

Photo acknowledgments:

- Gratitude is expressed to all archdiocesan departments for furnishing photos
- Special thanks is offered to the U.S. Army Corps of Engineers for making available numerous photos
- The work of the *Clarion Herald*, especially staff photographer Frank J. Methe, and the Office of Archives of the Archdiocese proved indispensable
- The photos and materials from the Building Office added much to the book
- The efforts of Andre Villere Jr. are most appreciated
- Cheryl Harper, Catholic Mutual Group
- United States Congress Office of History and Preservation